THE CALIFORNIA BLUES

A Musical Journey from the South to the West Coast

WORKBOOK PRESS LLC
187 E Warm Springs Rd
Suite B285 Las Vegas NV 89119 USA

Website: https://workbookpress.com/
Hotline: 1-888-818-4856
Email: admin@workbookpress.com

Ordering Information:
Quantity sales. Special discounts are available on quantity purchases by corporations, associations, and others. For details, contact the publisher at the address above.

ISBN-13: 978-1-965732-56-4 Paperback Version

978-1-965732-57-1 Digital Version

REV. DATE:08/04/2025

For Tom, Hardy, Martha and Caitlin

With thanks to my brother John Cooley, who has sung and played guitar as long as I can remember, and to Ronnie, Joe, Jimmy, Sugar Pie, Lowell, Cool Papa, Robert and Terrible Tom, who told me about the blues.

CONTENTS

AUTHOR'S INTRODUCTION

This book documents the migration of African-American blues musicians from the South to the West Coast, primarily Oakland, during World War II. They came to work in the defense industries and they brought with them the music of the South, music that was African-based, rhythmic, melodic, and created a blues that became urban, straightforward and diverse.

Most of the migrants came from rural areas and went to cities to work, and their music reflected the less harshly segregated and more fluid society into which they assimilated. This book, made up of oral life histories of the musicians, seeks to analyze their music in the context of their lives as they settled in, worked and lived among heterogeneous populations.

Between 1942 and 1945, 340,000 African-Americans settled in California; 140,000 of them in urban areas other than Los Angeles. Most of them came from Louisiana, Texas, Arkansas and the Mississippi Delta. Restrictions on housing and union bans in San Francisco forced many to move to Oakland, where they lived in mixed neighborhoods and could travel freely on public transport and circulate in public. In the mid-1920s the wages were more favorable in California generally than elsewhere in the country, and African-Americans could buy homes. The restricted residential covenants of the 1920s limited the neighborhoods where they could live, but real estate was available to them. The racism they faced and the piracy of their recordings were prominent subjects in theses oral histories.

The vibrant music scene in Oakland is little known today because it disappeared during the 1960s redevelopment project. Today Seventh Street lies in the shadow of a post office and under a Bay Area Rapid Transit railway line, its clubs and stores shuttered. In the day, every great blues figure performed there, from "T-Bone" Walker to Billie Holiday. Twelve miles away in San Francisco, what was known as the "Harlem of the West" in the Fillmore District was the place where all the jazz greats congregated and performed. Bop City and the New Orleans Jazz Club were just two of many clubs that offered all-night music, food and dancing. West Oakland and the Fillmore District were two of the few neighborhoods in the Bay Area where African-Americans could go for entertainment and they thrived. Most of the musicians lived and worked for a time in Los Angeles as well, playing downtown and in the beach communities.

There is a little documentation about these music communities. The story in this volume is told through oral histories taken with several prominent blues figures whose careers began in the 1940s and continued for several decades. They or their parents moved to the region from the South, and all of them performed on Seventh Street. Some of them are still performing, touring in Europe and playing in local clubs.

The list of topics covered in the oral history range from early childhood years and family to writing and performing the blues and experiencing racism. Subjects were sought who could document the 1940s to the present time. Most of the blues dealt with love gone south: the loss or unfaithfulness of a partner, loneliness or alienation, but they frequently focused on tougher subjects: violent racial confrontations, life-threatening illnesses, arrest and incarceration.

The oral history process is as follows: once the digital audio files for an interview are transcribed, the interviewer checks the text and corrects errors with a very light edit that assures that the text does not become an extension of the editorial voice. What might be considered errors of interpretation or analysis or even "misrememberings" are not altered, so that the narrator's words stand as recorded. The transcribed interviews are sent to the narrators for review. Narrators are encouraged to retain the informal, conversational quality of the interviews, and in all cases only minor additions and corrections were made, and no portions of the histories sealed. The resulting book is an oral history with multiple voices telling a story that spans several decades, very similar to the University of California Press' 1999 Central Avenue Sounds. As music historian in the Oral History Office of The Bancroft Library, I began the blues project in the 1990s and invited prominent bluesman and bandleader Ronnie Stewart, and American history teacher Joe Mathews to participate as interviewers. The National Endowment for the Humanities funded the project.

The volume has been organized as follows: Part 1 introduces the blues community in Oakland, profiles the subjects and excerpts song lyrics and thematic materials from the music and the oral histories. Among the chapter headings are Early Years, Grandparents, the Church, the Music, Seventh Street, Oakland, California, Racism, Recording the Blues and Piracy, and Writing the Blues.

In the second part of the volume are the full texts of the oral histories, which were recorded from 1990 to 2010. The interviewees discuss their childhoods and families and the journey from hard times in the South to new lives in California. They discuss their styles and processes of composing. They are candid about personal relationships, failures and successes.

It is hoped that this volume will invite more interest in blues music in California, a subject that has been almost completely neglected to date. The musicians tell the story in the best way it can be told, of a time and place where the blues thrived.

Caroline Cooley Crawford, Music Historian
The Bancroft Library, University of California
Berkeley, California, 2019

CHAPTER ONE—THE CALIFORNIA BLUES: MUSIC OF THE MIGRATION

Blues is a feeling. It's all about what happened in my life or to someone else's life, which is the true facts and a feeling. When you've been mistreated, you're not the onliest one. Someone else in the world has been mistreated–that's the blues. It's all in your feeling and the feeling is a true part of life.

Jimmy McCracklin

Billie Holiday, Big Mama Thornton, Charles Brown, Aretha Franklin, Jimmy McCracklin, Ivory Joe Hunter, Pee Wee Crayton, Saunders King, John Lee Hooker, Lowell Fulson—these are only a few of the names advertised outside the blues clubs in West Oakland in the years during and after World War II. The community around Seventh Street, blues central, had long been populated by African-Americans, Slavs and Europeans, but during the war the African-American population in California grew by several hundred thousand as families came from the South to work in the shipyards. The Oakland blues developed a new role for electric guitar as well as distinct performance style, rooted in the traditions of Texas, Louisiana, Arkansas and the Mississippi Delta. Louisiana-born guitarist Lafayette Thomas shaped the style as did Bob Geddins, a signal figure in recording the blues in the 40s, who defined it as a "slow, draggier beat and a kind of mournful sound." "T-Bone" Walker was another signal figure whose bent blue notes, thirds, fifths and sevenths, created a guitar sound that simulated human speech—that guitar could talk.

Blues and jazz first traveled by railroad from New Orleans to California in the early 1990s, at the same time as the music was developing in New York, Chicago and Kansas City. But the story of the music in California has been little documented, and the rich scene in Oakland, shut down by government-sponsored urban renewal projects in the 1960s, has been almost completely neglected.

This volume is an attempt to tell the story of the California blues, with an emphasis on the Oakland blues community, through oral history interviews with some of the major players: Lowell Fulson, Charles Brown, Jimmy McCracklin, Johnny Otis, "Cool Papa" Sadler, Earl "Good Rockin'" Brown, Sugar Pie DeSanto, Robert Kelton and "Terrible Tom" Bowden. The full histories of Sugar Pie DeSanto, Tom Bowden and Robert Kelton are not included, but excerpts appear in the text.

The blues musicians whose histories appear here wrote and performed songs that became all-time blues hits and the signature songs of music legends. Lowell Fulson made a gift to B.B. King of "Three O' Clock Blues," and Elvis Presley and Eric Clapton covered Fulson's "Reconsider Baby." The Beatles recorded Jimmy McCracklin's "The Walk," the song that earned McCracklin an invitation to appear on Dick Clark's *American Bandstand.* McCrackin also penned "The Thrill is Gone," made famous by B.B. King. Charles Brown's "Merry Christmas Baby" was covered by Elvis Presley, Bruce Springsteen and Sheryl Crow. Johnny Otis wrote Etta James' 1955 "Wallflower," and performed in and produced the first recording of Oakland artist Mama Thornton's "Hound Dog." Sugar Pie DeSanto's "I Want to Know" topped the blues charts for months and landed her a contract with Chess Records. Keith Richards adapted some of the Oakland blues for the Rolling Stones and spoke about the blues artists in a BBC interview as the real geniuses of their time.

In addition to the clubs where blues were played, there were African-American owned businesses: a bank, a pool hall, a pharmacy, a grocery store and record stores. The headquarters of the Brotherhood of Sleeping Car Porters was located there, and an African-American labor union organized in 1925 by A. Philip Randolph to improve the wages and benefits of railroad porters, who were required to work hundreds of hours per month in order to receive a paycheck. Christ Holy Sanctified Church on Seventh Street gave Saunders King, the son of pastor Judge King, his first paying job. Located in a Victorian house, the church was known as the Seventh Street Mission until it relocated to the northern part of the city. The sanctified churches held on to many African traditions and touched the lives of every blues figure in this volume.

The Lincoln Theater started as a vaudeville house in West Oakland in the 1920s and eventually became the center of live music and community events. Paul Robeson and Billie Holiday graced its stage, and its talent shows launched many musicians' careers, including that of "Terrible Tom" Bowden.

The best known of the Seventh Street clubs was the Slim Jenkins Supper Club, considered by many to be the most elegant club on the West Coast. Jenkins came from Louisiana in 1891, settling in Oakland after World War II. In 1933 he established his club at 1748 Seventh Street on the very day Prohibition ended. Before it was closed down in 1962 to make way for a gas station as part of the city's redevelopment project, it was a performance venue for Billie Holiday, Louis Jordan, the Ink Spots, Duke Ellington and Sarah Vaughn, and sixteen-year-old Aretha Franklin opened there for B.B. King.

Jenkins gave young musicians, including Texas-born Ivory Joe Hunter, their first stages. He helped make the Platters famous by improving their wardrobe and booking them at his club. Jenkins had a strict dress code: his clientele not only "dressed," they had to wear hats in order to enter. Jenkins was six feet five inches tall and wore a three-piece suit with matching silk tie and pocket handkerchief. Although he never owned the property, he built the supper club into the top venue along Seventh Street and added a grocery store, bar, and banquet room.

Esther Mabry went to work for Jenkins soon after she arrived from Palestine, Texas, in 1942. Soon she was working as a cook at the supper club, serving biscuits and syrup, greens and beans, salt pork and fried chicken. Sixty-five cents bought a full meal in those days, and servicemen packed Jenkins' club. Mabry established Esther's Orbit Room in 1962; the Orbit Room moved to make way for redevelopment and was the last surviving Seventh Street Club, closing its doors when Mabry died in 2012. Mabry said: "Seventh Street is the only place you'd ever want to be."

Many of the Seventh Street clubs were supported by Charles "Raincoat" Jones, a loan shark who collected West Oakland real estate. "Raincoat," so-called because he was said to have arrived from Georgia in 1878 wearing nothing but a raincoat, was a veteran of the Spanish-American War. He helped many Black businesses survive, among them *The Sun Reporter*, a Black newspaper

The man who is said to have created the California blues was Bob Geddins. Geddins composed and co-wrote many songs, but his primary importance was as a record producer and coach. Born in Martin, Texas, in 1913, he came to California in 1933, settled initially in Los Angeles and after a 1943 visit to the Bay Area, he decided to move to Oakland.

Geddins took a job as a welder at the Kaiser Shipyard in Richmond, established Rhythm Records, and by the late 1940s he was the leading blues and gospel record producer in the Bay Area. He was one of the first African-Americans to own a record label, and he developed several more labels, among them Big Town, Down Town, Cavatone, Plaid, Veltone and Irma, named after his wife.

Geddins ran a low-budget operation, selling records from the back of his car, and often had to lease his recordings out for lack of capital, which meant that artists such as Lowell Fulson, Sugar Pie DeSanto, Jimmy McCracklin, Johnny Heartsman and Roy Hawkins eventually turned to more established companies. Some blues artists thought Geddins made money off them by claiming their music; others like Fulson credited Geddins with launching their careers: Geddins claimed that because he didn't copyright the work, large companies to whom he leased productions, such as Chess, Aladdin, Modern and Swingtime, often refused to return the master copies to him and he never profited from the huge sales.

Geddins shaped the sound, working with the singers in rehearsal sessions to draw out certain words in such a way that the most mournful possible music was produced. A sadder sound in a mellower context was what he had in mind. He wrote or co-wrote songs about hard luck, troubled relations and general misery: "Why Do Everything Happen to Me" (covered by James Brown and B.B. King), "Fool's Paradise" (covered by Sam Cooke and Charles Brown), and "My Time After a While (covered by Buddy Guy). The recording of Lowell Fulson's

"Three O' Clock Blues" was his first big hit, placing high up on the Billboard race record chart. Geddins reworked a 1953 Jimmy Wilson song into the popular "Tin Pan Alley." The song was his personal statement about West Oakland.

Went down to Tin Pan Alley

See what was going on

Things was too hot down there

Couldn't stay very long

They tell me Tin Pan Alley's the roughest place in town

They start cuttin' and shootin' when the sun goes down

Oh, tell me what kind of place can the alley be?

Every woman, I guess, Lord, the Alley takes away from me

If Geddins shaped the sound into a slowed down, mournful blues, Louisiana-born Lafayette "Thing" Thomas contributed equally. B.B. King admired what he called Thomas' wailing electric guitar, and lamented that he never could produce the sound. There is general agreement that the music became less strident than the music of the Midwest or East because of the sunny weather in California, and that the songs had a shared background in the southern church. The blues brought what Chris Strachwitz, who recorded and documented the blues, has called "the drive and thrust and excitement of Sanctified Church rhythms. It wasn't "the screaming Mississippi sound," as Charles Brown defined "the boomy, boomy blues," and Strachwitz thought that might account for the attention the regional blues received.

Thomas recorded countless times with Geddins and performed in Jimmy McCracklin's band for nearly four decades before his death in 1977. His solos featured sound-volume warps and brilliant high trills, and the name "Thing" referred to the stage acrobatics with his guitar, a major element of "T-Bone" Walker's performance style.

Born Thibeaux Walker in 1910 in Texas, Walker pioneered the electric blues sound as well. He is credited with being the first to use the electric guitar in a blues combo. His parents, Movella Jimerson and Rance Walker, were both musicians, and as a small child he played guitar, banjo, violin, mandolin and piano. Ranked by *Rolling Stone* magazine as number sixty-seven on the list of the hundred greatest guitarists of all time, he influenced virtually every blues musician of the time. Oklahoma-born guitarist Robert Kelton recalls: "I remember "T-Bone"' Walker very well, that's right. He had his style of guitar, and nobody else had it. He used mostly bass, and all the bass had to do was play what he asked him to play, and he would sing his song and fill in with his guitar. The show part was holding the guitar here, behind the head. He was a good musician, and he knew how to wake the people up in the cabarets. Two or three songs and he'd have everybody in there rocking with him. He didn't play to satisfy himself; he played to satisfy the people who were paying. That's the way he operated." Among Walker's greatest hits is "Stormy Monday," released in 1947.

Oh they call it stormy Monday

But Tuesday's just as bad

Lord, and Wednesday's worse

And Thursday's also sad

The eagle flies on Friday

Saturday I'll go out to play

Sunday 'go to church

And I'll fall on my knees to pray

Blues styles, adapted to the urban environment, were diverse: Boogie-based blues from Texas and the southwest, with fixed bass figures in the left hand, were common, as exemplified by Lowell Fulson's "Reconsider Baby," issued in 1954. The song is considered among the all-time best of the Oakland blues.

Well, so long

Oh, I hate to see you go

So long

Oh, I hate to see you go

The way that I will miss you

I guess you'll never know

You said you once had loved me

But now I guess you've changed your mind

Gospel music had an influence on the blues as well. Blues writers drew from gospel performance practices in songs such as Jimmy McCracklin's 1961 hit "Just Got to Know" which fuses a religious melody with a twelve-bar blues:

I want to know, I just got to know

Why do you always play around

If you have the same feeling for me

Then why don't you settle down

I think you want me for conveniency

If I'm wrong please tell me right

I know I been in the dark a long time

But one day I will see the light

A blues-infused ballad style, as in pianist Charles Brown's mournful 1945 "Drifting Blues," developed too, an after-hours blues in which the frustrations of life came to the fore and the articulation of the lyrics was the most important element. Lowell Fulson describes it as "a soft, modern type of blues."

Well, I'm drifting and I'm drifting

Like a ship out on the sea

Drifting and I'm drifting

Like a ship out on the sea

Well, I ain't got nobody in this world to care for me

If my baby would only take me back again

Cause, darling, good for nothing

I haven't got no friend

Blues singers sing about love and loss, hard times and good times. They sing about things they have had taken from them, about social injustice and racism and the longing for a promised land. The blues is not just about one thing, it is rather a state of being, of coming to terms with life. African-American in origin, the blues originated in the South after the Civil War, influenced by work songs, spirituals and white folk music. The blues musicians of the 1940s and 50s didn't always have formal musical training. They went to church with a grandmother or another relative, sang in the choir, played the organ or the guitar and wrote their lives as the blues.

Loss of love and loneliness and what seemed like a life of endless problems are a focus of Charles Brown's 1951 hit "Black Night":

Nobody cares about me

I ain't even got a friend

Baby's gone and left me

When will my troubles end?

Black night is falling

Oh, how I hate to be alone

I keep crying for my baby

But now another day is gone

Those who came to the West Coast from the South looked for a golden future in California, but they often wrote about life back home, as in Jimmy McCracklin's 1954 song "Arkansas," which expresses nostalgia for the rural countryside he grew up in:

I don't want the city woman

She all too fast

Give me a slow country girl with a lot of class

So I'm going, it's just a hop a skip and a jump

Arkansas, here I come, it's just a hop, a skip and a jump

"Cool Papa" Sadler was the rare bluesman who wrote about politics and the environment, about the ruins of California farmlands, the homeless and disenfranchised in cities, about his personal suffering from diabetes. As he said, "My blues don't say a lot about losing my woman or losing my money. I sit around and write songs like "Resource Blues." They are building in the country, like the San Joaquin Valley. That's a source of food...right there in the San Joaquin Valley. Now you go out there you see building complexes-that's a resource stolen from the people."

They're filling our farmlands up with buildings

I'm going to sit and have me a concrete meal

For bread, chew on bricks

And for meat, I eat on steel

A year ago, I took a ride off in the country

You know the fields was full of corn

All I see out there now is brand-new houses

Lord, all the vegetables is gone

Lowell Fulson was an important part of the scene. Bom in Tulsa, Oklahoma, in 1921, his grandfather had escaped from slavery and lived on a Choctaw Indian Reservation, where Fulson was raised. His violinist grandfather was a major Influence in his life, as well as several uncles who played guitar. In his early years he picked cotton and played guitar in the local Holiness Church, a church derived from 19th century Methodism. Later he joined Tex Alexander until he was drafted and stationed with the U.S. Navy and West Oakland. Bob Geddins recognized Fulson's mastery of the electric guitar, and style similar to that of "T-Bone" Walker and worked to foster his career, signing him to record on his Big Town and Trilon labels before Fulson went on to Swing Time and eventually to the Chess Brothers Checkers label and the Bihari Brothers' Modern label.

Fulson claimed he made a gift of his first recorded song "Three O' Clock Blues," to B.B. King in 1948 because only King played his records on the radio in Memphis, and it is generally agreed that the song launched King's career, "He is the onliest man who can take my songs and beat me singing them", said Fulson. Fulson continued to play his big white Gibson guitar well through the rock and roll era, performing at festivals. He died in 1999.

Jimmy McCracklin, born in Helena, Arkansas, into a family of seven sisters and two brothers, met Walter Davis, a famous blues singer from whom he learned to play the piano, at an early age. He hoped to have a career as a boxer and claimed to have trained for a time with Archie Moore, but an auto accident ended his hopes, and he decided to concentrate on the blues. He served in the US Navy, moved to Los Angeles and then the Bay Area in 1947, where he owned several clubs over the years, including the Savoy in Richmond.

McCracklin claimed to have written more than a thousand songs, including "Think", "My Answer", and "Shame, Shame, Shame." If most of his songs were about soured relationships, McCracklin often focused on social problems, as in "Hate Will Change the World":

Someone in heaven

Please help us on this earth

Take away hate

And make a first

If our voice is not heard

Hate oh hate will destroy the world

McCracklin began recording with his Blues Blasters for Bob Geddins in 1947, but his star was launched when his lighthearted "The Walk" made the top ten on the charts in 1958. The song was recorded with the Blues Blasters by Checker Records and led to a performance on Dick Clark's famous "American Bandstand." Recorded but not yet released by the Beatles, it remains a popular blues tune:

Well, I know you heard of the Suzy-Q

And I know you heard of the chicken too

I know you heard of the cha-cha-choo

Cause The Walk is a dance that you can do

You just walk, you just walk

Oh, you walk, yes, you walk

Yeah, you walk, it has to walk

McCracklin's claim that he was the sole author of "The Thrill is Gone," which became B.B. King's signature song, is confirmed by B.B. King in a documentary film about McCracklin entitled "Jimmy Sings the Blues." McCracklin toured in Europe well into his nineties and died at the age of ninety-one in 2012.

Charles Brown was born on the Gulf Coast in Texas City, Texas, in 1922. He was raised by his grandparents and encouraged by his grandmother Swanee Simpson to study piano and perform in the church where she was the first female choir director in Texas. He earned a college degree in chemistry at Prairie View College, worked as a chemist during the early years of World War II and moved to Los Angeles, where he won a contest playing Earl Hines' "Boogie Woogie on the St. Louis Blues." He was first hired by Ivie Anderson to perform at Ivie's Chicken Shack and later joined Johnny Moore's "Three Blazers."

Between 1947 and 1961 he had several song hits: "Driftin' Blues", "Black Night", and "Merry Christmas Baby." The first two were lamentations about lost love; the third blesses the rare relationship that endures. He shared performance billings with Ray Charles, who became a devotee of Brown's warm, smooth style and claimed that everything he knew he learned from Charles Brown. Brown quit music for a time and with the help of Bonnie Raitt and others rebuilt his career in the Bay Area in the 1980s. He disparaged the "low-down blues", saying, "I never wanted to sing nothing about killing a woman. I had a more sophisticated style." He died in 1999.

Johnny Otis, drummer, blues pianist, vibraphonist, singer, bandleader and impresario, was born white, the son of Greek immigrants, but decided while growing up in a Black neighborhood in Berkeley in the 1920s to embrace Black culture. He said, "There is a richness about Black culture. The people from the South had brought that, their marvelous blues culture with them. And their whole culture of how they cook. We had the food, and we had the way of life. The way the young men walked and the way the young girls walked. The way we talked and the humor and the music."

Born in 1921, he launched his career as a drummer with Count Otis Matthew's West Oakland House Rockers in 1939. He left the Bay Area in the 1940s to join Harlan Leonard's Kansas City Rockers at the Club Alabama on Central Avenue and played drums with several other big bands in Los Angeles. His 1946 "Harlem Nocturne" was a hit, followed by "So Fine", "Double Crossing Blues" and "All Nite Long." His songs were mostly upbeat, cheerful even when describing a breakup as in "Double Crossing Blues." By 1950 ten of his songs were top sellers on *Billboard Magazine's* lists. Otis discovered numerous blues artists such as Etta James. He wrote her 1955 hit "The Wallflower", "Little Richard", "Jackie Wilson", "Hank Ballard", and "Big Mama Thornton."

On his Blue Spectrum label, he recorded and performed with Charles Brown, Louis Jordan, and Big Joe Tumer. He broadcasted "The Johnny Otis Show" for fifty years, first from Los Angeles and later from Sebastopol in Northern California. Otis continued leading a blues, jazz, soul, gospel and rock revue until recent years, and hosted "The Johnny Otis" show for fifty years, first from Los Angeles and later from Northern California until shortly before his death in 2012. His "Willie and the Hand Jive" was covered by many musicians, including Eric Clapton, in 1974:

I know a cat named Way Down Wille

Got a cool little chick named Rocking Millie

He can walk and stroll and Susie Q

And do that crazy hand jive too

Mama, mama, look at uncle Joe

Doin' the hand jive with sister Flo

Grandma gave baby sister a dime

I do that hand jive one more time

Haskell "Cool Papa" Sadler was born in Denver, Colorado, in 1935. His parents had come from the South and supported his desire to play guitar and write songs. He left Colorado in 1949, performed in Los Angeles for several years, and ended up in the Bay Area, where he formed a band at the Oakland House of Joy. His musical style was a combination of rough country and more mellow urban blues. Cool Papa recorded with Flash and Fantasy Galaxy, but most of his songs were never published and he received little money from the recordings.

His writing was focused on social and political issues such as the desecration of the environment and the plight of the homeless, and he tried to enter his name on the presidential ballot several times. "If I was President", outlined his platform:

If I was President

The first thing I would do

You wouldn't have to go hungry

There'd be plenty enough of food

If I was President

There's one thing for sure

Say if I was President, there's one thing for sure

You'd have a roof over your head

Wouldn't be forced to sleep outdoors

He and his wife Jane, who takes part in his interview, had to flee the South as a mixed-race couple, encountered racial problems in Los Angeles as well, moved to Las Vegas and Reno and finally settled in the Bay Area, where he performed in local clubs and schools until his death in 1994. In the 1990s he was invited to tour in Europe, and when the plane touched down in Copenhagen the King of Denmark walked out to the plane to welcome him.

Earl "Good Rockin'" Brown was born in Arkansas in 1931 and raised in Dallas, Texas, by a single mother who sang in gospel groups. He heard Louis Jordan play, signed up for saxophone lessons, and never looked back. In 1943 he moved to Richmond, where his mother went to work in the shipyards, and at the age of sixteen he joined Lowell Fulson's band, recording the blues hit, "Every Day I Have the blues." (The band included Ray Charles, piano, Billy Brooks, trumpet and Stanley Turrentine, tenor saxophone). He toured with Ray Charles and Muddy Waters and performed often at the Apollo Theater in Harlem. He lived with his family for six years in Alaska in the 1950s and 1960s and claimed that it was the only time in his life that he was free of racism. He died in 2019.

Tom Bowden was born in 1938 and grew up on Wood Street in West Oakland. He shined shoes outside of the Slim Jenkins Club for pocket money. He sang at talent shows at the Lincoln Theater and became a tough fighter, which earned him the title "Terrible Tom." He sang at Esther's Orbit Room, won one of the talent contests at the Lincoln Theater, and by the early 1950s was performing throughout California. He remembers the boarding houses along Seventh Street that were home to US servicemen and a close-knit community where people socialized on front porches and doors were left unlocked. Bowden shared California stages with Aretha Franklin, Richard Pryor, Etta James and Ray Charles. Bowden lives on Wood Street and performs at local clubs and blues festivals.

SPEAKING OF THE BLUES: EXCERPTS FROM THE ORAL HISTORIES

When the musicians talk about the blues, they describe the music in urban, hard-core terms, with references to difficult lives, or love has gone wrong.

Lowell Fulson: Any time with human beings—you can go back as far as you can go—there has been trouble. And wherever there is trouble, there is blues. Blues is just a person who is not happy. You and your husband quit each other. He don't look as good as he did yesterday morning, or whatever, and you go to brew about it, sulking at him, and he's snapping at you. Somebody's got the blues, and if you don't do something to correct it pretty soon, he'll be by himself. That's the blues. Music corrects it. Put your mind thinking. You build one house, it burns down, build another one. You can get out and sing the blues, whatever you can sing. Sing in the shower and you'll feel better, things look better to you when you walk out of there.

Sugar Pie DeSanto: God graced me. Blues has always solved problems. Just grab a song.

Haskell "Cool Papa" Sadler: I wrote about my leg being gone, onstage. I sang it before it was written. "I ain't got no kidneys but I still got balls!" About how the world is changing, about the homeless, and they're going to the moon in the spaceship like they did yesterday, leaving things here in the condition it's in. Poor man, about as far as you can go,what can you do? You tried and tried and tried and every time you think you're going to do something; the bottom falls out.

Earl "Good Rockin'" Brown: It's something you cannot fake. It's got to come from the heart. The blues is one thing where we can say, "This is OURS! This is our culture. What else can we say is ours?"

EARLY YEARS: GRANDPARENTS, THE CHURCH, THE MUSIC

Although most of the musicians came to the West Coast from different areas of the South, there are common themes in their lives. Grandparents were significant in their upbringing, and involvement in the church, usually at a

Sanctified Church, had a major impact on their exposure to music. There was usually a father or uncle who preached or a hymn-playing aunt or mother. Church-goer families pressed the children into service not only as singers but in the fields. Life was universally difficult for them. Below are excerpts about their early years.

Charles Brown: My grandparents, Conquest and Swanee Simpson, reared me in Texas. My grandmother was really into music, because her people were into music. We had a choir right there in our family. We sang and we was up sided. They was Sanctified. They just start off singing if they're happy; you'd have to catch them. I was able to play in any key, so I'd catch them, whatever they did.

Lowell Fulson: My grandmother was Cherokee. My grandfather, they called him Choctaw Freedman, because he was freed under Indian law, because he fought in the Civil War with the Indians. I was twelve years old when he died. Nobody bothered me coming up as a kid in Oklahoma. I'd be out there hustlin' on the guitars—they didn't bother me. I walked and acted like a man. I didn't have a whole lot of kid in me. [laughter] We had a Methodist Church and a Baptist Church and the Holiness Church they called it, and that's where most all the music was. It gave the kids something to listen to and something to do. It was something to keep them out of devilment just to hang around there and listen to the old heads play and talk about it. And if you learned to play that and the songs they sang. You could play just about anything else, now.

Jimmy McCracklin: My dad had cows, hogs, chickens, and all that stuff. That's why I made "Arkansas." I made it to the true facts of actually what sent down, as I was a kid coming up. We didn't have to buy meat. We raised our own cow. We did it all. We had to work. You know, the old man kept us working. We learned how to work and I'm proud of it now. Learned how to make our own living and everything. We didn't get nothing free. Pick cotton and chop cotton, pull cow and pick peas, we did it all. I believe my dad had about eighty acres. You want to know if we ever went bare-feeted? Okay, I'm gonna let you answer this for me: "Is an elephant heavy?"

Earl "Good Rockin'" Brown: Hard work—I can remember my relatives; they all went to the cotton fields, see? And I wanted to go with them, and they said, "No, you're too small. You'll be in the way, you stay home." And when I got older and realized what they was doing. I said, "Thank GOD I didn't have to go to the cotton fields."

Lowell Fulson: My grandmother wanted me to learn a lot about Fats Waller. She was crazy about his style of piano playing. So she went over to Galveston, Texas, and went to this music shop. She said, "I don't want the church folks to know that I like this kind of music. She bought "Lulu's Back in Town." She bought "Honeysuckle Rose" and "When My Dreamboat Comes Home."

Charles Brown: I started in the school dance band. Then I had a teacher, and he taught me the blues. I read a little but mostly I played by ear. Influences were "T-Bone" Walker and Lowell Fulson. That was my roots, that was the records they had. Lightning Hopkins and Muddy Waters.

Jimmy McCracklin: I wanted to be a fighter, I thought I did, and inasmuch, I left and went to St. Louis and got started in the boxing game. I won, there, three Golden Gloves. That's when I met Archie Moore. He's the one who influenced me in coming to California. But I got hurt in a car wreck. My shoulders got hurt, and was advised by a lot of people, say "You can sing until you get to a hundred you can't fight that long." So, I just picked up the blues. I used to watch this old guy, Walter Davis. I used to look at him playing and listen to him sing the blues. It just got into me.

Sugar Pie DeSanto: My mama, that's who taught me my music. She was a classical pianist, and she played ever since she was a very, very little young girl. She was a monster. She never read a note. Later on, I started hanging out with my soul people. That's when I started picking up the blues. Etta James and I grew up together. Johnny Otis named us. (Sugar Pie's original name was Umpelia Banton; James' was Jamesetta Hawkins).

SEVENTH STREET, OAKLAND, CALIFORNIA

The Bay Area was a place of promise and excitement in the 1940s. This is the way Seventh Street looked to those who landed there:

"Terrible Tom" Bowden: I shined Count Basie's shoes [on Seventh Street] yeah. Told him I'd sing with his band one day, too. That's another story. But that was my greatest desire. That was at the Showcase. I did "Every Day I Have the Blues" with Count Basie.

Lowell Fulson: I had seen the bright lights, and when I got back there in Oklahoma, I said, I can't stay here, wasn't enough NOISE! So, I came on back— that was along about the last of May in '46, and I stayed right around there in Oakland, Vallejo and San Francisco. Oh, my beginning was right up there. I was walking around from Seventh to Eighth Street and I heard some music playing and said, "Where's that coming from?" So, I went up there and Bob Geddins had a one-man press pressing records, in his garage. I think it was the Rising Star Quartet. When they got through there, I picked up this old guitar saying, "Man, I want to play and sing." So, I'm singing the blues, and they said, "Fine." That was what they wanted.

Cool Papa: Oakland was great for the blues. Slim Jenkins and House of Joy, Manhattan, you had the Morocco, you had the Club Rumboogie, which is the Continental Club now. I put a band together for a little club on Seventh Street.

You know the House of Joy? Little Willie John used to come there. Bob Geddins. I knew Sonny Rhodes like my brother. Frankie Lee, Mississippi Johnny Waters, Ted Butler, Johnny B. Goode.

Charles Brown: Slim Jenkins, if you didn't play what he wanted you to play, you couldn't get a job there. He wanted you to play the blues. He was nothing but the blues, and the people coming there came to hear the blues. I played up and down Seventh Street, from the Southern Pacific to Seventh and Washington in Oakland. Slim Jenkins had the main club there, and there was another club called the Down Home Club, in fact, they had about ten clubs up and down Seventh Street. Any time you had to have the blues, you'd be on Seventh Street.

RECORDING THE BLUES AND PIRACY

The Oakland blues musicians knew little about copyright laws and publishing. They passed their recordings around, hoping to get a contract, and too often their songs were claimed by others who took out copyrights and reaped the profits from million-dollar sales. This was the case with McCracklin's "The Thrill is Gone." It is generally acknowledged that he wrote the song, but someone else took the copyright and profited from the proceeds.

Cool Papa: In the early days I did these recordings for Flash label and first thing I know it was sold. Bob Geddins took me out there and we dubbed it in Johny Otis' studio. I didn't get nothing for that. The way they used to get you they still get you same way. First thing they'd do, they'd bait you with a new car. Nice apartment. Figured you came from working class of people or something of the sort. Apartment in your lap. You can't say no to that and there aren't no ties you think, but they keep a bookkeeper. At the end of the year they'd come to you for x amount of thousands of dollars for their services. Oh, they'd taken care of the apartment, bought you new clothes, new Cadillac, and all that kind of stuff, Buick, something, and they'd cut the song you wanted to cut and that song could make a million dollars. "Tell you what we'll do, we'll go back in the studios. We'll do it again and call it even. You'll get gigs out of it." In them days that's the way they did it. You'd get nothing and you were so glad to get out of debt.

Jimmy McCracklin: It was about 1948 when I started making all them dubs. We used to run to the studio; it didn't cost us but two or three dollars. I'd come up to an old man and say, "You want to hear this dub?" "Yeah, leave it here, I'll listen to it." You got about twenty or thirty-five dubs stacked up on there, and they'd take them and sell them. They took advantage of it. We knew nothing about copyright and publishing, all that stuff. In them days, ninety percent of the average Black musician, blues singer trying to get out there and get a name for himself, all he really cared about was getting his name on the label. What they'd do, they'd take the Black guy's stuff, put it out, put their name on it, publish it, sell it as in-house publishing, while we didn't know how to do that. And see, people like Bob, and the Bihari Brothers, and we be walking down the street, smoking a cigar, like we done did a great thing. We have, for somebody else.

TOURING THE BLUES

The Oakland musicians toured the US and were always in demand in Europe. Sugar Pie DeSanto and Jimmy McCracklin toured there well into their eighties. Cool Papa remembered a European tour that started in Copenhagen. When the plane touched down, he looked out the window and saw the King standing on a red carpet. His royal highness had come to welcome Cool Papa personally.

Charles Brown: We went to playing at tobacco warehouses in the Carolinas and the Virginias. On down into Georgia, Alabama, Mississippi. We had a lot of fun and met a lot of people. People were GOOD down there they just open their doors to you, oh, man! There are some good people down there. I lost my drummer down there. One of them girls took him off there and I haven't seen him from that day to this. And of all places, Hattiesburg, Mississippi.

Cool Papa: I was astonished by Europe, I really was. The places that you play at big old auditoriums, marble stairs, brass rails, teakwood, ivory all over the place, and what I like about Europe they came to see you! I don't care if B.B. is playing next door, they come to hear YOU! I went to Copenhagen, Amsterdam, all over Norway and Sweden, went to Germany and ended up in Iceland. I'm telling you they'd have a line around the block. You play your heart out all night long and a lot of people told me I made their day. That's my million dollars. That means I'm doing my job and I've done something.

Lowell Fulson: When I met Big Joe Turner, we teamed up, and that ran for ten years. They called us the Big Three: Lowell Fulson, Big Joe Turner, "T-Bone" Walker. We went to every state big enough to caravan in this United States, going South and North. We went to New York in '61, 62. The Apollo was all right. But couldn't keep from shaking because I was so scared. Moms Mabley was the emcee. I refused to go back to the Apollo because they worked you too hard.

RACISM

Racism has been a constant in the lives of African-Americans. It followed the musicians from the South to the West Coast in a form less explicit than in the South but equally pervasive. When I first interviewed Jimmy McCracklin in the 1990s, a cross had been burned on his neighbor's lawn in Oakland.

Johnny Otis: Racism doesn't care how excellent a human being you are. Either trained or an innately fine person. Racism cuts all that down. In the North, they just wouldn't give us a room. And in the South, there was nowhere for us to eat, and also in much of the North, the same thing. So we wound up eating cold cuts, or, if it was a big enough city where there was a Black community, we'd find a Black restaurant. And if it was big enough there might be a little Black where we could stay too.

Lowell Fulson: We were in Atlanta doing a concert. Stan Kenton and Dizzy Gillespie played a concert, and me and Dinah Washington and Earl Bostick played the regular dance. And they had a rope in that big, old auditorium, and we got to jumping up and down and playing that music and before we knew it nobody knew WHERE that rope was! They thought they had to be there to guard things, you know. Keep the Blacks separated from the whites. But they didn't have no luck that time.

Cool Papa: I got busted a lot of times, just for being a musician. They'd hold you for suspicion, just something to hassle you with. They didn't find nothing because wasn't nothing to find. They didn't have no proof, they just said they did and you were suspicion. They'd bring you through the lineup and all that kind of mess. They got me for that a couple times. I had trouble with the police back in Los Angeles because I mix married then. Back in the early 50s they just wasn't ready.

Earl "Good Rockin'" Brown: The Klu Klux Klan people came on the bus hollering obscene names to us. Ray Charles was standing on the other side of me. We all had our hands up against the bus. Our manager was a three-degree Mason. He shook the policeman's hand...and then he whispered something into his ear, and this man say: "We want everybody just go on home. We're going to escort them on through the town." They put out their torches and turned off the lights and we was escorted through Macon, Georgia, and on our way. You'd be surprised. Since Martin Luther King's passing; you would hope things had gotten better. But things have gone backwards.

WRITING THE BLUES

And finally, this is how they wrote the blues:

Jimmy McCracklin: Supposing I would know a friend and I would see that friend was doing all he can in doing the right thing, and someone maybe he's in love with is using him. That could have been me. It could have happened to you. You got to have something to write about. So, if it's happening in my life or in somebody else's life, that made me want to write about it.

Sugar Pie DeSanto: I write about the life I've lived, things I've gone through in real life; marriages, divorces, whatever. It's put in a song, and it's how I've lived. Al my writings pertain mostly to me. They make for good stories.

Lowell Fulson: It don't take me long to write no song. I get my mind made up, I see that my life and other folks' life, I'd write a song within two days. But see, writing a song ain't all of it. The meanings of what you writing, and putting the right melody to it is what counts. My songs changed from two guitars to a twelve-piece band. You know, there's got to be some changes made along that. Yes, I had to change. If I didn't I would have stayed in the chittlin-switch mode which was an old beat-up piano, couple of little guitars, a harmonica.

Cool Papa: I'm going to write about the President. I hope he is going to do something. I believe he'd like to do it, but it don't work like that. Congress doesn't work with you, you can't get too much done. The President loves the blues and that's good sign. A darn good sign.

Interviewer: Caroline Crawford

Date: October 24, 1995

Location: Charles Brown's apartment at Harriet Tubman Terrace in Berkeley, California.

Charles Brown
Credit Caroline Crawford

Brown wore a sequined cloak and cap during the interview, during which he sat at the piano and played to illustrate the conversation.

Crawford: I'd like to start at the beginning and ask you to tell me about your life in Texas from your birth in 1922.

Brown: I'm from Texas City, Texas, a small town on the mainland. Galveston is right across from it, like a little island. Everyone claims Galveston as the town, rather than Texas City. We would all go to Galveston to do our shopping— my grandmother, who reared me. My mother died when I was six months old and my father was killed by a train when I was going on six years old. So, my grandparents, Conquest and Swanee Simpson, reared me and my grandmother was really into music, because her people were into music. Her brother was a preacher, Reverend James Harrison. He was out of Wharton, Texas, which was sixty miles from Texas City, and he had his church. He had his own church, called Prosperity Baptist Church, and he was also the choir director of that church.

My grandmother was the choir director of Bible Chapel Baptist Church in Texas City, so she had the choir there and she played the piano. So, they would run contests to see which choir could beat each other. So, my grandmother would always beat him, because she even could sing bass. She could sing soprano and bass, and she had the chorus, with a cappella singing. They'd go into Wharton and with that harmony, at that time. Because people weren't used to good harmony. She had that, and that's what made her really prominent. So, when we came up, she wanted to put me in the same position she was in, as a pianist with the church. Well, my mother told her when she died to take care of my little boy. In fact, that was her favorite daughter; she had that in mind to do. So, her idea was to give me an education, if she could and lived long enough, and music. She said, "Well, you'll have a white-collar job. You just get up in the morning, you go to work, maybe at eight o'clock, and you're back home at four." She said, "Now, if you do the music and you do that, you go maybe work four hours a night and you make good money." She said, "But I don't see you doing that; I see you playing for the church and the school." I said, "Thank you, grandmother." So, as we went along, I used to walk, then being six or seven years old, with the choir. Just like a little boy who's interested in being something in the church for years, when he gets older. So, she brought me up into that. So, then I did that.

When I got to be maybe six years old, she thought she'd take me to this music teacher. Because I was even taller than the average little boy of six, so she even put me in school; I went to school at five years old, a kindergarten school, and right on into the regular school. So, she took me to this music teacher when I was six years old, named Miss Jones. My grandmother would sit there to see what she was teaching me, so she could help me when I would practice at home. But Miss Jones spent more time trying to get my fingers right on the piano and hitting my knuckles. She'd say, "Put your fingers in here. Put them in here." So, when the lesson was over, I think it was thirty minutes to an hour, they'd ask you for $5.00 my grandmother would say, "Charles, how do you like Miss Jones?" I said, "Mama, I don't like her because she hurts my knuckles." She said, "Well, I'm not going to take you back to her anymore." She said, "I'm going to teach you all I know, and then we'll find a good teacher in Galveston, Texas, and we'll let you go take music under her."

So, she taught me what she knew, because she played with the church. But she said, "Those notes with those flags on it, I don't know what they are." Because all the songs, years ago, used to be half notes and whole notes. So, they had to do what they had to do with it. She only played accompaniment. All right, she did that and she taught me, and I got the chance to learn more about the basic things in piano. So, when she heard about this girl named Janice Felder, who was a concert pianist. She had gone into Raleigh College, and she got a master's degree in piano, scholarship, because she did these scholarships with different schools. They had who was the best pianist; she won every one of them. And quite naturally, she was playing out in Dickerson, Texas, which was about twenty miles or so from Texas City. She was playing in a big church; Reverend Cole was the preacher.

My grandmother wanted me to go out and hear Janice Felder and Reverend Cole. So, we went out there. This woman could play a piano. With that man singing those spirituals like the blues. Women were falling out and shouting, and the men was crying. I mean it was just interesting, just to see that. The way she played that piano, it was way beyond what you would hear today. She was just that great. She was way ahead of her time. Tall, thin, ladylike and she was doing her master's. She was young. I guess Janice must've been maybe in her early twenties or so. I was about maybe eleven years old.

So, then my grandmother went and asked her, and said, "Janice, my little boy loves the way you play, and I do, too." She said, "I really want him to take lessons from you. Do you give piano lessons?" She said, "Miss Simpson, well," she said, "I'm pretty busy," she said. "But why don't you bring him over to Galveston?" She gave my grandmother the address and she said, "Let me see what he does." My grandmother took me over. They had a lesson for $5.00 an hour. She saw my fingers, that I'd already got the basics, so it wasn't a problem, no problem. It's a matter of holding your hands in a certain way and how to do your exercises. Of course, I hadn't gone through how to exercise with both hands. Then she took me in as her pupil and I began to learn a lot from her, in classical piano. Then my grandmother wanted her to teach me some of the sheet music, because she loved Fats Waller. My aunt, one of her daughters, had a little place called Hollywood, where she had jukeboxes in there. And on a Saturday night, the church sisters would come over there and they would sell ice cream and pound cake and cook fish. So, they would sell that to give it to the people.

They'd sit outside, even though they were in there dancing, and they'd come in and buy this stuff for the church. So, Saturday, returning to the church what they had made that Saturday night, and they were seeing who could raise the most money in the church. That's why they did it. So that was wonderful. So anyway, my grandmother wanted me to learn a lot about Fats Waller. She was crazy about his style of piano playing. So she went over to Galveston, Texas, and went to this music shop. She said, "I don't want the church folks to know that I like this kind of music.

Crawford: They thought it was sinful.

Brown: Yes, sinful. So, she bought a box of sheet music. She bought "Lulu's Back in Town," she bought "Honeysuckle Rose" and "When My Dreamboat Comes Home." These are great tunes that Fats Waller had done on the jukebox.

She said, "Now, you've got to learn these." So, she took them to my music teacher Janice for her to teach, because Janice could play anything. She wanted to know how to get into playing a little jazzier, how to take those chords and do something with them. But I haven't got into that yet. All I was getting into, the sharps and the flats and how to do my exercise and read the notes.

Well, that went on, and finally when I got a chance to go into high school, I was well groomed about the piano because I was taking classical piano. So, there was a fellow named Mr. Costello James, who had the physics department. He was a saxophone player, too.

So, he played out on West Beach for a lot of the Italian places. He found that I could read well. And it was hard to find piano players available at that time, so he said, "Well, Charles, I can give you $18.00 a night to play in these places, and it'll help you when you get ready to go to college."

So, I did that on the weekends, Friday, Saturday and Sunday. Of course, school was Monday, Tuesday, Wednesday, Thursday, Friday, so Friday night, I would go over there and play. And I learned to read a lot of those stock arrangements, but I could never really solo yet, unless he had it written up there. Like a lot of Count Basie or "Beer Barrel Polka" and all of those songs, which was very popular with the Italian people. And "Roll Out the Barrel." You know the polka. That was a great experience for me.

Crawford: Where were you playing then?

Brown: That was in Galveston, Texas, out on West Beach. It was a lot of Italian clubs out there. See, West Beach was really for the colored folks to play, but they had white people's places out there, and they didn't go into them.

They had their own businesses, but the colored people would use that beach. They couldn't use East Beach, because it was for the whites. It was segregated. But everybody would do the little beach walk and go out there, go in the water. They didn't care. But the clubs was doing good because the white people came to the clubs; they didn't go in the beach.

Well, that was a great experience. So, I had that experience, when I went to college. So, when I finished high school–I played for vespers in high school, along with another girl named Bessimer Bradley. We were the two best piano players at the time, because I had really improved myself for reading. But it was really good. So, when I went to college, I had the experience of playing with Mr. James, with the band. See, he had a little group playing for these things, so I had that experience. But I was kind of country when I went to Prairie View (Prairie View A&M College), because you knew a lot of people'd come into the city and they were dressed all fine, and we didn't have but one outfit. My grandmother bought me just a blue suit, because it was a military school. They had uniforms so everybody would be classed the same way.

Prairie View College was a military school. Those guys who had great clothes, they had to wear those military uniforms, just like everybody else, so they couldn't show off how great their parents had bought them different things and how their parents were much over our country parents. So we figured we were on an equal basis with them.

But my education, I was very smart and I liked chemistry and mathematics. I wasn't so much in English. I didn't care for English, really, because of all of those theses that you had to write, and you had to write different things that they want you to do in English. I thought it was just too much time. But I had to do it, so I did it, to make grades. When I went to college, I had to take English, too, American history and whatnot. I didn't like history too much, but I had to conform with what was required. So, the first year I went to Prairie View, I didn't make too good of grades because I wasn't used to it. I had to go to conferences and find out what did I needed to do and how to study, because high school was quite different from college.

So, I called home about what to do. Then I started making A's and B's, all through my senior year. I got to write a thesis. I majored in chemistry; I minored in education and mathematics. But now, when I did that, music, I took one semester of advanced piano because I was playing better than the kids who were taking four years of piano, because I had that background. If you have ten grades of piano before you go to school, it's like ten grades of high school, or twelve grades, then you're advanced enough to go into higher things with music. I wasn't in the Prairie View band yet. But one day I was going into notation and terminology, my seven-thirty class. And when I came out, I was just touching the piano, because they had these beautiful pianos in this music school conservatory, where the teachers taught the kids.

Crawford: At the school.

Brown: Right. And so, I'm doing the classes; they had them up there, too. Like taking notation, terminology, how to read, knowing about music description and different signs and things. Well, I was just plain practicing one day. So, this fellow named Mr. William Henry Bennett, who was over the Prairie View orchestra, came in. I was just practicing. He heard me practicing, and said, "Boy, where you from?" I said, "I'm from Texas City." He said, "You play the piano real well."

Said, "We could use you. You a freshman?" I said, "Yeah." He said, "Well, the main pianist is a senior and he's going to be going out this year and we're going to need somebody to take his place." He said, "Why don't you come to rehearsal?" They had rehearsal on Thursday night, and to see what they did, so I could kind of be in line, if I did take to it. So, the guy was named B.H. Rhymes, who was the pianist of that orchestra. And I went and listened. So, after Mr. William Henry Bennett told him that I would be the next one to take his place, he started trying to show me what to do when they took solos. He showed me what to do and how to play those solos like Teddy Wilson, that was with Billie Holiday. He could play that, and he showed me how to do it. I caught on real quickly, how to do it. Said, "When you take a solo, you do this. You do that. And then the band comes back in."

Well, I took all that in mind, what to do, and I started trying to do it. I wasn't good at it, but I kept on till I got good at it. So, then he was sick and we didn't know it. He had breaking out of his skin and they said it was really syphilis, which [there] was no cure at the time. But you're not supposed to be in school with any kind of disease, but his people had plenty of money and they were hiding it. And he was taking these spinal shots and everything, to try to offset that. They said it's spinal tapping and whatnot. But it didn't do any good. So, one day I came down out of my eight-thirty class and he was at the piano, because he was studying for his concert, for his graduation, his thesis, with the Concerto in B-flat minor, by Tchaikovsky, for two pianos, with the pianist Mr. Fuller, who was his teacher. That was his thesis, and he was there practicing.

So, when I came by and he had been practicing, but he had stopped practicing, I guess, and was laying on the piano like this. So, I said, "B.H.," I said, "What's the matter?" He said, "Charles," he said, "I feel like I'm going a long ways from here. I'm never coming back." I said, "But you're going to finish this year." That must've been around, oh, May, because school went to June. I said, "Well, what's the matter?" He said, "Look at me." He said, "All these boils." And he said, "If I bust one with a white fester, another one makes a sore." He is the first guy I've seen, had a record player, portable, in school, because his people had plenty of money. I had told him, I said, "Ooh, I wish I had something like that." So, he says to me now that he remembered. He says, "Charles, you can have that record player." He said, "Because I won't be here." I said, "What do you mean?" I said, "No," I said, "I don't want that record player, B.H., I don't want it." He says, "Oh, no," he said, "because I'm going a long ways from here. I'm never coming back."

So, I went and told Mr. Fuller, who was his teacher. I said, "B.H. must be really sick." And I said that somebody should do something about it. So, they had a Wednesday for the teachers' showings of the pupils, and he played for his thesis with Mr. Fuller. We went to see it. And he played that concerto, do you hear me? He put his whole soul, with two pianos. So, after that, they took him to Houston because he was sick. But he played over the sickness. And they took him to Houston. And when they took him to Houston, those people had treated him so bad. His mother and father had died and left him a lot of property there. On his sickbed, they wanted him to sign things over to them if he died. He said. "Well, you talked about me, so I wouldn't sign a thing for you."

A lot of this stuff went to the state, because nobody got it. I didn't go around there, because that wasn't my business then, because I was too involved in what I was doing. So we went to his funeral and everything. But that started me, really, into knowing how to solo. That experience that I had with the band. On days off, we'd take our lessons where we had work to do. They had little jobs to play in Dallas, Texas, that they booked through Prairie View. They booked the little towns like Bryan, any type of club to play, and we made a little extra money; it was $18.00 a night, that you made. So our monthly payments were not but $18.00 a month.

Crawford: For tuition.

Brown: Yes, for tuition. Well, I thought this was great because I could help her pay my monthly fees. And I could save a little. My books were kind of high, but could offset the books that you had to buy, so it took a lot of weight off my grandmother and my grandfather.

So, everything was working good. I went all through school with that. I played with the band all through my senior year. So that gave me a great experience. I was playing real great then I was ready for anything then, because I had the experience. All of the principals would come out when you get to graduation, your diploma, and find out which person they wanted to teach in their schools. The principals would pick who they wanted. So a fellow named Mr. Archie, out of Graytown, Texas he said, "Mr. Brown, I want you to be in my school, Carver High School. I want you to be over my chemistry department and then you could play music with Miss Calma. We all finished school together." So, I got the job that September. I got the job that September, going into school as a teacher. He put me over the science department and eleventh and twelfth graders, a homeroom teacher. So that was an experience. I was only nineteen years old. So, I taught in that school the George Washington Carver High School—very close to Houston. It's only mainly water, the Gulf of Mexico, and the Galveston Bay runs right by there. So they're right on kind of a mainland coastal route, Baytown and all of them.

So, I worked there. I worked there from September until around about January of 1943. But then I found out that the pay wasn't so good; it was only $90.00 a month. And my rent took up most of that; I only had $5.00 left out of it. Well, my grandfather helped me out, because he was down in Texas City, which wasn't far. He'd come up and give me a little extra money, because the $5.00 I had, when we'd go to church, the preacher would say, "All the men stand up, put $5.00 in the collection." So that took my $5.00; but my grandfather kept my front there, by giving me money.

Crawford: So you kept going to church all the time.

Brown: Well, on the weekend, see, they expected all the teachers to go to church. When school's out you have your Saturdays free, but on Sunday, you're supposed to be in church. Monday's back to school. It was Baptist church. So, I'm just saying they expected you to go to church.

Crawford: Tell me your grandparents' names. And what they did.

Brown: My grandmother was Swannie Simpson. And my grandfather's name was Conquest Simpson. My grandfather was more of a dredge boat worker, longshoreman. My grandmother was mostly into the church and the choir directing and what not and playing the piano. I knew them well, because that was Mama and Papa to me. My grandmother died my junior year, '41. Because I finished college in '40. So that kind of took a lot of life out of me, because I loved my grandmother. I always said that if she died, I didn't want to live. There were things that happened, even in dreams, that she came back and said that,

"You should go on, because I tried to live as long as I could." It's not a thing that I tell people. They won't believe it, so I don't even talk about it, because they would say, "Oh, I don't know how you could see that." But I did see things.

Crawford: That she was with you.

Brown: When my grandmother died, they all came down to Prairie View, because she was supposed to come down there that Sunday. But that Saturday night before she died, I had all these weird things whispering in my ear, looked like, saying, "You better go home tomorrow. You're going to die tomorrow." I heard these things. I said, "Oh," and I went to the high school. I went in and met Dr. Franklin. I told him, I said, "Something's wrong with me. I'm going to die tomorrow." I thought it was really me. He said, "Mr. Brown, we don't find nothing wrong with you, but we're going to keep you overnight." So, he did keep me overnight. And you know what they do; they give you medicines and try to conservate you. But then I said, "If I'm going to when I got up that morning to go to vespers, to eleven o'clock vespers– die tomorrow, I want to get up in the morning and go to vespers, in college." I said, "This'll be my last time to sing in the choir, because I think I'm going to die." I really thought so.

So, my grandmother was supposed to come up there that same Sunday to see me, because she had told me she was coming because she was bringing me these boxes of pineapple upside-down cakes and chicken and potato pie, in a big box. Enough for my roommates to eat, because they were waiting for that big box to come.

But anyway, so when I was up in the choir singing, I saw my uncle, which was my grandmother's son, my mother's brother, standing in the door. He had come in. I saw him, I said, "Oh, they're here now." So, I felt relieved when I saw him. So, when it was over and I ran by and I said– Uncle Dick is what we called him, whose pictures on the thing right there now. I said, "Oh, I'm so glad to see you." He's back on my dresser; I'll show it to you. I said, "I'm so glad to see you." I said, "Well, did Mama come?" He said, "No, she didn't come." I said, "Well, okay," because she told me she was coming. So, Papa's out there in the car, because he didn't come into the vespers. It was letting out and all the kids were going out. So, I went out into the car and my grandfather had his head down like this. So, I said, "Papa, how you doing?" He said, "I'm all right." I said, "Well, where's Mama?" Said, "Well, she's at home. But you know your Mama's been sick." I said, "Well, why did you leave her to come up here?" He said, "Well, all the daughters back there, they're looking on after her. It ain't that serious, I don't think."

So, all that really hit me. But something told me, I bet my grandmother's dead. So I ran across this campus to go to my dormitory. I said, "Mama's dead. I know she's dead." And I ran to my dormitory, and they followed me in the car. They jumped out and went to my room and everything. I said, "You tell me, ain't Mama dead?" He said, "Oh, no, she's not dead. She'll be all right. We're going to take you home." I said, "Well, I need to go now because I could help her." I figured I could do something; but actually, nothing you could do.

But so when I went to get blue clothes, my military uniform–I was going to wear it back there–he says, "Get that blue suit." I said, "What do I need–" Said, "Well, you might have to use it." Because that's the only suit I had. I got the blue suit and I said, "Is Mama dead?" "Oh, no. Well, you never know what's going to happen, so just have it here." So we got in the car and I kept on inquiring. "Well, what did she do?" "Oh, well, she went to the doctor last night," and so on and so on. "Her kidneys didn't move and whatnot and they drained them out. Said, "it looks like she's going to be okay." But see, her kidneys went out from high blood pressure. Actually, they didn't have the things they have today, the dialysis machines. They said that she aged to look like she was eighty.

Mama was a good-looking woman. She was Indian-looking, part Indian girl, out of North Carolina. She had that beautiful complexion like Indians, with the little wrinkles. You know how Indians look with their little wrinkles and complexion when they smile? You can see. And she didn't have a gray strand of hair in her head. She was only fifty-five then. So when I got near Texas City, I said, "Is Mama really dead?" But I prepared myself. I said, "If she's dead, I'll try to hold up, because my aunts," who were her daughters, I said, "They'll want to see that I'm holding up and being strong, so they won't be hollering so much." So I made up my mind. Said, "Yeah, your mama's dead. So I've got to be strong." So when I got to Texas City, they were standing in the door, looking at the car. When I got out, they were looking to see, was I taking it. But I was trying to be strong. So late in the day Miss Carr, she said, "You've got to open up and cry, get this out of you. You can't do this. You can't hold this in you all the while." But I said, "Oh, I'm all right." She said, "No, you've got to cry. You've got to get this out of you." See, because it affects you. But what was really hurting to me when I got out of that car, my grandmother used to greet me, say, "Here comes my baby," with open arms, and hug me and smiled, because that was her heart, was me.

Crawford: So sad for you.

Brown: When I missed that, it almost tore me up. So we had an old cesspool toilet out in the back. We didn't have the running water, like they have here, because we'd have to go across the street to get running water out of the hydrant, because we didn't have it at our place. You had to go get buckets of water and get enough for the bath and whatnot. We had an old big cistern that would get the rainwater, and the tadpoles was in it, so they would boil it and use it for bathwater. But this particular time when I got home, I went out to this privy outside and I sat in there. And did you know– this is what I wanted to tell you; this door opened, just like I'm sitting here, my grandmother stood at that door, and she said, "Plummy," she said, "Now, don't you take it so hard about me." Talking to me just like I'm talking to you. She said, "I didn't go to your mother's funeral." Okay. So, it went on that way. So, I ran in the house, hollering and screaming, telling my aunts, "Mama's out there. Mama's out there. And she told me this about my mama, that she didn't go to the funeral." Well, they knew she didn't go to the funeral, so they had to figure out she was really there. And really, the howling took place. Everybody was yelling out there. You should've heard that house, that day my grandmother died. They'd taken her to the undertaker, the funeral home already. She wasn't up there. Everybody's hollering and crying and they would try to console them. You know they cook, have coffee cooking. We had an old oil stove, kerosene stove and everything. We didn't have electricity; we had lamps. And my grandmother always would get the good lamps, because she would sit up in the window and have the lamps on and look out the window. And she used to always tell us, when I'd come home during the summer, she said, "Oh," she said, "the grass is so pretty and green out there. See, look how pretty it is out there." She said, "But one of these days, I've got to go join my other children." She said, "You all ain't going to miss me." I said, "Mama, you can't leave us!" said, "We're going to miss you when you go." She said, "Oh, in a year, you'll forget about me. Because things will be turning over in your life, that you won't think about me hardly anymore." When you get to thinking about this, after a certain time, you may think about it, but it's not as prominent in your life as it was when they were living there.

Crawford: You don't forget.

Brown: You don't forget. So then as that went on, I started trying to take care of my grandfather, because he was still working, trying to send me to school. I really wanted to go back to school then because that was my junior year, when she died, and she didn't get a chance to see me finish. So, my duty was to go on and finish, to try to do what she wanted me to do, to be a schoolteacher. So that was my encouragement.

So, in 1942, when I finished, my job was to be a schoolteacher. I got the job, as I told you, in Baytown, Texas, called the Carver High School. So, all that went along a while, and when I found I wasn't making enough money, I was looking for a better job because I said, "I can't help my pop. I can't give him nothing out of this. He's still trying to help me."

So, when the government put out an advertisement about junior chemist, people who had finished college, there was an opening for junior chemists in civil service. So, I put in my application, which I passed. I had a choice to go to Pine Bluff, Arkansas, [or] Maryland. I chose Pine Bluff because it was closer to Texas; I could go back home, which on my day off, I wanted to go. So, I passed the examination, and I got the job as a junior chemist. It was $90.00 every two weeks, which was $180 a month, which was much better.

I left school to go take this job with the government. So, when I went to Pine Bluff, it was in mustard gas manufacturing. They had an interview for me. I have to tell you this. I didn't know anyone in Pine Bluff. The train brought me there early that morning because they were taking a lot of soldiers on those trains. I got off at Pine Bluff. Sitting in the station, it was cold because it was getting round about February. It was so cold, and I didn't know what to do. I said, "What am I going to do?" Because I had an interview that same morning at seven-thirty.

There was a taxi driver. I forgot his name. Herman was his name. Yeah, Herman. He came up there, he saw me sitting there with my luggage, and stuff. He said, "Boy, where you going?" I said, "Well, I'm supposed to be a junior chemist over here. I have an interview in the morning." He said, "Where you staying?" I said, "I don't have nowhere to stay." He said, "Well, I live in a place, 520 North Cedar, with Miss Bullard. Maybe I could take you in; she might have a room for you." I said, "Okay."

So, he took me over to this 520 North Cedar, to Miss Bullard. She told me, "Yeah, come on in." Said, "I've got a room for you." So, she said, "I'm going to fix you breakfast in the morning." Because it must've been around one o'clock or two in the morning then, and I had to be up at seven, to go.

Then they told me how I had to catch this bus to go into the arsenal, because I had an interview and had to go to what they called the academic building and wait for them to come get me on those little Jeeps, to go to the interview. So, when I went into this building, I told the lady I was Charles M. Brown, and I was there for an interview for the junior chemistry job. It was real cold, so they had one big heater in there, on the white side, that was just– all the heat was just coming out of the Black side. Wasn't even burning.

So, I sat over there. I know it was from seven o'clock that morning, seven-thirty, till eleven, she hadn't called me. So, I went back up there, and I said, "Miss," I said, "How come you haven't called me?" She said, "I'm not going to call you because you're sitting on the white side." She said, "Now, if you get back on the other side, I'll call you." So, I went back on the other side and she called, and this little Jeep came by to pick me up for the interview. So, I went to the interview, and they were majors, and all of them, they were asking me questions.

They're sitting around in a big circle there around me and they asked me where was I from? I told them, Texas City, Texas. They said, "What do you think about prejudice?" I said, "Well, I'm not prejudiced," I said, "because I learned to appreciate a person on the basis of what they have to contribute to civilization, barring race, color or creed."

They said, "Well, you don't seem to be from Texas," saying that.

"Well, another thing we want to ask you." Says, "We have some people who're working in this mustard gas manufacturing." It was hydrogen disulfide. So, they had to know how much sulfur come in those machines in sulfur and hydrogen, so they make this mustard gas. Smells like mustard. They said, "The people may not have as much education as you have." Said, "What would you do if you found out that you have to take orders from fellows who may not be educated as much as you are?" I said, "Well, I'll tell you one thing that I have learned. I took military science, and I learned to obey my superior officer. Makes no difference between what he was." That really shocked them. "You've got a job."

They said, "Now, we're going to tell you this. Mustard gas is very dangerous." They said that you have to really keep yourself good clothing, don't get burned, because it goes against your record. Said, "We're going to have a guy to teach you the format about how to draw samples, a guy from the University of Missouri." He taught me all that and I learned it well.

Crawford: Were you producing mustard gas?

Brown: No, you had to run samples from the vats, those big things, to know how much sulfur was in there and how much hydrogen. You had to get a sample every so often, so they know just how much hydrogen was coming in, so they [can] make the mustard gas. That's what we did. I had caught on real well. He said, "You have to use carbon tetrachloride, CCL2. So, when you get a burn, you have to clean up those tables so you don't get mustard gas on you." I never got burned. I was very smart about being careful. But one day, I don't know, I don't ever talk about it, but this fellow from the University of Missouri, we got to be very good friends. He liked me quite a bit because I did the samples and he said, "Charles, if you want to go eat today, I'll wait till later, because I'm not hungry."

But this particular one day he wanted me to go eat and I didn't want to go. I said, "Well, you go." He said, "Well, no, you go." So, when I came back from lunch, they said, "Your friend is in the hospital." The gas line blew up on him and it went all in his eyes and face." So, I went out to the hospital to see him. These blisters, ooh, he was ruined. It looked like his eye was popping out. He was just in pain, he panicked. He didn't even know me. He died. They evidently said it could've been set for me, because I'm a Black guy. Or colored. I don't believe it was, but it could've been.

Crawford: Did that go on?

Brown: Well, possibly it did, because see, I was the first Black junior chemist out there. They couldn't understand that. On my day off, I was at home and Miss Bullard was fixing some soul cooking.. and here comes these guys on my day off, knocking on the door where I lived at. Oh, five or six of them, in this car. And they were at the door.

So, Miss Bullard went to the door. Said, "Is Charles Brown here?" She said, "Yes, he's here." "Well, we want to talk to him." So, Miss Bullard came back there and told me. She said, "Don't you go out there," she said, "because they might kill you." I said, "Oh, Miss Bullard, I'm not scared of them." When I went out there, there was some of the guys who was working on the same floor. They said, "Oh, we want to take you over with us, over in the piney woods, and have some beer with us." I just went and said I'm going to go, because I wasn't no drinker, but I wanted to show I wasn't scared. So, I went over to this place out in kind of like the woods, and they had a little beer joint out there. They said, "Come on, go in here with us. We're going to have a beer." I said, "No, you bring me my beer." I said, "Simply because I'm not supposed to be in there, and you know it." They said, "We respect you for that." So, they bought me a beer, and I did drink it. And we got to be very good friends, and they took me back home and nothing ever happened. They became great friends of mine. Even on the floor that I worked on, they all seemed to like me, you know what I mean? They said, "You're a little different from the rest of them."

Then I go along and I did well, until I had a run-in with the second lieutenant. He had the clothes up there for the whites and the clothes for the colored. So, the clothes for the colored was kind of raggedy. And I had this information from the major, not to take any clothes that are not good, because you can get burned. So, when I went there this particular morning, I said, "I want a forty-six." He wouldn't go to the shelf. I said, "I want one off that shelf up there." He said, "*You're* not going to get it, neither." He says, "That's for the whites."

So he got to talking that he wanted to kill or hurt me. And they were holding me and guys were scared. The Black guys were scared, because here I'm running in. But I'm still a civilian. He had no control over me. So they went and told the major and the major came down there. He told him to give me the things. I forgot his name.

He said, "Whatever Mr. Brown wants from that shelf, you give it to him." "Yes, sir." I had no more trouble out of him when I'd go down there. But I figured that the tension was there. I wanted to leave. I said, "Because no telling what they might do to me."

So, I wrote to Washington, D.C. and told them I wanted to be put into another place, as a junior chemist. I said, "I'd like to come to California," because my friend was out here, as a Doctor of Psychology, Dr. Lawrence Jefferson. He was studying at UC in Berkeley. He had a place at Barrington Hall, so he said "Well, if you come out here, you can stay with me until you find a place and you get your job." So, they transferred me out here to the western research laboratory in Berkeley. But when I got there, that job was taken. So now, I don't know why it was taken; but now in the meantime, they classified me 1-A and then I knew it wasn't going to be long before they called me. So, I did little things to keep going out here. We would try to get a little job working in San Francisco.

Crawford: Playing?

Brown: Yes. We saw these pianos. We were going all up and down the Market Street to see what we could find, and we saw the Pepsi-Cola service center, where the servicemen had a big grand piano in there and someone was trying to play it. So, we walked there and we started playing boogie-woogie, me and Lawrence. He played well, too. And oh, they started jumping. We played and all the soldiers, oh, they were just dancing. So, we went up there and asked him, "Didn't he need some piano players to play that piano upstairs and one downstairs? So, he came down, "Let me hear you."

So, he heard us play and the soldiers was carrying on, the sailors and whatnot, and Marines. He said, "Well, I can give you a job, $60.00 a piece a week." So, we took that. That kind of helped us, because it was near the summer and we had that.

So, we worked there for a while and here comes Xavier Cugat. One of his talent scouts was looking for us to play on a Xavier Cugat show out here at the base, out from San Francisco. Hamilton Field. They were having a big show with Xavier Cugat and they wanted us to be on this show for the soldiers. Well, we didn't believe it. He said, "I'll meet you over here tonight and give you the directions." So, when we got through playing, we slipped around and went another direction and peeked around the corner, to see if he was there waiting. And he was.

But we said, "We're not going to go in that big place because we don't know that guy." Because we're young. So, we didn't come over there, so he never saw us. We didn't go to that Xavier Cugat show. I guess it would've been a great thing, had we done it; we didn't do it. So now it was, we went on down. The International Settlement used to be very popular in San Francisco. They had a place called the International House, where a lot of the merchant seamen would come. They had a band playing there, so we'd go over there. This guy called me to do a number, because Lawrence told him I could play the piano. And I did.

Crawford: Was that on Market Street?

Brown: That was on Kearny. Kearny Street, running up to North Beach there. Kearny, near Columbus and going up that way. So, we played, so that was a venture for us. That's where I got clipped. I had two wallets in my back pocket, with my little money in it. Standing up at the counter there, I got clipped off both of my wallets and didn't know it. When I went to reach and get money, I didn't have nothing. I started crying. Lawrence said, "What's the matter?" Because we didn't have no money to pay. But somebody paid for us, and we told the man we got clipped in there. Well, they were used to that. So, the man let us go and we went on, we got out of there.

So, we were wise to being clipped now, because I'd never been clipped before. So, we said, "Now we know what to do. We ain't going to go in there no more like that. I'm going to keep my wallet where I know where it is." Because the back pocket, you think ain't nobody would go in there. So that went on. So, in the meantime, I called my draft board and told Mr. E.V. Roach, who was the head of the draft board in Texas City, that I needed a little more time because I was trying to find an essential job, but not in the service. So, he said, "Well, Charles, we'll classify you in another class. Wait until we call you." But in the meantime, I volunteered, and I went back to Houston, Texas, into the induction center. When we left that morning, my aunts were all crying because they knew that boy ain't coming back.

Crawford: How many aunts?

Brown: I had three living then. Aunt Alice was her name, Alice Matthews, Ethel Paine; and Rosetta Nelson. So these three were living. My Uncle Dick was my mother's brother; he was James Simpson.

I had enough money to come back to Houston because Papa was there. So, when I went in, they said, "Can you read this?" "Oh, no, we can't read. I don't know what that is." So, when it got to me, I read it. I didn't pretend I didn't want to go. The others were pretending they didn't want to go. So, they went through all the examinations. When they got around to the heart specialist, they all went in that direction. So, they said, "Mr. Brown, did anything go wrong with your heart." I said, "Well, I had asthma." He said, "Well, Uncle Sam doesn't want a liability; they want assets." And he wrote, I think, D-I-S-Q, which means disqualified. But I didn't like the guy, and I said, "What does that mean?" He said, "You're disqualified, man." And he told me to follow that line going out that way, going home. Oh, my heart just beat for joy because I said, "Oh, now I can pursue what I want to do." Because I wanted to come to California again and see could I get into the music industry, playing in some hotels and making money, because a lot of the men were in the service, who could play piano, I imagined. I figured I had a free way to go then, because wasn't many men out there. A lot of music; and nobody to play too much, because a lot of men were in the service. So, I went back to Berkeley, and I got a job in the shipyards, trying to make some money in Richmond. That was good, as an electrician trainee. I'm making good money, and it kept me up on my money.

So then after I'd saved up enough money, I decided to go down to L.A. So,

Lawrence bought some train tickets on the Santa Fe, right at 40th and San Pablo, to go down to L.A. Okay, we get on this train. Before we got on this train, we bought the tickets. The conductor saw us buy these tickets. I put the tickets up in my bosom, and my extra money I had in my wallet, because I'm onto people, clipping you because I had it up here this time.

So here comes two Mexican guys. They say, "Did I see you working in Moore's shipyard?" And which I was working there. He said, "I remember you." He was talking to me and he was distracting me, talking. This guy had gone up in my bosom and got my wallet and those tickets. I didn't know it. So when we got on the train and the conductor was coming around for the tickets, we saw them sitting up where you could look through the doors and see them sitting up there, and they were waving at us. But they got off at the next stop from Berkeley, from San Pablo, whatever the next stop was, the train stop. They got off the train. But they had my wallet and my tickets and money.

So here comes the conductor, says, "Where's your tickets?" We went to feeling. my wallet wasn't there. I said, "Well, you saw us buy the tickets." He said, "Yes, I saw you buy them, but where are they?" I said, "Well, those two guys came up, the Mexicans. They must've clipped us." And we started crying. Honey, we boo-hooed, because we didn't want to get off this train because we were going to L.A.–

Crawford: You were on your way.

Brown: He told us, said, "Well, I tell you what I'll do. I saw you buy the ticket." But we go to the men's vestibule. "Go and sit in there." So, when we got to L.A., we didn't have a nickel. We had to walk all the way from the Union Station up to Fifth Street. Then when we got to Fifth Street, we didn't know nobody, and we didn't know where a soul was. We were hoping we'd see somebody. We didn't have no money, no nothing. So here we saw a fellow that was in Prairie View and taught school too, named Walter Clark. He said, "What you all doing down here?" He said, "I'm so glad to see you." Said, "We just got off the train." He said, "Well, I've been up here a long time." He says, "I'm out here with the Wings over Jordan." That was a group. Gospel. He was singing with them. I said, "Well, who else is out here?" He said, "the principal's daughter that was in school [where] I taught; her daddy was the principal, Mr. Tom Archie. She lived at 984 East 50th Street, so we walked all the way down there. to East 50th Street, from 5th Street. Well, we were laughing and talking and we were hungry as the dickens. When we got [there], they was all glad. Because old classmates, glad to see you.

She cooked some scallops, and I never will forget those scallops she cooked. We were so hungry, ate that. And oh, we had a good time playing the piano and carrying on. So, this was the venture. I sent for my papa to send me some more money and he sent enough so we could go back up to Berkeley. So, I went back up to Berkeley, but now I wasn't satisfied, because I wanted to come back to L.A." I'll make a synopsis how that got to be.

So, then I came back to L.A. to find a place, but where I stayed in Pine Bluff with Miss Bullard, on 520 North Cedar, she had told me that she had a brother living in Los Angeles who was a preacher, a Reverend Driver. And she told him about me being a piano player, too, and that if I ever wanted to come out to California, I could come stay with him. This was 1943.

Crawford: So, your time in Oakland was very short then.

Brown: Very short. I had a very short time to stay here.

Crawford: Do you remember any of the clubs?

Brown: I didn't play none of that, because I didn't know anything about Slim's or nothing, because I was young. The only thing we knew about it– I told you about going to the International Settlement. I didn't go to any of the nightclubs here because being a young student. You didn't venture to those things. Because Lawrence didn't go to them and I didn't either. But I went back to L.A. searching. I didn't even look for a job up here. I wanted to be in L.A. because Rachel Dell played the piano and she was going to UC, working on a master's degree, and I figured I could get more information down there, of where to play.

So, I went back down there, and I stayed with Reverend Driver. I told him to meet me, when I went on the train, because I didn't know what he looked like. He described himself to me, that he was a little Indian-looking man with a foxtail coat on. He had a church called the Saints of All God in Christ, at 22nd and Grove. He told me what he looked like when I got off the train, and I told him what I would be looking like tall and thin. So, when I saw him waiting for me, well, we kind of met; it was just where we said we were. He said, "Are you Charles?" And I said, "You're Reverend Driver."

So, he took me over to his house. He said, "My sister always talked about you. Nice fellow." So, he had a church, and he didn't have a pianist. So, when I went there, he wanted me to play for the church, and he would pay me. So, I did, because Sanctified people, they didn't have any music.

Crawford: What did you say, Sanctified? That is, an association of Holiness churches?

Brown: Yeah. They was Sanctified. They just start off singing if they're happy. You'd have to catch them. So, I was able to play in any key, so I'd catch them, whatever they did. They'd start off and I'd catch what key and play with them. Then when they start another song, I'd do that, too. But I was jazzing it up, because I really didn't know the songs; but I could follow what they were doing. It was routine church songs, but they were a little faster than [Baptists], because they did this. (claps) Everything was this, this, that. Because they'd get happy and shout and everything. So okay. I stayed then with Mr. Reverend Driver for a month or so. And my cousin who was a preacher out in Watts, California, named Reverend Sam Taylor, he heard that he had a cousin in California, and he heard about me, about me playing down in Warren, Texas, from my uncle, too. He said, "I'm going to get that boy." That's what he told me. He said, "He ain't no Sanctified church member; he's a Baptist."

Crawford: Tell me the difference. I'm not clear about it.

Brown: Well, the Sanctified people have a way of doing Holy Roller. They roll and they get happy, they do their little dances. And they have unknown tongues that they have, that comes, they say, from God. They get happy...with these unknown tongues. But that's when you're really supposed to have the spirit. And so they would roll, some of them would roll on the benches. They'd roll.

Crawford: That is what we call the Holy Rollers?

Brown: Yeah, the Holy Rollers, right. But now, the Baptists would just sit up straight. Now, they would shout, but they didn't have all that extra thing. None of them would get up and do nothing like the dancing. It was just a matter of just shouting, [claps] boom, boom. If you fall down, they would try to take you out of the church.

Crawford: Do the Baptists prohibit dancing?

Brown: Well, nobody was supposed to do anything that they thought was satanic. Just like the Catholics. They dance, but not the sign of the cross. You couldn't use the sign of the cross. If you dance, as long as you dance a way not crossing your legs or something. That was a sign of the cross. But the Baptists just didn't go for anything that was sinful, they thought they had to do with drinking or dancing or hearing that kind of music, because they say the Lord's music is just as joyous as the devil's music.

Crawford: The blues was supposed to be the devil's music.

Brown: Yeah, that's right. So, whatever you did. So, my uncle came and got me and I'm thinking about he has a big, fine church like Reverend Driver. So, I told Reverend Driver, "I have to leave. My uncle was here." He was living with my cousin. I called him Uncle Sam. He took me out to Watts, and said, "I'm going to feed you, boy. You don't have to worry about nothing." So, they were working at Terminal Isle extra. He was preaching, but he had extra money because it was paying good. So, when I got there to his house, I said, "Where is your church?" He said, "My church is right next door." Another house. He had five little members. And I had to play there. But he was feeding me; I had to go and play. The collection was sometimes like $3.00.

Crawford: But didn't people learn about the music there and they decided they would come?

Brown: Well, no, because he was doing the preaching himself, but he had his own little church he made up. So, he had only a few faithful members, because he wasn't no big preacher. He didn't have a great big church like the preachers got all these members. There are some people who like to be secluded from the big churches; they wanted to be in a little place where everybody could be together. Some people just didn't want to be in a big [church]. So, he had those same members. Quite naturally, they would come maybe five or ten; not ever more than ten members. So, I played for the church, but I got tired of that.

Crawford: You played hymns?

Brown: Yeah, hymns and things. So, he had an old big Buick and he had his daughters, Meg and all of them, and they would go down to town and we would ride on the rumble seat. He had a big old Buick with the rumbling seat. We'd ride down there. He would go down to LA. and say, "Let's go down to L.A. I want you to see this L.A." So, when I went down riding in the rumble seat with him, oh, just going through town and looking at L.A.

Crawford: You are going on tour soon. Where are you going?

Brown: To Germany. Cologne, Germany, which is Köln, in German.

Crawford: I know how they love you over there.

Brown: Oh, they love me there. Then I go to Paris for a week.

Crawford: Where are you going to play in Paris?

Brown: It's a club. I don't know the name, but Danny Caron knows the name of it. See, Danny does all the groundwork for me.

Crawford: Acts an agent?

Brown: No, he's my guitarist, but everything comes into him. I have an agent, but he does the groundwork that doesn't bother me, so I don't have to worry myself, because it's just too much for me.

Crawford: Wonderful guitarist, too.

Brown: A great guitarist. But he's very up on it and he's very intelligent and a nice guy. That's not our whole band; that's without the horn.

Crawford: Are you taking the trio?

Brown: We're taking the trio and the band and a horn. But when we go to Paris, we're only using the trio because the place is smaller, and he doesn't want it; he only wants the trio.

Crawford: What's the place?

Brown: I don't know the name of it. I don't know the name of it. Danny knows the name of it; I don't know it. But it's a place in Paris, yeah. The guy's been doing it for so long, but he can't afford to pay for a band. Our trio is just as strong as a band; we can play either way, so it don't matter. We've been to Paris. We've played the Hotel Meridian, we played all around Paris. We played down there where all the big rich people go, near the waterfront. We played a lot. In fact, outside of Paris, we played at a lot of other places in Paris. Then we played Germany; we played Italy, we played Madrid, Spain; we played Finland, to the North Sea Festival; we played Montreux, Switzerland.

Crawford: I know that one.

Brown: So I've been on all the nicer things. The blues can only go so far. You have to be in the current. See, I'm a borderline case, that I can play anything. But what we do is stick with our vocal things, the ballads. So, you stay away from that fast stuff. It's more of a creativeness for your ballads. The singing part of the jazz and jazzier type of things. We call it balladeer. So, it stays with that, rather than trying to (vocalizes quickly) and every minute is fast. Everybody's showing how well they are into their music or how much training they have and how fast they can play.

Crawford: Outplay you?

Brown: Yeah, that's right. So, it goes out of one ear and out the other. Yeah, there are people with that talent, say, oh, yeah, they play really good; but it doesn't do anything for the heart. When you hear a song that relates to something in your life, a love song, it makes you feel a little different. Now, you go to hear jazz for enjoyment. When you're not thinking about anything, you just want to go and listen to music and you're not really heartfelt about anything. You just go because I want to see what this guy does, see how good he is, so and so.

But when you go to hear a singer, you want them to really put you in a mood where you can reminisce of the things of your love and your life or whatever happened in your life. And songs can do that to you, whereas (jazz) music can't. Jazz can't, because it's too fast. You just look at it and listen to it because of the creativeness of the artist who performed it and how good they are. Like I tell everybody, I say, "Everyone's a king on their own throne, or a queen." You can't compare to say this one is better than the other one, because you have a kingdom, just like kings do. Every person has a kingdom. So, the kingdom that you have, the people who love you for your kingdom. They love that other person for their kingdom. But never the twain meet, because you've still got your kingdom. I analyze it like that. I analyzed it to that musical cake. A musical cake can make it good for the people to eat it and say that it's a good cake. You've got to put sugar, flour, butter, vanilla flavor, and many other little things that will make the cake really good, in how much you put in it. That's the way music is. It has to be a variety of little things to make the people really enjoy the fact that they want to eat it and listen to it. So, when you have things that you put the wrong ingredients in it, they say, oh, that ain't so good. I don't like that. That's the musical cake. That's why certain things in certain songs will not go, because it's not presented musically correctly. So, when you find somebody you can really create a good musical cake, people buy that to eat it.

Crawford: Are European audiences different much from what you play for here?

Brown: Well, now they're about the same because actually, now the people who really come to hear you are people who really want to hear you. Because the United States is messed up with so many variety ways of music—like the rapping and the things. Look like the people really go for something that's vulgar, sexy. Just like they have this woman doing all these nasty things. And they crowd in to hear the nastiness of things. Anything classy, you don't find them going. Just sing about church and things. People who go, who're the devil's people, they go in crowds to things. But the Christian people have a hard way to go. Well, it's the same with music. Anything that's offbeat, according to society, that they can make society come down to their wants and needs, then they figure that that's the way to do it. Just like you take rapping. I think that they've got guys off the streets who never had an education, they don't know; and they pick them up because they're doing this. They give them a little money and then they make them a start.

And it's terrible. It looks like little monkeys. They can put them on the Grammys and these guys, who I figured they'd have all this great money– I don't know who has it, but it must be some people who are from that kind of class that has the money. They make them a star, because they want their things to sell as much as the other. The people, when they hear it, they get so used to [it], the young people figure that this is the way to go. So they are [vocalizes], with the things up here. They don't hear anything of good music.

Crawford: But that's why it's so nice to hear your show, like the other night. It was crowded with young people. [at the Café du Nord in San Francisco]

Brown: Young people.

Crawford: They were loving it.

Brown: I don't go there often, I just go when I have little breaks. The man said I've done a great business for him, just coming there. They think I'm Prince or somebody, because they crowd in there like that. It's amazing how they enjoy it. But what I'm saying is, everybody has a right to what they like; but America doesn't seem to keep the roots in mind, of what America is about. Here the guys have written great songs, like the Gershwins and the Richard Rodgers and things, for the American music, for people to listen to, to introduce people like Quincy Jones, who played the Detroit sounds. And they said they're going to make that American music, and they brainwash the people with these types of things. That's not American music. When we were down there to play for the Kennedy installation, we were on the stage when the vice president and his wife came on the stage. If you ever saw that, you'll see me back there on the piano. They took the railroad station, Union Station, and made a place where they have different parks. Oh, it was beautiful.

I'm just saying what the people call the Motown sound is not American music. And what they call rhythm and blues is not rhythm and blues, what they call rhythm and blues. But you see, they used to have gospel, soul. But the only thing they could find, when rhythm and blues people were not strong enough money-wise to keep their things going, then the Grammys took up the rhythm and blues and said that when Whitney Houston would sing, it's rhythm and blues. And it's not rhythm and blues. They make jazz and blues secondary to the things that they have now, when American music was based upon jazz and blues generated, created here. They make even at the Grammy awards; they have the people come in the daytime to get awards. You can't go to the night sessions, and they put you onstage, because all the guys with the tuxedos on and the light flashes on them, they're getting paid 20,000 for the lights to flash on them. So, what they used in the Grammys, they say, "We invested so many million to get seventy million." They only give those people pots. Little pots. No money. And the record companies are pushing their artists; that's all they're doing. It's not what really, the people like. But they put this on the basis of this is a high-class thing. When blues and jazz should be on the shows, too. I mean the night shows. Say B.B. King won. They'll show his picture, well, he won in the first part of the thing, but not–

Crawford: But they don't focus on that.

Brown: They don't focus. And it makes you sick. Because even I told Mike Lynn, I said, "The categories that they put people in now is not the categories that it should be." They are talking about traditional blues. Traditional blues go back to people like John Lee Hooker or Muddy Waters. We're not considered traditional blues.

Crawford: Charles Brown.

Brown: No. Nat Cole, we were considered variety artists, because we could play the blues, but we could play pop numbers, too, ballads; whereas blues. artists, they only know twelve bars. They can only sing twelve bars.

Crawford: Regular twelve-bar blues.

Brown: Twelve-bar blues. See, and they try to put them on something else, a standard, they cannot sing it. Where we can. But we do our own bluesy way of doing it. But it just makes me sick. That's why I say I kind of stayed out of that picture. Because what I went out of the picture about, which you should know, is because my agency, I was the number one leading. After I left Johnny Moore, I was the number one–

Crawford: With Morris?

Brown: No. We were with them at first, with the Three Blazers.

Crawford: That's right.

Brown: But then when I went on my own, I went with Federal Artists, then with Billy Shaw Agency. It was the hottest thing, after I left Johnny Moore, because when they found out that I was doing the vocal and my style was very prominent, and all the record companies who was drying up, after Petrillo put a ban on the big band, the small companies were springing up. So, they had Modern Music, they had Exclusive Records, Excelsior Records. Anybody who was anybody was springing up, getting the little groups. Like Nat Cole had set a pace with the trio, that they found out they don't need no whole big band.

Crawford: Why did he do that, Petrillo?

Brown: Well, they weren't paying the things into the union that they thought these companies should be paying. So, he banned it, so that they couldn't make no more records.

Crawford: So, there would just be live performances.

Brown: Well, yeah, live performances, but they couldn't record. So, when they found out they could do it, these other companies started coming up, which Petrillo didn't have no control of.

Crawford: The smaller groups.

Brown: The smaller groups.

Crawford: Well, so were you a member of the union then?

Brown: Yeah, I was a member of the union then, because I was going with William Morris Agency.

Crawford: We should back up and go back to Los Angeles, when you first got there, what your impressions were.

Brown: Well, when I went to L.A. I was looking for work. When I left, I told you I came back, worked for the church; then I went out to Watts to work with my cousin, with his church. I didn't like that. So, I was going to find out some way I could get into L.A. and get a job and kind of get away from Watts,

California. So, I looked in the paper and I saw jobs available, elevator operator, at the Broadway Department Store on 4th and Broadway in L.A. at that time. So, then I said, "I'm going to go see if I can get a job, and I can get into Los Angeles," because I didn't know nothing else to do. I wasn't in the music field. I didn't know nobody, and I didn't know who to contact. I didn't know anything about the musician's union, where it was. But what I did, I went and passed the elevator operator examination, and I started running an elevator. The captain said all the ladies started wanting to get on the elevator; they liked my voice. I said, "Going up please. Going down, please. First floor, please. Second floor, please." And all these ladies were trying to get on the elevators, so the captain said, "Charles Brown," said, "The way these ladies like the way you talk," said, "You're going to be captain here soon."

But then during my lunch period, I would go up to the fifth floor in the Broadway Department Store. They had a music department up there, where they sold sheet music and the guys played the songs, for the ladies to buy sheet music. So, I heard him playing some song and I knew I could play those songs with a little addition to them. I would go up there, looking and looking. I said, "I can play that for you." I played it and their eyes opened. I jazzed it up, too. The lady said, "Well, I want that song." They said, "Where are you working?" I said, "Well, I work on the elevator." Said, "You should be up here with us." I said, "Oh, no. I'm working in an elevator." I said, "It's not time for me to be up here with you." Because they didn't have that, working up there with the white guys. But they liked me. So then I began to kind of search what I could find to do in music. I heard that they had an amateur show, I think every Wednesday night, like the Apollo, down at the Lincoln Theater, 25th and Central.

Crawford: Oh, Central, that was the big music place.

Brown: Central Avenue, yeah. So, we went on and so I thought I'd go down. I'd practice up real good, to learn this "Boogie-Woogie on Saint Louis Blues," that Earl Hines had made, that was a great record. So, I practiced that real good and I said, "I'm going to go down there and see if I can win a prize, and maybe somebody might see me and give me a job playing the piano." So, I went to the amateur show, and I went on there, and they asked me what my name was; I told them Charles Brown. I wouldn't say Texas City, Texas, because I thought nobody would know. I said, I am from Houston, Texas, because that was a big town. So, everybody who was from Texas, a lot of people from Texas, Louisiana, out there they just cheered me, before I even sat down at the piano. I sat down there; I was tall and thin and kind of nice looking. So, I sat at the piano and I started playing this thing [vocalizes], and the house started rocking. Well, the band joined with me. Johnny Otis was in the band; he was playing drums.

Crawford: Johnny Otis?

Brown: Mm-hm. Bardu Ali, who had formerly been with Chick Webb and Ella Fitzgerald, he was over that band for the Lincoln Theater, just like Apollo Theater had a house band. So, I played and they joined in with me. So, when I got up, oh, they really gave me the wonderful applause. Then they wanted me to go back and play again. So, I went back and I did. I said, "I'm going to fool them." So, I did *Clair de Lune* and part of *Warsaw* Concerto, and then part of the theme of *Rhapsody in Blue.* And sure enough, the house came down. Oh, they kept clapping, so I went off the stage; the guy got me off. So, he told other people, he said, "You know what? You should all go on out there, because he already won." So, everybody went out there after me, they said, "Boo! Boo! Boo!" So, then the people who were ahead of me, that they didn't boo, they let them come out there and they put their hands over their heads. But they put their hands over my head and I won. They put me out front. So, I think it was $25.00; whatever it was, I got it. And in the audience was Ivie Anderson's husband, named Marque Neal. And Johnny Moore was in the audience, too, and Eddie Williams. So actually, they saw me. I told them where I was working. There was a broadcast, so I told them I was working the Broadway Department Store, 4th and Broadway, because they ask you where you're working. And here comes Marque Neal. Ivie Anderson's husband gets on the elevator. Because now he wants a pianist in the place that Ivie Anderson and he had bought, called Ivie's Chicken Shack, where they had dinner music and they had little wines and dinner wines and whatnot. So, he got on the elevator.

He said, "You're Charles Brown?" I said, "Yeah." He said, "I was at the amateur show, and I saw you play, and I would want you to come into my place. Have you heard of Ivie Anderson?" I said, "Yes, she sang with Duke Ellington and I love her "I Got it Bad and That Ain't Good."

He said, "Well, that's my wife." Said, "We've got a place down on Vernon and Central, if you're interested." Said, "What time you get off?" I said, "Four o'clock." He said "Well, I'll wait for you, and I'll come and get you at four and we'll go down there." Said, "If you like the place," he said, "I'll put a tuxedo on you and I'll take you to the union and I'll get a union card. So, he picks me up and we go down to Ivie's Chicken Shack. He had this wonderful spinet piano, blonde, and he had a little spotlight up there and then booths around, where people sat and ate. It was a really nice little setting and cute.

He said, "You'll be making a lot of tips." So, when I saw this place, I said, "This'd be the ideal place for what I want to do." He said, "Because all the Black movie stars come here. Ethel Waters, Hattie McDaniel, Ben Carter, Mantan Moreland and a lot of others. Hattie Noel and all them come in here, Noble Sissle and his wife." Lawrence Brown and his wife, who was with Duke Ellington, played the trombone; and the young Bobby Short, who plays up in New York now.

Brown: We got to be all great friends. So, everybody who came to L.A., who was going to make a picture, would come out there. Ivie Anderson had her crew come out from the Circle Bar, where she's working, on Highland and Hollywood Boulevard.

Crawford: Oh, she was still singing?

Brown: Oh, yeah. Well, she was working in the club in Hollywood, because Hollywood Boulevard had just numerous clubs, like New York. It was just like Harlem in New York. They were like 52nd Street in New York.

Oh, you'd go down Hollywood Boulevard, they had the Circle Bar, they had Kid Ory, they had the Suzie Q; they had the Swing Club; they had the Florentine Garden, with Arthur Lee Simpson. Out there on Sunset, they had the Trocadero, where "King Cole" was working. But it was just all these things. Hollywood was just like New York. That's why they didn't worry about New York, because the movie stars and the servicemen frequented Hollywood Boulevard. And they used only Black entertainers to do the music. Only Black. You couldn't sit in the places. It was only for strictly the movie stars and the servicemen. So that was okay.

Crawford: It was more for the white audiences, on Hollywood Boulevard?

Brown: Yeah, it was mostly the movie stars, and then the white audiences and whoever, because Hollywood was full of people that were stars that you didn't know who they were. But they would come into the clubs and sit. The music you played was strictly background music for them to talk trash. It was interesting. But they used Black entertainers for the dancing, or bands would play. So, it was really interesting. And they paid you good money. So, my venture was really, if I could ever get down on Hollywood Boulevard, that's where I would want to be. So, after I played for Marque Neal, then the government sent a thing out there that those companies had to pay for. If you paid your money, you had to take out taxes. For whatever your check was, they had to take out Social Security, I guess, and whatever comes out of it. So, Marque Neal, that was okay; but I wanted to increase my salary so I would get to the same amount of money, because my tips were very good. My tips would be $200 and $300 a week extra.

Crawford: Oh!

Brown: I was making money, and I was just saving it in a big old sack. I had one of these big old sacks from the bank, I'd put money in. I had more money than I ever had, and I was saving. I was saving so Papa would be proud of me. Now I could kind of help. It let him know that I was doing some good.

Crawford: Helped him.

Brown: I wanted finally, one day, I could bring him out to California. So okay, that went along for a while. But when the government put this in, Mr. Neal told me, said, "Well, look. If you want a raise, you have to talk to my wife, Ivie. She'll be in tonight." So, when she came in that night and I had a chance to break, I said, "Miss Anderson," I said, "since the government is putting this tax on the thing, I would like to get a raise so I can make nearly the same money." She said, "Well, I don't know about that," she said, "because probably when I get back from Mexico City, I can think about it." It was the way she said it, so nasty. I said, "Miss Anderson, I want to tell you something. When you get back from Mexico City, I will not be here." That's when I left. So when I left, I got a little job working at Lincoln. They were crazy about my piano playing, so I got a job doing the piano for the chorus girls' routines, before they went on the stage. Like rehearsals. They were paying me $60.00 a week.

Crawford: Where was that?

Brown: That was in 1943.

Crawford: And where?

Brown: In L.A., right at the Lincoln Theater. Because the theater had a chorus line, too. We got to do that rehearsal with the girls on the chorus line, every show they made. So, they want you to play the music for the show, for them to learn tap dance. Whatever routine they wanted to do, they had to go buy music, so they hired me to play for that. So that went on for a little while, and then I wasn't satisfied with that. I had saved up this money, so I said, "Well, I want to kind of move up in L.A." I said, "I want to go where the movie stars are."

They told me Sugar Hill was where Ethel Waters stayed, and they told me where Ben Carter lived at Harvard. Hattie McDaniel, off of Washington Boulevard, near Western. Then Harvard and South Hobart, all right in there, came up between Adams and Washington Boulevard. So, I went looking for me, a place to stay. So, I found a place out there, at 2118 South Hobart, with the Reverend Davis family, Charles Davis family, senior. So, I got the place out there. So, I didn't have a job, but now I'm looking. I've already got a gist of things.

So Bardu Ali, who had the band, they were moving on to 1st Street, because they had moved the Japanese people. They took all those clubs from them, out on 1st Street, off of Main there, and they gave them to the colored people, because they put a lot of them in prison camps, the Japanese. So, they had a place called Chef's Playhouse. And Chef's Playhouse was a place the Japanese had, but they'd given it to the colored to use as a nightclub. So quite natural, the theater was closing because they claimed that it wasn't doing as good as it should've been doing. They said they had to move into Chef's Playhouse and bring the shows down there. So Bardu had the band; he asked me did I want to play.

They wanted me to come and play with the band, and he offered me a certain amount of money. I said, "No, I want a hundred-and-some dollars a week if I'm going to play down there." But he said, "We're not able to pay you that," so I didn't play. So, the next venture was, I stayed kind of dormant, until Johnny Moore and Eddie Williams came looking for me. That was when he had the Three Blazers. So now I'm still not doing anything now. I'm living up there, across from Ethel Waters, and not working. But I had enough money saved so I could kind of take it easy, because the rent wasn't but $20 a week, and so it was easy.

So, I hear this Reverend Davis's son calling up the steps, said, "Charles Brown," he said, "Johnny Moore and Eddie Williams are down here to see you about a job." I said, "Johnny Moore?" He said, "Yeah." So, I put on my robe, and I came down to talk proper. I said, "I'm Charles Brown." He says, "I'm Johnny Moore, with the Three Blazers. I'm the lead guitar; I'm Oscar Moore's brother, who plays with Nat Cole." And Eddie Williams said he was a bass player. Said, "We were looking for you." Said, "We went to every house to try to find [you]. We heard you lived in Sugar Hill, but we went to every house to try to find out where you lived." And said, "We went to this white lady's house," and asked her, "Do you know Charles Brown?" She said, "No, who is that?" He said, "Well, he plays the piano and he's a young guy." She said, "Well, I don't know about that, but I hear a piano next door going crazy every other day." That's what I did there, because I was practicing playing piano, when I had time, and she heard it.

They came then and there I was. So, when I went downstairs the guy told me Johnny Moore and them was down there to meet me and probably give me a job; he's with the William Morris Agency. So, I came downstairs, and they introduced themselves. They said, "We heard you play at the Lincoln Theater, and we were interested in you playing with the trio." He said that "Garland Finney, who was my piano player, died of a heart attack. And see, we were looking for another pianist and we thought you would be the one." So, he said, "Well, do you think you could take the job?" Said, "Where do you play?" I had studied Art Tatum's books; Art Tatum, on piano. "If I Had You," and I loved Helen O'Connell; I had learned one of her songs, "Take Me," and "Embraceable You," during the World War II. I would marvel at her singing, how she said the words and things.

So, they asked me to go into the big living room and try it out, to see what I knew. I played these things for them, and they said, "Man, that's what we want." Said, "But I tell you what, you have to put that left hand behind you with the trio, because when Johnny plays the lead guitar, you have to comp. When you play the lead, he comps." Said, "But we'll have to train you how to do that." He said, "You see how Nat Cole and they do?" I said, "Yeah, I've seen some of that stuff." And he said, "Well, do you sing?" I said, "No." He said, "You don't sing, with beautiful teeth?" I said, "No." "Don't you sing so good?" I said, "Well, I used to sing in church, and I did sing in funeral homes," because I was always asked.

When I was a little boy, I had a high voice. So, they said, "Well, let me hear you sing a number." So, I did "Take Me" and "Embraceable You." "Man, that's what we want." Said, "The man who owns the Talk of the Town, where we're going to audition, he wants the singer to be in the trio, and he doesn't want any ladies; he wants all men out there." So, he said, "Well, if we can practice that, we'll be making $600 a week; we'll divide it, $200 apiece, if we pass the audition."

So, the audition's supposed to be that September of '44. Okay. When they left, Reverend Davis' son–he's a preacher; he's living, but the other family's dead– he said, "Charles," he said, "This may be a good break for you." Said, "You should call Johnny Moore and tell him that you're interested." I said, "Oh, they're too old for me." Now, I'm young, you know what I mean? Because they were older. I was looking for somebody more on my order, because I'm young. He said, "Don't pay no attention to that. Why don't you call him? This may be the best break in the world for you to have."

So, I thought about it. I called Johnny Moore, and I told him I was interested. So, Charles told me, said they had a piano out in the garage, because they had an apartment over the garage; they had a little room out there with a big upright piano, said we could rehearse out there. So, we started rehearsing for the audition. And we got it down pat, singing and everything, and we went out to Beverly Hills and the Talk of the Town. They had twenty trios out there, for the same job. Johnny Moore's manager from the William Morris Agency told Johnny, when we got ready to go up there, about the eighth trio. He said, "Charles, show those teeth..." He said, "And smile." I guess that's why I smile all the time now, because he said to.

And sure enough, when we went up there and played, and we heard the other trios; they sounded very good. We didn't think we were that good. We thought we were okay, but what we heard the other guys do, we thought they were much better. Actually, I did, because they had more experience than we had. But we had our stuff together. Our theme song was Warsaw Concerto, the theme of– [he sings the melody] So when we did that, I went up there and I introduced Johnny Moore and the Three Blazers, and my name, and we went into our little work, what we had practiced. So, Mr. Vandergriff was standing back by the door and looking. We thought he was after us, that we had done something wrong. He said, "I don't want to hear no more trios." Said, "Johnny Moore, can you all open up here next week?" John said, "Yes, sir, Mr. Vandergriff."

And did you know that was really the start of things. We got so popular. So anyway, Mr. Vandergriff hired us, and all the movie star columnists started coming out there. Our tips were really great. Sometimes we'd do $500.00 a night. And people are giving us $100 bills. Monty Sontag, who owned all of Sontag's drugstores, he came out there and wrote a check. He wanted us to play "Summertime" for him. And we had these ladies who had the limousines and stuff, with the chauffeurs, come down. And we'd go from table to table, after a certain hour. I'd sit at a table and sing, while the bass and guitar would be walking around. It was really interesting.

So, we stayed there, was doing real well. Finally, ASCAP [American Society of Composers, Authors, and Publishers] came in, and they wanted for Mr. Vandergriff to pay money for using their songs. He said, "This is a democracy." He said, "We can use anything we want to use and don't have to pay nobody nothing." But they insisted that he should pay some money. Mr. Vandergriff said, "We'll fix them."

So, he closed the club up and made it into an after-hours place that you had to have a card to get in, so he could recognize the people, if they would send the ASCAP people in there, so they couldn't get in there. Which was a kind of handicap to us, because he figured well, some people would bring people in with a card, but they brought other people with them. So, they would ask us to play something, and they'd be friends of Mr. Vandergriff, and we could play. But when the people who really liked us that we knew, he wouldn't want us to play for them.

So, Johnny Moore just got sick and tired of it. After we'd stayed there, we had made a pretty good record there. He said to Mr. Vandergriff, "I don't think it's fair for you to let us play for your people, and when our friends come in, we can't play for them." He said, "Well, I tell you what. Since you don't like what I'm doing, see, all you characters, you're fired." So, Johnny Moore said, "That's good."

So, when we left there, and while we were getting ready to go, because we're going to get two weeks' money, a fellow who was Italian [was] sitting there. He come in there with his girlfriend every night, to listen to us play. He had a club called Lou's. His name was Lou-something, with an Italian name. He said, "Did I hear him say he fired you all?" Johnny Moore said, "Yeah." Said, "Well, you can open my club next Tuesday," on La Brea. I think La Cienega and La Brea. Yeah. No, it's La Cienega, off of Beverly Boulevard. La Cienega and Beverly Boulevard. Or either La Brea. I can't remember, but it's out there near Beverly Boulevard.

So that was all we wanted. So, we started working out there. And oh, the crowd. We started getting a fabulous crowd of white people coming to see us, who knew where we were. So, they had another woman working out there, named Lil [Lillian] Randolph. She was in the Gildersleeve show (The Great Gildersleeve). Gildersleeve was a very popular television show at that time. So, she was out there singing all these risqué numbers, nasty numbers.

So, she would sing. "Selling nuts. Anybody here want to have some hot nuts?" So, Johnny Moore said, "Look, you're a disgrace." Said, "You shouldn't be singing those kinds of numbers, those risqué numbers." "I looked at the clock, the clock struck one. Come on baby, let's have some fun." Johnny said, "Look, you shouldn't do those."

So, she got really peeved about Johnny Moore criticizing her. So anyway, she knew she was on television, where we were not on television. She meant to get revenge. She came that day, and she said, "Did y'all see me on the Gildersleeve show today? It was such a great show, and I was at that show. I hope you all saw it." Johnny Moore said, "Yes, I saw it." Said, "You had that pan of hot biscuits, carrying it around." [laughs] Because that's all she wore. A maid, you know what I mean? Said, "That was no credit, to be on the show. Anybody could be a maid." So, it really made her mad and she quit. So that's all we wanted her to do, was quit. So, we had the whole show to ourselves.

Then we became really popular. Billy Berg, who had the Swing Club in Hollywood, wanted us to play. The Suzie Q wanted us to play, down in Riverside. So, we were playing all the fabulous places.

Then finally, this guy who owned Jerry's Joint on Sunset Boulevard, he was very rich and he came to hear us and he said that he had a club up in San Francisco called The Backstage, that he wanted us to go up there and play. And he offered us $1100 dollars a week.

So, this is way up from what we started. So, Johnny Moore asked him, "Well, when do we start?" We started working here, from one until five in the daytime. So, we worked from one until five in the daytime. So that's when Billie Holiday came in. She was working in what they call the Tenderloin District; but that was a very fabulous San Francisco area.

Crawford: The Tenderloin?

Brown: Oh! There used to be nightclubs, round there.

Crawford: What clubs do you remember there?

Brown: Well, I don't remember the name of them, because see, we were only working at the nightclubs. Because there were a lot of clubs, like New York, that you didn't even know the name of them. They were off-brand, but they were very popular because people will frequent it, like New York. See, San Francisco was like New York.

People'd go down in the clubs and whatnot. And then they had the North

Beach working. Well, we were right off of Powell and Geary, which is right there at that circle there. There's a lot of sections there. So, this club was very fabulous. It had great entertainment.

Crawford: The Backstage?

Brown: Yeah. Day and night. It was just like a day, from one until five, and then the others came in at night. So, we worked there. So, this particular lady came in there one day we were playing. Well, she sat there with her dark glasses on and a little white dog she had, and a white girlfriend was with her. Johnny Moore, he whispered to me and said, "That looks like Billie Holiday sitting there." So well, I didn't believe him, because well, I had never seen Billie Holiday and didn't know what she looked like. But I had heard the records. So, I didn't believe Johnny Moore, so I wanted to go see if this was true. When we came off the stage, we all went over there. She was real hip. So, Johnny Moore introduced himself and Eddie Williams, and I say, "I'm Charles Brown, the vocalist." She commented on how well we played, and she said, "You, young man," she said, "I think I told you that the other night, said you're going to be a great star one of these days." And I tell the people I'm waiting for that day. But this is what really encouraged me. Now we've even met Billie Holiday. So, when we got our break to go to New York for the jukebox operators, because our records were selling so on the jukeboxes, they wanted to meet us, off of 10th Avenue, what they call–They used to call it some other name; I can't think of it. But it was 10th Avenue, where all the jukebox operators used to have the jukeboxes. New York. So then when we went to New York, we couldn't play at the Apollo Theater. They thought we weren't strong enough, because Nat Cole had set a pace there.

Crawford: You know Nat Cole.

Brown: Oh, yeah, because he used my piano. Because see, Oscar Moore was a brother of Johnny Moore, so we all were together there. We practiced over there at 945 South Normandy, in L.A. He had to use my piano for all these things of practice, when Nat didn't have a piano.

Crawford: Because he traveled from New York.

Brown: Yeah. Well, in other words, they had gone to New York. I think that it was Stan Kenton and June Christy and them. Carlos Gastel became their manager, so he was managing Stan Kenton and June Christy. So, Nat Cole did go to New York; then he took a picture. When he went to New York, he played the Capitol Theater. I think the Capitol Theater, on Broadway. But when we got a chance to go to New York–the William Morris Agency booked us—we couldn't get in the Apollo, so they booked us at Renaissance Casino, with the Louis Russell Band. So that was on 136th and 7th Avenue, somewhere up in there.

But we were going to prove to Frank Schiffman [at the Apollo] that we could draw. And when we did play there, they had the fire department all up the street. You couldn't hardly get to this club, to this big theater, something like an arena. Quite naturally, Schiffman says that he didn't have nobody hardly in this club and asked Johnny Moore will he come to work for him. Johnny Moore told him yes and he went in with the agency, and then that's how we got into the Apollo Theater.

Crawford: What was that like?

Brown: Well, the first time it was interesting because one thing about it, they tend to heckle you when you don't do good. But they didn't heckle us because I had my little star, and we looked great. But when we worked there, we had the zoot suits on. That was popular. But Schiffman made us go to a tailor.

Crawford: What year was that?

Brown: That was 1946.

Crawford: And when you came to San Francisco, when was that?

Brown: The first time I came to San Francisco, that was '45. When I'm talking about Billie Holiday coming? That was the early part of '45, because we hadn't made a record then. When we played The Backstage, the first record we played was with Ivory Joe Hunter. He was living here in Oakland, and he came over there to hear us and he wanted us to play behind him.

So, we made two songs behind him, "Blues at Sunrise" and this other number. So now we're familiar with Billie Holiday because she came to see us. So, when we went to New York, we went looking to see if we could see Billie Holiday on 52nd Street. Because she was popular then on 52nd, so we felt great that we could go around there. So, we went down there at nine o'clock at night. We thought it was like California. Johnny Moore ordered me a Singapore Sling, which was the thing to get you turned on quick, it was a drink during the war that was very popular, mixed up with different kinds of rums and whatnot.

I was feeling good and everything. I didn't know, because it tastes like punch to me. And all the time it was affecting me, and I didn't know it. So, we waited there, and we'd say, "When is Billie Holiday coming on?" Well, we heard this voice around about close to eleven o'clock, the show started. We heard somebody come in the door. "That's Billie Holiday now." And immediately, she went to the dressing room and changed, and they introduced her and she came out there on the stage.

I think this guy playing the piano played for Billy Eckstine, just before he died. This white girl was sitting at the table right over from us, like that. We were sitting here, and Billie Holiday was standing here, right in the front. Not no elevated stage, just on the floor. She had the rose in her hair, and they introduced her. This white girl was just keeping up so much fuss. They was trying to make her shut up. "Shut up. Bilie Holiday's on." Finally, when she did that, Billy Holiday gave the signal for her piano player to start. And when she opened her mouth, she sang this song about "I Wonder Where Our Love Has Gone." "All I know is I'm in love with you..." and baby, you could see the house change. That woman was something else.

Oh, the magic she had! Then she had that little sassy way of doing things, and we just craved for Billie Holiday because we'd seen her. So then that gave us our inspiration. Now we've seen Billie Holiday. We didn't get a chance to go back and say anything to her. I didn't get a chance to go say anything to her till I went on my own in '49, when I left Johnny Moore. I have to tell you this. It's so much to tell, good gracious. It's a long story you're having: it's almost a book.

We had planned to write a book.. We've got four chapters. And so many things happened that's funny, during the time we played the Talk of the Town. I'll tell you this, we don't want to put [them] in the book.

But you always find one person who deviates from the norm. There's this guy coming up. We're playing all these songs, and Monty Sontag drunk said, "Can you boys play 'Darktown Strutters Ball?" Johnny Moore said, "No, we don't play that kind of number." "What about "Way Down on the Swanee River'?" Said, "We don't play that either." "Darkies Work on the Mississippi?" "We don't play that either." "What do you all play?" "Music." So, he said, "You know what? He went back and told Mr. Sontag. "You've got some sassy niggers up there."

Johnny Moore really upset him when he said that. And we never had no trouble with that man, never saw him again anyhow, because we always keep in mind who we did see. But these are little things that happened that was funny. Jokes and stories. Okay, I'll be back here on the 10th or 11th of November. We've got to travel. Our last date is the 9th. So then you can find out what you left off at and your kind of monitor where we left off at, and then I can go from there.

Crawford: Because that's a long session for you.

Brown: Yeah. Now it's coming down to where you can come on your own. I left Johnny Moore and when I left Johnny Moore, how the agency sued me for wanting to go see about my grandfather. Then I went on the blackmail list with the union. That was in the fifties. And then when they did that, I couldn't play no more. And that's why my popularity died, because when you're not out there performing no more, they forget about you.

I loved my grandfather and so I said, "You know what you can take with those deposits? Take them and do what you want, because I'm going to see about my grandfather." Well, he took sick, and he died. Later on, well, they sued me for $40,000 that they knew I couldn't pay. So, I was blackballed by the union, so you're forgotten in a year. So, I just went out into oblivion. Well, I maintained playing, still playing.

Crawford: Were you writing songs already?

Brown: Oh, yeah. I had written songs. Well, I wrote "Merry Christmas, Baby," but I got no credit for that. That was in '47.

Crawford: Well, everybody knows that's your song.

Brown: Mm-hm. But I gave it to a guy named Lou Baxter, who was having a throat operation. He needed money. He gave me his little satchel. He said, "Charles, I need to get $500." And that's what they would give you if they used your song. So I told him to give me his satchel, so I saw "Merry Christmas Blues," but it gave me an idea. I said, "Nobody say 'Merry Christmas Blues.' "I said, "Merry Christmas, Baby, everybody will say. So, I'll fix the word." And they liked the way I fixed it, so then they recorded it. But when we recorded, he put Johnny Moore's name and Lou Baxter, not mine, because I was just secondary to Johnny Moore, who was the leader. Except Johnny Moore couldn't hardly write his name, let alone write a song.

But they didn't put my name because he figured, well, you're young and you don't know. So that's the way it happened. Then I didn't do no more till 1960. I did "Please Come Home for Christmas," which they used in "Home Alone," and I just got it back, after twenty-eight years, because within the twenty-eight years. they said I sold it out. But I outlived everybody who was claiming things against me, and I got back in the union because everybody was dead. It's a long story to tell, but the Lord blessed me to still be here, for some reason. Because all the people who had things against me, they're not here.

Crawford: How about recording? I know you did a lot of recording for Aladdin. You said something the other night about Philo Records. What was the story you told?

Brown: Well, Philo Records was before. It was the same company, but it was called Philo before they changed it to Aladdin Records.

Crawford: To Aladdin.

Brown: Philo was in the Philharmonic Auditorium building. They had it on 5th Street, and they just named it Philo, part of philharmonic, see? It was just related to the Philharmonic place; they had a little record store.

Crawford: I see.

Brown: Yeah. See, they had a little record store down on the Philharmonic Auditorium. Because the music teacher I took lessons from, advanced piano II, was Mr. Alexander Comba, who was a second violinist with the Los Angeles

Symphony. So, I took an advanced piano with him, when I went out there. How to hold a technique and how to get speed, like this, the curving fingers. If you notice how I play.

Crawford: Oh, yes.

Brown: Here. Because that's the way he taught me how to get speed, which a lot of people don't know. You'll see some people playing like this, and that's not the way to play. You get this.

Crawford: Power.

Brown: Mm-hm. So, these things you learn over a period. The guy gave me this picture the other night, of Franz Liszt, because he said that was his favorite piano player. He's a fan of Franz Liszt. So, I got that. So, you can do that. You can kind of document what you do have, and then you can know where to start for your other things and then get it down.

Crawford: Well, let's see, a couple of more questions about "Driftin' Blues." I wanted to ask you about your own music.

Brown: Well, "Driftin' Blues," I did that when I was twelve years old, before I ever came to California. My cousin, she's just dying last year. When my grandmother would go out in Texas with the choirs—I told you that they had the battles of the choirs, who had the best choir. Well, they would sing, and they had a quartet called The Taylor Four; they were really good. And they were playing the piano, too. So, everybody was in when they heard something that was kind of bluesy or something, they wanted to try to play that. So, the reason I remember was my grandmother went to choir rehearsal, so that we would slip out. They thought we was in the band; we'd go down to the honky tonks, look through the cracks and listen to their sounds. So we heard this lilting melody [vocalizes] And then we said, "We're going to make some words with that." Said, "We'll shock everybody." It starts, "Driftin', walkin' and driftin.'" That's what we had at first. So, when we did that, that's how "Driftin' Blues" came about.

Then when I came out to California, we always reserved that number and played it. But it was getting to be real popular on 1st Street, where I told you they moved the Japanese out. We were playing at a club called the Copa Club. It began to get so popular that Philo Records came down to hear about this song. When they heard this song, they wanted to record it. I'm just making it short. And that's how we recorded "Driftin' Blues." And then it made a great big hit, as the best record, best race record of 1946. So, that was part of how "Driftin' Blues" came about.

Crawford: What were race records? Were those blues records, per se?

Brown: Anything the Black people did, colored, was race. Louis Jordan was tops on the race record list. That was on the Billboard as a separation from the white music. They had pop, then they had classics, and they had race records, which was strictly Black folks. We moved Louis Jordan out of first place, then we got to be number one. Yeah, so with "Driftin' Blues," the juke, see, what the juke boxes were playing told the story of what the Billboard chart had. Because they'd get what those operators would tell them, what was really number one in the race records.

So "Driftin' Blues" got to be number one because it satisfied the demands at the time. Servicemen in the era there, was going overseas and people were drifting from place to place, trying to find jobs. Just the words related to a lot of things happening in the World War II, so it made a hit. Because they had never heard no good blues number that related to— It wasn't risqué. Because all the blues, years ago, used to be risqué. "Mama, keep your dress down," and "Hound Dog" and funny things like that. People were going for that. But when you came up with something more concise and constructed, that told a story, then that's what made us popular, because then we got a chance to have our own style.

Then everybody thought of copying after us, with that same— Ray Charles coming up, he was trying to sing like me. A lot of other record companies was trying to deceive the people, trying to imitate my voice, because I had a high voice.

Crawford: I heard that one of the record companies, think it was Philo Records, turned Ray Charles down when he wanted to record something, because they thought he was copying you. [Charles is on record as saying how much he learned from Brown]

Brown: Well, that's probably why. So, when Atlantic took it, and when Atlantic thought that they could get me, they wanted to fire Ray Charles. And when they did put me on the East/West label, which was a branch of Atlantic, Ray Charles and them, found out I was on that, they said, well, they didn't want to be on Atlantic. So Atlantic called and said put me on a different label, in order to enhance that particular East/West label. And I see where EastWest label is coming out now.

But I only did—How many numbers did I do? I did "We've Got a Lot in Common," that I did with Ray Charles, singing about "When Did You Leave Heaven?," which is very beautiful. And Ray Charles, man, we got really hot. They didn't want me on their label. But then I told them I didn't want to be on the label if I couldn't be on the top Atlantic label, I didn't want to try to make an East/West label, because those disk jockeys would throw it aside. Because if you weren't on the main Atlantic label, who's East/West?

So that's why I got away from them. So, when I got away from them, I started recording again for– I was freelancing. Then I did a thing for King Records. And then we did "Please Come Home for Christmas," and that made a big hit and that started me out again.

Crawford: Are you recording now?

Brown: Yeah. Oh, yeah. I just got through talking to PolyGram—they signed me. He just called me this morning. We're having a session November the 18th. And I'm using two women, great women. I'm using Etta Jones, a great singer, and Irene Reid. They're going to do two. She's in New York; we're going to fly them here. That's who I wanted. We were going to get Bonnie Raitt, but see, those companies don't want her to leave. We don't really need Bonnie Raitt. We don't need her help now.

Crawford: She helped you out a lot, though, didn't she? I've just seen your "Merry Christmas, Baby" on YouTube.

Brown: Yes, she did. She did. She bought this for me.

Crawford: It's beautiful.

Brown: All that, Bonnie Raitt. A lot of other things I have here, Bonnie Raitt bought. On my birthday, every birthday or every holiday.

Crawford: When's your birthday? You didn't tell me when you were born.

Brown: September 13th, I was in the hospital this time, when my birthday came, and we talked about an hour. That's her picture right there.

Crawford: Oh, that's great. That was in '90, that she found you, discovered you, really, again.

Brown: Yeah, in '90. She came to the Vine Street Grill, where I was doing a showcase. In Hollywood. I hadn't been there... But everybody was so elated that I was back, and I was doing so well and singing, they said, "You shouldn't retire, because you still got it. You never know." So that's the way it all happened. She told me that she knew the owner. So, when I got the life achievement award from the Smithsonian Foundation, I mean the Rhythm and Blues Foundation, they were all there. Bonnie Raitt hadn't got no Grammys then. But after that, she got Grammys. She told me that I'd be the first one on her show, because she thought I was Mr. R&B, nobody was like me. Sure enough, when she got the four Grammys, they began to organize a show; they wanted to find me. And that's how I got on to the show.

Crawford: You had troubles at times with record companies, over royalties. When did you get that squared away?

Brown: Never got it squared away.

Crawford: Never did?

Brown: Only thing now, that's why they give you the $15,000 grant, because the companies hide a lot of stuff that you could be rich with. Because we didn't know. We didn't know nothing about no royalties. All we knew, we wanted papa and mama to see us up on that stage, what they thought about. And we made a little money. It was good for that time. And we had a few little things, like they would give you a Cadillac, the record companies. Said, "I don't want this one no more. I use it, but you can have it." So that's the way. That was your royalties, I guess; that's what they thought they were paying you. But they kept the money. But we didn't pay no attention, because that was it.

So now the companies got shamed, when they brought it to the front. Atlantic Records never paid Ruth Brown much; because see, she sets Atlantic Records. And finally, they gave a million dollars to this little Ruth foundation. They started off this foundation that they give. Now money's in their galore. Capitol Records, millions of dollars. So that's why they can give out these awards to so many people every year, because the money's there. They got an award, where if you get sick and you end up way back in the fifties or something, or forties, you go to the hospital, they pay for it.

Crawford: Oh, they do?

Brown: Oh, yeah. You send them the bill. Whatever the bill is, they'll pay.

Crawford: And you're still a member of the union? Musicians' union.

Brown: Oh, yeah. You can't play without being a member of the union. I'm a union member, I'm Local 47. Yeah, oh, yeah. You can't play nowhere without being a union member.

Crawford: What percentage of ballads to blues do you play?

Brown: Well, I only play the blues that were very popular, like "Black Night" and "Driftin' Blues." I play more ballads than I do blues.

Crawford: You didn't play a lot of blues the other night.

Brown: No. I get away from that. I can sing them; I've got many blues I made that I could really sing. But like I tell the kids, I have fifty years of songs in my head. We have to reach and get what you want to do. Because you try to find out the numbers that would be more into what you want to be like now.

Crawford: You care a lot about words, I know.

Brown: Oh, yeah.

Crawford: You told me that when I first talked to you on the phone.

Brown: Yeah. I always like to say my words, because it's like dramatizing, so that people can understand you. We hear a lot of things today, you don't know what they're saying. The music is great, their voices are great, beautiful voices; but what is the story? You may hear one word that you recognize. And I say I'd hate to be like that. Maybe I'm just old. But if you really listen to it, even the choirs that sing these spiritual songs, they're just saying sound and hollering and screaming, and you don't know what they're saying.

If I had a group, their diction would have to be good because they're singing where you could say the words and every word would come out. That's why I like Etta Jones and Irene Reid. You understand every word they sing. And Nancy Wilson. Aretha used to wouldn't say her words, because they're hollering. Natalie Cole finally caught on, where she'd come on hollering. But she'd try to get like her daddy; that's how she won the Grammy. Because she was hollering and screaming, like Aretha Franklin and them. People didn't like it. So, she had to cool down. So, Nat Cole won the Grammy for her; she didn't.

Crawford: That's interesting.

Brown: See what I mean? See?

Crawford: Because he was her father, or because he taught her?

Brown: He didn't teach her, she just capitalized on the fact, because she had been into a dope situation before. She just found out where she could really exploit the fact. And I guess her husband told her, "Get back into your daddy." when they found out that they could do this with her. It made Houston, Whitney all mad because they weren't singing those standards. And when she come back with Nat Cole behind her with that thing that tore everybody's heart out. just to see him. Because see, he was loved by a lot of people.

Crawford: Yes, still is.

Brown: And by doing that, being the daughter, she used that. Which was really to her advantage. Because I think the mother, they said they didn't like it because they can't go to the front again. But who cares? If you can make money, bring it. But he didn't get a Grammy, but he got one for that. She got it. So, it's a lot of things that people want to hear.

[End of Interview]

Interviewer: Caroline Crawford

Date: April 18, 1993

Location: Fulson's home in Palmdale, California

Lowell Fulson
Credit The Bancroft Library, University of California, Berkeley, archives

Crawford: You were born in 1921, and we've been talking about your early years in Oklahoma, where your uncles played guitar and listened to blues recordings.

Fulson: Yes. I messed around with it without them knowing too much about it until I was about twelve years old. I was pretty good. I played in church, and stuff. Played what you would call—well, some of the churches didn't have all that much music, but the Sanctified Church, as they called it, did.

So, we had a Methodist Church and a Baptist Church and the Holiness Church they called it, and that's where most all the music was. But it give the kids something to listen at and something to do, because it made it pretty interesting for even the guys who didn't even learn to play or didn't try; they had a lot of fun listening. So, it was something to keep them out of devilment just to hang around there and listen to the old heads play and talk about it. My grandfather, he was a violin player, but I never did see him play, because he was an old man when I was born. His last boy was my dad, and he'd put it up.

Crawford: Did he write songs too?

Fulson: No, no, no, I don't think so.

Crawford: In church, you sang the hymns mostly?

Fulson: I played with what they sang, you know. And they would say "Glory, Hallelujah!" and all of them sanctified songs. And if you learned to play that and the songs they sang, you could play just about anything else, now. So, you didn't learn to do much picking: you learned your chords. I got me a book on the notes on the guitar—the position of the hands. When you make G how you put your fingers in a certain way. C a certain way, and so on and so on.

Crawford: And then did you join a band?

Fulson: No, there was no band. I just fooled around and played with my brother there until I was about seventeen, eighteen years old. I didn't play in schools–they had schools down there, and they had programs. Then I got big enough to play in that, and I thought I was getting pretty good. And then I wound up somehow in Oneida, Oklahoma, in about '39, '38, and that's the time I joined the string band, Dan Wright String Band. And it was easy. I had an old boy sitting in the first chair–it had about twelve, fifteen pieces sitting in the first chair–who showed me quite a bit. The rhythm was pretty good; some of the songs my timing wasn't so good, so they worked on that. So, I got to be all, right. Then I learned some of them country and western songs. That's mostly all I played–"Silver Moon," songs like that.

Crawford: Were there clubs then?

Fulson: Yes, Tex Alexander came through there during that same year, in '39, and he wanted a guitar player. Well, during that same time I was playing in a band, but we played in the afternoon, and everybody was through about when it was dark, five, or six, or seven o'clock.

So, then we'd go down to a place what they called the Bottom. And all the blues singers, harmonica blues and everybody, they'd meet up down there. And that's how I met Tex Alexander. He was down there singing. I picked up the old guitar.

Crawford: And you went on into Texas with him?

Fulson: I went on into Texas with him; Western Oklahoma and Texas, and that was a circle we had, you know. That went on for about a year, and I'd gotten married, and I was through with music for a while, I thought. I never could turn it loose, though, so I left Oklahoma and went back into Texas. Me and Tex Alexander and them broke up, and so I went on my own. I had some people down there and I went there, and so I'd play at these Saturday night fish fries; everything is done in the house. No night clubs.

Crawford: Private homes?

Fulson: Yes! But they made it wide open, you know. You'd buy what you wanted and have a ball. Dance and everything else. They'd have one big room there; it'd be the front room, and from there to the front yard—that's where you played and entertained the rest of the guys. They'd be doing other things, you know, around there.

Crawford: So, you were hired privately?

Fulson: Well, yes. Five dollars a night, you know.

Crawford: What were the county balls?

Fulson: Those were plantations, and I never experienced that. We didn't have those kind of balls in my home state. No, we just played in those guys' houses, like I said. They had a county boss up there whatever they called him big boss man, or whatever it was. He was there, but he didn't concern me, because I didn't work for him. I didn't work for him, but they knew when to close down, and he'd know how late they wanted to keep up and what nights. They shouldn't be up much past ten o'clock, because they had to get up and go to work.

So, they was happy, and I was happy. I'd made my little five dollars, you know, so some guy who was working all day wasn't making but six. And I'd come out on Saturday night and entertain; well, he didn't mind me doing that, because everybody was having a good time.

Crawford: Did they always dance?

Fulson: They always danced. Somebody would always be dancing—I don't care what you played or how fast or how slow they would be dancing.

Crawford: Were you drafted, or did you join the military?

Fulson: I was drafted. I was drafted, and I lived in Gainesville, Texas, then. I was drafted in '43, and they sent me out here until I finished my boot camp, in Maryland, and I didn't stop playing. I played right on, on weekends when they had a show.

Crawford: Did you play for the Army?

Fulson: No, they had a special job for me, storekeeper and cook, keeping the food for the officers' quarters. What they called the BOQ, bachelor officers' quarters. But I did shows for the chaplain on board ship going overseas, you know. I had my guitar.

Crawford: You went to Guam?

Fulson: Yes, I went to Guam. And I'd get a bass in. In that ship's company, I didn't have to move out until I was up for discharge. But we'd go to Fleet land and entertain the soldiers and things with the Red Cross. We also had recreation on our command. And they pulled me five pieces out of a color band. So, they were better musicians than I was, but they couldn't sing the songs. I had more experience, but to me they were better, because I'd ask a lot of questions and I learned a lot from them guys.

We did all right. The Chaplain loved that, because in the village I would load up the carryalls and take them to food in different places, you know. I was in service, and I wasn't getting paid by the service for playing guitar. I was getting paid for what I was sent there to do, and that was to see that everybody had plenty of food and didn't run out of rations.

Crawford: That was pretty good duty, wasn't it?

Fulson: It was all right.

Crawford: You probably had the key to the larder.

Fulson: I had the key to just about everything on there.

Crawford: How long were you abroad?

Fulson: About a year and a half; I was over there until the war was over. I got over there in '44, around the first of '44, and I got back to the states December 5, '45, I got discharged.

Crawford: Where did you play on weekends during that time?

Fulson: I wouldn't play nightclubs; the military wouldn't allow that. The MPS, they set me on top of a car. People all gathered around right down there in Oakland on Seventh Street, and they was having a ball. Sirens came, and I didn't know what was happening either. Sirens coming, lights blinking, and that was the MPs and SPs, military police and shore patrol.

Crawford: How did they find you?

Fulson: All that noise I was making down there, traffic all stopped up. They knew something was going on that they didn't authorize, you know. So, they says, "What's going on here? What are you doing, sailor?" So, I said, "I'm playing me some blues, man," and they are listening. I tell them to listen. They said, "But you are blocking the traffic. You see the traffic up there?" And I said, "No, I hadn't noticed." They said, "Well, you're going to have to–," And they stepped up and said, "You can't touch him. Don't touch that man!"

So, he said, "Well, if you all want to hear him that badly, get him off the streets. Because we're going to lock him up."

Crawford: You were in uniform?

Fulson: Yes. [laughter] But, they were real strict back there during the war. You couldn't [do that].

Crawford: But if you had left, could you do what you wanted?

Fulson: You could do what you wanted to do in the bounds of the regulations. So, I could play [San Francisco] parties. That's how I met Bob Geddins, the guy I cut the first record with.

Crawford: Yes, I wanted to talk to you about Bob Geddins.

Fulson: He said, "You're pretty good. I'm going to record you when you get out. You coming back out here when you get out?" I said, "Yes, if we're going to make a record." I was just joking. So, I had seen the bright lights, and when I got back there in Oklahoma, I said, "I can't stay here; it wasn't enough noise!" So, I came on back that was along about the last of May in '46–and I stayed right around there in Oakland, Oakland, Vallejo, and San Francisco. I haven't been nothing in Los Angeles yet. Oh, my beginning was right up there.

Bob Geddins walked in on me one time. I was out of the service, and a lot of the people that I knew was gone. The war was over, and they was going back to different places, and some of them would be on the streets sometimes. I remember one club I'd go to all the time. I liked this old guy. His name was Dodo, that's what everybody called him. That was even the name of the place down there close to Willow Street some place

I walked in and Bob Geddins looked at me, and he didn't say nothing. So, the next day I was walking around from Seventh to Eighth Street, and I heard some music playing and said, "Where's that coming from?" About this time of day, about four o'clock. So, I went up there, and he was there, and he had a one-man press pressing records.

Crawford: In his garage.

Fulson: In his garage. I think it was the Rising Star Quartet. Same boy that put out "Tin Pan Alley." Jimmy Wilson. They were recording their group. So, when they got through there, I picked up this old guitar, saying, "Man, I want to play and sing," and I had the blues [album]. They said, "Fine." That was what they wanted.

So, I'm singing the blues. "Is that you, that sailor who was here about a year or so ago?" I say, "Yes, I was here." "I told you I'm going to cut a record. You want to cut a record?" I say, "Yes." "If I tell you I give you a hundred dollars–." I said, "Let's go." And it started from that.

Crawford: You launched the Big Town label for Geddins?

Fulson: Yes. I guess I did. First thing I did, I cut "Three O'clock in the Morning," oh, four or five tunes. It got me to going, and I got so hot people was calling me, and my little nights there went up from ten to twenty dollars a night, and I just kept studying. And in '48, '47, '48, I went to work in Mare Island Shipyard during that time. Got a job as storekeeper there. Decommissioning ships there, you know. But it wasn't food; it was nuts and bolts when I was storekeeping, putting the used ones on, how to clean them and put them in different bins and take them where they were going to take them.

So, one day I went there, and I had me a little house out there in Chabot Terrace, and all them big, fine cars pulled around my house, that little shack I had [laughs]. "Hey, man, we want you to come to Los Angeles." Well, that was Jack Lauderdale. He had Swingtime. So, we made a deal; he threw a little advance money on it, and I had an old '36 Ford, and I got in it and drove from Oakland down here.

So, we went in the studio—I didn't know anything like these musicians said, "Gosh, these guys are sharp." One of them heard me, said, "You don't have to play with us, we play with you." [laughter] This was in L.A., Bigtown then. But then they made the change, after the label got so big, they woke up to it, so he had to change it.

So, first record I cut for Jack Lauderdale, "Trouble, Trouble." A couple more things I did for Bob. Messing around there. Jimmy Chandler was the first real band that I had in the studio, the big studio. But he was a little too jazzy for me. That type of music just plain didn't fit my voice, me, and my music either, because I didn't like it.

So, I told him, "I just like it plain." He said, "Well, we'll put this record out." So he put the record out, and the record sold pretty good. And "Black Widow Spider" sold more than that. And he brought in Lloyd Glenn, so Lloyd Glenn sat down at the piano, picked me out right good: "I know just what you need." He was a soft-spoken guy. So I did, and we went on, and he said, "Well, you got some ideas. What you want to do?"

Well, I had me a band in Oakland, see, four or five pieces up there, so I'd come up for my band, play on the weekends and work in the day.

Crawford: Who was in the Oakland band?

Fulson: Earl Brown, the same guy I brought down here. Earl Brown on the alto sax, King Solomon on the piano, Con Carson on the drums, Floyd Montgomery on the bass. But Earl was the onliest one I brought down here to record. I liked the way he blew on the horn and the things my brother and I had coached him the way to blow. We had Louis Jordan records, and all that stuff, and holding those long notes on that alto sounds pretty good.

Crawford: You and your brother had been working for some time out there, a pretty long time.

Fulson: Yes. He was my second backup guitar player, but when he got on there he didn't fit in too good because he knew it. But he didn't fit in, and I'm glad he didn't because I didn't want him. I wanted him to coach me, "You ain't good enough—you think you're better than I am, but you aren't. That's me talking.

Crawford: I hope you're an older brother. [laughter]

Fulson: I'm the oldest. Yes. I said, "You just hold my money while I make it, because I'm going to make me some money." So, he says, "Okay." So, we go in, and they say, "So what you want to do?" I said, "Man, this old boy got a good song called 'Memphis Lamb,' and I'm going to cut it, but I'm going to have to write it to fit me."

So, I picked out a few words and messed around, and we cut "Every Day I Have the Blues." And it hit *big*, so big I didn't have another song I could put on the other side. So, Jack wanted the record so bad it didn't make him no difference, he just played the one side. Blank, you know, to advertise it.

So, Lloyd Glenn said, "I'll put something with it, and put it on the other side." So, he sat down with his piano, him and the same group, the [Old Time Shuffling]. That's the group he had, and we went on from there. Which wasn't peaches and cream; there was a lot of studying and a lot of hard work. I learned that. And I finally moved to Los Angeles after I had the blues so much. That was my group, and I wouldn't cut it unless I had them guys.

When I got to playing, I had Lloyd Glenn, Billy Haddanot on bass and Bob Hargon on drums, and Big Tiny Will played rhythm guitar. And that's all I wanted for the time being. We did "Blue Shadows," and that was a big hit. They wanted me to cut a Christmas song, so I cut "Lonesome Christmas," and then they were ready for me on the road; they wanted to hear some. So, there was a kind of demand for me to go out on the road.

Crawford: Who recorded "Lonesome Christmas"?

Fulson: Me.

Crawford: No, I meant which recording company?

Fulson: Oh, that was still Swing Time. I stayed there from about '48, '51,'52. '52. I turned them loose—well, we didn't understand each other. So, I turned them loose, and I didn't record for couple of years, because those records was still going so good until I didn't need to. I thought I may come out with something that would break the sales, slow down the sales. So, he agreed with that; he said, "We'll just push this long as we can."

Crawford: You worked with Ivory Joe Hunter.

Fulson: We toured together; we didn't work with each other. He had his own show and his own band that he'd bring on; I'd have my own show and my own band. I did that with a lot of guys, and I wound up having twelve pieces. And furnished the music to the booking (agents) for almost all the groups they had there: Drifters, Dominos, Stanley Turrentine.

Crawford: Ray Charles was in the band?

Fulson: Ray Charles was on the piano. Floyd Montgomery was still with me on bass. He's a good road man on bass, but he wasn't good on records. He played too harsh.

Crawford: Harsh?

Fulson: He was rough, not a good sound for recording. All right for the house.

Crawford: Did you play acoustic for a while?

Fulson: My first record was acoustic guitar. But I couldn't get the sound I wanted, so I went back, and this Holiness preacher had a good guitar, a Gibson, and he didn't know how to play. He hung around that same shop where Bob Geddins was, so I went back to the electric guitar. I cut mostly the "River Blues"; and several other songs I cut for Bob Geddins. I said, "I'm going to put a little electric to this, but I'm going to turn it low," I said, "and make me do a little better." Which I did. It made me slide up and down the strings like I wanted to pretty good. So, I was teaching them to play, and he let me use his guitar till I bought me one.

Crawford: That was a Gibson?

Fulson: His was a Gibson. He had a good one. The first electric I bought was an Epiphone, which we call a cousin to Gibson. Just about as good as Gibson. So, I used an Epiphone for a time.

Crawford: I remember in "Longest Train Running" you said that Bob Geddins helped you a lot with your phrasing.

Fulson: He did. He did. He helped quite a bit. I'd started singing the blues. And he said, "No, Lowell, that's not the blues. What church did you belong to?" And I said I was a Holiness singer. He said, "No wonder you can't sing no blues. You ever go to the Baptist church and listen to hymns?" I said yeah, and he said, "Can you sing those hymns?' I said yes. "That's what I want, man!" So, we tried a couple; they came out just right, what he wanted.

Crawford: He knew what he wanted.

Fulson: He knew what he wanted, and he'd get it out of the artists. But when I got with Jack Lauderdale and Lloyd Glenn and them down here, we just smoothed that out. We just smoothed everything right out, and I sang like I wanted to, because he wasn't in the picture no more.

Crawford: He must have been sad to lose you.

Fulson: Well, he didn't mind; he figured he had enough records to last a while. He knew he couldn't hold me, not with the setup he had. He couldn't get out of Oakland with his records. He'd put them in the car and go around Oakland, Richmond, Vallejo, San Francisco. Set them on his car.

Crawford: He did the whole operation, and working night and day, I guess.

Fulson: Yes, and that press, he had that press just about all night to have enough left for the people, they was buying them so fast.

Crawford: Who do you most remember from Oakland?

Fulson: Well, there was Ivory Joe and Saunders King. They was about the onliest guys I knew that had any big records out. Ivory Joe, he lived in West Oakland. I don't think Jimmy McCracklin was playing then. If he was, I didn't hear no records till later years. Of course he had a little night club here, and he had me playing in his night club for a while.

Crawford: Did you know him well?

Fulson: I knew him pretty good but I didn't know him real well because we walked on different sides of the street. He had his bunch that he went to–he was a fighter, a prizefighter, and I think he spent his time mostly around doing sports, you know. Old man Simmons had him. They tell me he was pretty good; I never did see him fight. I knew the family he had, his wife, and she booked me in North Richmond all the time.

Crawford: She booked you?

Fulson: Yeah, that was in the forties.

Crawford: What clubs do you remember from the forties?

Fulson: Brown Derby and the Savoy, the Astor House, and Vallejo, the Showboat in Vallejo. I played nice places there.

Crawford: Slim's?

Fulson: No, I wasn't graduated enough to play Slim's. But I was up the street, and I can't think of the old boy who had that club, but I'd go in there. And Christie's Grill on 12th Street. And Poplar or something like that down there in West Oakland. We had a lot of things going on down there.

Crawford: What about "T-Bone" Walker, his style?

Fulson: I thought that was the prettiest thing he did when he came back with that "Bobby Sox Baby" and the way he swung with the big bands. I thought that was really something, because guitar players couldn't hardly get work. If you did you got it at a chicken fry or chittlin switch [laughter] or some honky tonk club, you know.

Crawford: What was the Oakland sound?

Fulson: You could identify Oakland pretty much with Ivory Joe Hunter and Saunders King. He was like between Oakland and Frisco. It was blues, but it was more than blues, blues ballads and kind of swing.

Crawford: It's been described as a more mournful sound.

Fulson: By some singers, I guess it was. I don't know. Ivory Joe, he didn't sing mournful songs. Saunders King didn't either. I was about the only one who sang any of them type of blues during that time with that mournful sound, because that's what Bob Geddins wanted, and he hadn't found anybody to sing the way he wanted it. And I was accidentally enough to get it partly like he wanted. Closer than anybody else to what he really wanted.

Crawford: Did you keep in touch with him after you went to Los Angeles?

Fulson: Yes.

Crawford: We were talking about life in Oakland, and you said it was pretty good.

Fulson: In Oakland, it was pretty good! It was pretty good; I blew a lot of the places I was playing at. I couldn't go back in there no more because I was going in there with an agent. So, I couldn't go into the Savoy no more, and the agents didn't fool with Slim Jenkins', just the local clubs and the guys wanted to be jazz players mostly, you know, played around there.

There wasn't a lot of jazz on that side of the Bay; it was mostly really, really blues. This boy of Tin Pan Alley, he came out with a song. I forget what it was.

Crawford: "Roughest place in town"?

Fulson: That's right, "Tin Pan Alley Blues." But everybody was kind of curious after I was gone a year, and they'd just hear about me; didn't see me. And I think the people just came out to see what I looked like, you know, because it was a little over a year before I got back.

And what you might say is that I left walking, and I came back in a busload of musicians, name all over it and everything. So, it was–

Crawford: A celebrity.

Fulson: Yeah, I was kind of a celebrity. That's when I met Big Joe Turner. We teamed up, they had us teamed up, and that ran for ten years. Just about– they called us the Big Three: Lowell Fulson, Big Joe Turner, "T-Bone" Walker. And that's the way they wanted us to go across the country. Anybody else, they'd take them a little while and wind up with the three.

Crawford: Touring, you mean. Did you do much touring?

Fulson: We went to every state big enough to caravan in this United States, for going South. And North. We went to New York in '61, '62. Did we play Boston? No, Chicago and the Midwest was good, all over the Midwest. And New York and New Jersey were as far east–

Crawford: You played the Apollo in New York.

Fulson: Yeah.

Crawford: Was that considered the big time then?

Fulson: That was to see whether I could make it or not.

Crawford: Talk about that and tell tales about the Apollo.

Fulson: It was all right. But I couldn't keep from shaking and trembling because I was so scared, because they built the thing up, so I was a little shaky.

And when they said, "We're going to have to use your band to back up Clyde McFadder and the Dominoes and whoever else comes." I say okay. I say, "You talk with Ray and Stan, and they'll get your music out." They said, "But he can't see." I said, "Get the music." So, Stanley Turrentine would call off the notes, and he'd braille them off. First thing you know we had the show ready to go in no time, and everything went off real good. And by me having my own band I played what we know to play and I played the best I could play; didn't bother me any.

Crawford: And they apparently liked you.

Fulson: They did. They did. They called me back on the stand. Moms Mabley. She was the emcee [laughter], and she made it a little homier. "Now if you look too lonesome out there you just give them a good hand. He'll be all right." She make it more embarrassing than the people out there!

Crawford: That was kind of an icebreaker.

Fulson: Yeah. Yeah. I looked at her, and I went on doing my show. But I think they were more interested in the band that I had than me. But before the week was over I'd worked into it pretty good. They said I did all right the opening night. I said, "Well, I don't know." But to me even up to now I don't sound that hot. I just barely get a program over. But I work hard at it.

Crawford: How did they get audiences into big theaters like that?

Fulson: I don't know. Billy Shaw, Shaw Company, was handling it. We got all the theaters after that. The Howard in Washington, DC, the Regal in Chicago. the Circle in Dayton, Ohio. Then we went to playing to tobacco warehouses in the Carolinas and the Virginias. On down into Georgia, Alabama, Mississippi.

Crawford: And how was that?

Fulson: Didn't bother me any. We just had a lot of fun and met a lot of people. People were *good* down there; they just open their doors to you. Oh, man! There are some good people down there. I lost my drummer down there. One of them girls took him off past there, and I haven't seen him from that day to this! [laughter] And of all places, Hattiesburg, Mississippi.

Crawford: He didn't even say goodbye?

Fulson: No, nothing. Well, I got me another drummer.

Crawford: Did you play the same places?

Fulson: No, I refused to go back to the Apollo. They worked you too hard. I came out of that place, man, and I had to take off a couple of days. I told that man I had to rest up. Ten o'clock was the [tune up time] in the morning. You'd get there and that's to tune up and warm up for the first show around eleven o'clock or whatever time they had that day. You didn't go outdoors for anything that you wanted because they catered everything in there. And you'd go in there like nine or ten o'clock just dragging, and it'd be the midnight show and after before you got out of there. And like that for the whole week.

Crawford: Who were the audiences?

Fulson: Kids in the day, youngsters in the afternoon and children, and then the adults mostly came at night unless they'd brought some kids out. But the show was mostly built around for the youngsters, certain jolly stuff.

Crawford: You'd already moved to LA?

Fulson: I moved to LA in '49.

Crawford: How did life here compare with the northern part of the state?

Fulson: I hit it off in Los Angeles real good. Once I got in the studio and got lined up like I wanted to–that was my biggest problem, getting my stuff played like I wanted.

Crawford: Recordings? Did you have an agent deal with the companies then for you?

Fulson: No. No.

Crawford: You recorded with so many companies you can't mention all of them, but I remember Bob Geddins had trouble with Aladdin, it seems to me.

Fulson: All those guys came later. I wouldn't sign a contract with none of those guys because I didn't get a proper deal that I thought I should have had. And I didn't fool with any of them. They got their records from Bob, or bought them from someplace else. Of course in later years I did do sessions with Aladdin, but just one record, you know. Four, five. They released singles quite a bit then, moreso than LPs. During that time when you got an LP they just played it so much until they'd just take them and bring them back and then put them all in one. The 45s were mostly famous.

Crawford: What about Chess?

Fulson: I did Chess in the forties and fifties, '53, and I was playing then quite a bit. Matter of fact, I met Chess and them because they were the Swingtime distributor out there, promoting the records out there in the Midwest. And that's how I first met them. They told me to go down there and talk to them because they'd sold so many records. This guy out there in Los Angeles.

So, I did. They wanted to know, to use the saying, "Who you with?" and I said, "Jack Lauderdale," and they said, "They bust him out of business. You're not with him anymore." I said, "Well, I thought he'd be back." And they said, "No, he won't be back." [laughter] "The government got him somehow or another." Anyway, he couldn't cut no more records, whatever he did.

Crawford: You toured in Europe, and Europeans love the blues almost more than anything else. Why do you think that is?

Fulson: Well, that's something we have had so much fun off back in the forties and fifties. The stateside whites, period. Some days there'd be pretty much tension, and you'd just get over there in the corner and play until it wouldn't bother me. But they weren't like that about jazz and the swing stuff, Louis Armstrong and those boys. They were mostly brought up around it, the whites you know. But they still weren't listening to no blues; they were listening to swing and different types of stuff.

But when it came to blues, the regular blues, they didn't pay it any attention, and some time you'd have trouble keeping the blues on the radio station because they'd take it off. They'd take it off, saying it wasn't suitable. They'd turn around [interruption]. They'd turn around and Chess brothers would put it right back on, you know. He just went and bought him a radio station and [I'd] just take it right off of that, if I'm not breaking any kind of law. I never had any more trouble with that [tape break]. But that's something they never got to enjoy. But you could see them quite a bit in auditoriums, where they could get balcony seats [inaudible] through all the fifties and into the sixties.

We were in Atlanta doing a concert. Stan Kenton and Dizzy Gillespie played a concert. Me, Dinah Washington, and Earl Bostick played the regular dance. And they had a rope in that big, old auditorium, and we got to jumping up and down and playing that music. And before we knew it, nobody knew where that rope was! The rope was gone, and so was the sheriff. So was the police. Everybody left, and everything went off just beautiful. They thought they had to be there to guard things, you know. Keep the Blacks separated from the whites. But they didn't have no luck that time. People just went on and enjoyed themselves and had a good time.

Crawford: Well, now the audiences are as much white, aren't they?

Fulson: I think they're more white. And the young people that's the way they are in Europe. Europe reminds me of here in '51 when everybody went for it. And they have a ball. They have a ball. One thing, they could have sold a whole lot of records back then if their parents hadn't been in the way.

Now you take since television has been in, those little white kids nine, ten, twelve years old, on TV, and when they get sixteen and seventeen years old, they're old men about the thing. And they pick up what they want and sing what they please, and sometimes they get bawled out about it.

But they learn, and they begin to socialize with each other. And they just got acquainted through by music. And all this prejudice that you see that's going on now, back then when it was terrible, but you never did hear anything about musicians. They got along. Sometime you'd go back into those Southern towns, back in there, and you'd hear, "What's that white boy doing up there up on that bandstand? Get him off of there! He can't play on there."

Crawford: Is that a fact they wouldn't let them play in the bands? Forties and fifties?

Fulson: No, no, He couldn't play.

Crawford: That wouldn't be true now.

Fulson: No, that wouldn't be true now. I tell you, they mix together, they play their music together, laugh and drink out of the same bottle.

Crawford: Universal language.

Fulson Right. Right. [laughter]

Crawford: Did you play differently or write differently for Black and white audiences?

Fulson: No. Same old blues, and they liked them better than I did.

Crawford: Did the style of your songs change?

Fulson: Yeah. They changed from two guitars to a twelve-piece band. You know, there's got to be some changes made along that! Yes, I had to change. If I didn't I would have stayed in the chittlin switch route, which was an old beat-up piano, couple of little guitars, a harmonica [inaudible]. A lot of the blues singers now that *live* long enough to enjoy seeing the music coming their way, that sung that kind of music, that I didn't do so good with, that I didn't care about. But I like the challenge because it's hard to sing. You have to have the right type of voice to really rough it up. What they call the real Harlem blues. Moaning and groaning, like you mentioned a few minutes ago. You have to have that kind of voice. Muddy, Howling Wolf. Those guys had powerful voices that didn't need a mike. Just go to the party, jamming and playing.

Crawford: Your style is much more smooth.

Fulson: I didn't feel it. I guess I could have hollered as loud as anybody else, but I didn't have the voice. That old, big growly, raggedy voice! [laughter] That's what you need to put out them blues! Them type of blues.

Crawford: Which of your songs would you pick out?

Fulson: Well, "Reconsider Baby" was a pet, and I did love "Every Day," and I did a big band thing which I did like very well and never did come out called out "Black Gold," on Swing Time with a big band. That's the last time I heard it, and I don't know what ever happened to it. It was pretty good, and in later years, I did "Black Night," which was a favorite tune of mine.

Crawford: We didn't talk on your Indian heritage

Fulson: I don't have enough to even talk about it. Choctaw Freedman, my grandfather on my daddy's side.

Crawford: Oh, not Cherokee.

Fulson: My grandmother was Cherokee. But he was–they called him Choctaw Freedman, because he was freed under Indian law, because he fought in the Civil War with the Indians. I was twelve years old when he died.

Crawford: I have read that you were especially effective in adapting your personal style to the changes over the years. Was that a conscious thing?

Fulson: That was a conscious thing. I would check the record sales, and they wouldn't be buying what I was recording, so I'd change my style to something else. Like "Tramp," you know. I had a group wasn't getting any records sold. Nobody wanted to cut it, so I waited until everybody left, the arranger left, and I grabbed four or five boys that I knew very well, and we went in and cut "Tramp. They made fun of it and laughed at it, and the disk jockeys told them, "You better release that, man," so Bob trudged over there to Frisco, and they released it. It hit overnight. From then on, they quit telling me what to cut!

Crawford: Anything you'd say about your marriages?

Fulson: See, because I have never talked about my love life, nothing like that.

Crawford: Well, that has to be in the book.

Fulson: That has to be in the book. That's what I'm saying. A whole lot of stuff like that. God bless her soul, she's dead now, died five or six years ago, my wife.

Second and last wife, and the only one.

Crawford: We have a picture of her. Pretty lady standing right behind you.

Fulson: Yes. And I couldn't afford to tell my life story when she was around, because she just didn't understand anything, you know? [laughter]

Crawford: You had stuff to hide?

Fulson: Matter of fact, some of the stuff happened she wasn't born!

Crawford: Talk about the more personal side.

Fulson: Next time!

Crawford: Was there always blues? Somebody said the blues started with Adam, because he didn't have a woman.

Fulson: Any time with human beings 'you can go back as far as you can go' there has been trouble. And wherever there is trouble, there is blues. Blues is just a person not happy. Life's disgusting to them. They can't do what they want to do, and you can't call it happiness; you call it the blues. Just something that's disgusting to them.

You and your husband quit each other. He don't look as good as he did yesterday morning, or whatever, and you go to brewing about it, sulking at him, and he's snapping at you. Somebody's got the blues, and if you don't do something to correct it pretty soon, he'll be by himself. That's the blues. Then you got the blues.

Blues is everything you got, and you don't know whether you can replace it, what else you going to have? You can't shout, because you're not happy. So, if you can't sing about it, you talk about it, or jump off a bridge. Music corrects it. Put your mind thinking. You got that one you can get another one. You build one house, it burns down, build another one. Ain't nothing to brood about because it won't bring it back. You can get out and sing the blues, whatever you can sing; whatever you can hum. Sing in the shower and you'll feel better, Things even look better to you when you walk out of there.

Crawford: What did you mostly write about?

Fulson: Conditions of other people, more than myself. By me being a traveling man, a boy always in a man's way somewhere, because I didn't fool with boys my age. I got them, the tougher the better, because I knew I'd be protected better. I would be, and I was too—nobody bothered me coming up from a kid. I'd be out there hustling on the guitar; they didn't bother me.

I didn't associate with boys; my uncles and brothers and that's all. They talked kid talk. But I was a boy, and I thought like a man. I walked and acted like a man. I didn't have a whole lot of kid in me. [laughter]

My grandfather on both sides, mother and father, they'd taken me up, taken up to me, because they said I was quite advanced about thinking and understanding other people. He'd tell me lots. And there wouldn't be nothing I wouldn't ask him, either. The rest of the boys would be saying around, [whispers] but me and him would be sitting around there talking like I was his equal in age. [laughter] And sometimes he'd laugh and say, "We'll talk about that some other time." I'd say, "Okay." I'd be asking him one of those heavy questions that I'd want to find out about. I'd be sixteen years old.

Crawford: Did you have younger brothers?

Fulson: Just one. See, my father got killed when me and Martin was small boys. Maybe three years and five years.

Crawford: Well, that tended to make you serious right there, didn't it?

Fulson: And then my mother's dad was named Dave Wilson, and mothers, when they get to be widows, the first thing they do is run to their mom and dad, before they'll go to their in-laws, they'll go home. So that's why she stayed home, but grandpa'd come get me, and I'd stay with him. And then I'd go back over and stay with them, and Papa would take me.

Crawford: That's your grandpa.

Fulson: Go between two grandpas. And the uncle that didn't want me to play his guitar. He'd take little, short shots at me, you know. "You're not doing that right. Watch that. You step off deep water, and if you can't swim you can't get out," blah, blah, blah. Talk slang talk. I picked up what it meant, and I'm studying everything he was talking about. See it pretty good.

Crawford: Who encouraged you?

Fulson: Me.

Crawford: You just wanted to do it.

Fulson: Yes. It was a challenge to me.

Crawford: Was it fun?

Fulson: It was fun. Even up to now it's fun when I play. Things may not be so good after I get off the stage, but while I'm up there I'm having fun with it. And the people is having fun; that's what makes me have fun. When I see them.

Crawford: To have the gift, that's the best thing.

Fulson: Thank you.

[End of interview]

Interviewers: Ronnie Stewart and Caroline Crawford

Date: November 10, 2003

Location: McCracklin's home in Richmond, California. McCracklin sat at the upright and played and sang as he spoke.

Jimmy McCracklin

Credit Jimmy McCracklin and Ronnie Stewart

McCracklin: Now what is this for?

Stewart: The Oral History Department of UC Berkeley is archiving people about Seventh Street, about the music. This is our interview with the legendary Jimmy McCracklin. This is in conjunction with the Oral History Department of UC Berkeley. And we're going to be archiving all the history of great people like you, Jimmy. We specifically looking at the history of Seventh Street and the history of Oakland's blues. And we feel, from a historical standpoint, you are the man. You and Bob Geddins and a few others, is the most important people that ever come out of Oakland and also one of the pioneers of the West Coast blues sound.

What I'd like to do, Jimmy, you get a lot of interviews, but I want to start back in Arkansas, even before that. I'd like to know your parents' name, where were you born? We want to go back as far as you can, even before you played music. Could you start off with where were you born?

McCracklin: First, what I would like to do, Ronnie, is to thank you and Caroline for coming by. And thank you for thinking what you think of me.

Stewart: Oh, absolutely.

McCracklin: I was born in Arkansas and raised in St. Louis, Missouri. August 13, 1921. My dad, he was born in Louisiana, I believe, and my mother, she was born in Arkansas. They passed away about fifteen or twenty years ago. And that's the size of it. My mother's maiden name was Emma Coldwell. My father and her got together; I think they were together for about fifty-five years. She passed away first and he followed her. Being honest about it, she passed away going home from out here in California. She had a heart attack on the train, and he passed away in Arkansas about two years later. In this world, you know, we all gotta go some day.

Stewart: How many brothers and sisters, before we leave Arkansas?

McCracklin: Well, it was three boys. The oldest boy, he deceased, he passed away. And I have another brother now, the older brother, he's living in Louisiana.

Stewart: What part?

McCracklin: Well, I believe Shreveport. He was living in California, so he decided he wanted to go to Louisiana. We have a few people down there in Louisiana, and that's where my father was born. So, he's back in Louisiana now, and I'm still out in California.

Stewart: Doing well, doing well. Did you have any sisters, Jimmy?

McCracklin: Oh, yes. It was seven girls altogether.

Stewart: Seven girls!

McCracklin: Yeah, some of them deceased. And right now, I have three living sisters right now.

Crawford: Did your father or mother sing in church? Anybody musicians in your family?

McCracklin: No, they weren't in the musical business. My father was a deacon, and my mother, she was a star, whatever you call it.

Stewart: Eastern Star?

McCracklin: Yeah, Eastern Star. So, they both are passed away, and they kept us in church. We used to sing in the choir. The facts are, it was almost enough of us together, just the family, to make a choir out of it. I was very young then.

I don't remember ever having a piano or nothing like that in church. We sang religion songs, and we'd just get out there and sing on our own. We'd use our hands for drums...and the whole church would be with us, so we didn't need no musicians. That's the Holiness Church.

We'd do our own choiring and stuff at the house. My dad and mother, they would be the judge; they would sit back and listen and make sure that we did it the right way. We had harmony; we used to be beautiful, man. We would sing, and people would get upcited in the church and clap their hands. That's what I said, that was our music; our hands and patting our feet. That's the way we did it.

So, if you're doing it the right way and got the right harmony, you don't really need no big band or nothing behind you. At that time, there wasn't no such things as no bands in the South down through Arkansas playing church music and stuff. You didn't need that band! All you needed was voices. It was strictly spiritual.

Stewart: Did that help you in your singing today?

McCracklin: Well, it is still is in me, and I guess until I leave this earth it will be still with me. That's what I have to try to teach my daughter, and whatever, you know. She sings with me a lot of time I'm on the piano. Make sure she get the feeling in the harmony.

A lot of people don't understand, blues and jazz and all that stuff that come from the church, believe it or not. The church is what I would call the foundation. Whatever you put into music is nothing but a feeling. If you got the right feeling, you can get across with it, but without the right feeling...you can get across with it, but without the right feeling you can't. What I feel, I gotta make you feel it. This is the way I see life. And if you don't feel it and I don't feel it, I ain't doing nothing. Just making noise.

So, you got to have that feeling, and where I gets my feeling from, I do a lot of writing and it's about songs. Then I try to put the feeling to it with music that I accomplish that particular song. That makes sense to someone else.

I have over three hundred and some songs, that I've wrote in my lifetime, and it really gives me a good feeling to know that I have songs that have been covered by almost a hundred peoples. I don't just write songs for Jimmy McCracklin. I write songs for real life of peoples. I want my songs to connect with your life as well as it connects with mine.

Crawford: Have you written gospel songs?

McCracklin: Oh, yeah. But I never released a gospel song on my own. But if stay around I'm gonna do it. In facts I have a song now that I just wrote the last week. It's called "Ghetto City Life." I might do a little bit of it for you before you leave, see what you think about it.

Stewart: Did you ever play church music on your piano?

McCracklin: No, no. After I come to age of about, I believe, nine or ten, I left Arkansas and went to St. Louis, Missouri.

Stewart: Now, was this with the family or just you by yourself?

McCracklin: Well, I just went to St. Louis by myself because I had an uncle there. My mother's brother was living in St. Louis, so I went to St. Louis, and that's where I made my home until I got up to about eighteen or nineteen. And I started all my activity in St. Louis.

Stewart: Okay, so that's how the St. Louis connection came in.

McCracklin: That's how the connection of St. Louis came in, yes. But I was born in Arkansas, and I feel proud of it, generally.

Stewart: Yeah, my parents is from Pine Bluff. What part of Arkansas were you born in?

McCrackin: It's called Helena.

Stewart: Helena! That's where they have the King Biscuit Blues Festival

McCracklin: That's the King Biscuit Blues Festival, right?

Stewart: Did you ever listen to the King Biscuit's blues hour when you was a kid, or do you remember that?

McCracklin: Well, I used to when I was young, and Sonny Boy Williamson, and all of them guys–

Stewart: Right, it was on the radio.

McCracklin: But Arkansas, the last time I played there a couple of years ago, we had almost a hundred thousand peoples.

Stewart: At the King Biscuit Blues Festival?

McCracklin: Yeah, they reckon that Jimmy McCrackin was from there, you know. And they came out and showed their appreciation.

Stewart: Well, Jimmy, let me ask you this. Was you actually from a farm, or was you from a rural area or was you actually out of the city around Helena? Was you living did y'all have, like, a couple of acres?

McCracklin: Oh no, I was on a farm, you know.

Stewart: A real farm? Did you have animals, could you tell me?

McCracklin: My dad had cows, hogs, chickens, and all that stuff.

Stewart: Oh really? So, you're a real farm boy!

McCracklin: That's why the record come in Arkansas. That's why I made "Arkansas," I made it to the true facts of actually what went down, when I remember, as I was a kid coming up.

Stewart: Did you guys slaughter your own meat? Did y'all have hogs?

McCracklin: We raised our own hogs and chicken. We didn't have to buy no meat. We raised our own corn. We did it all.

Stewart: Did you have greens and corn and peas and vegetables?

McCracklin: You name it, yeah.

Stewart: Oh, really? So, you said they wasn't yours, but I bet you your job was to feed them and slop the hogs.

McCracklin: Well no, we had to work. You know, the old man kept us working. And we learned how to work, and I'm proud of it now. Learned how to make our own living and everything. We didn't get nothing free.

Stewart: This is kind of funny, but when you was like seven or eight, before you left, could you tell me your chores? I really want to dig into what Jimmy has done on the farm. I mean, what did you do in the mornings before you go to school?

McCracklin: Pick cotton and chop cotton, pull corn and pick peas, we did it all.

Stewart: Did y'all grow cotton?

McCracklin: Oh yeah. Oh yeah.

Stewart: Oh okay. Well, how many acres did y'all have?

McCracklin: I believe my dad had about eighty acres.

Stewart: Eighty! Oh, see, I'm thinking like one or two acres.

McCracklin: Oh, no, he had eighty acres. We've still got about seven acres down there now that was willed to my niece, after my mother and father deceased. We gave it to the niece, and we sold the rest of it and split it amongst the family.

Stewart: Oh, okay. That's cool. Did your father work a day job? I mean the farm was a job.

McCracklin: He was a farmer, he strictly was a farmer.

Stewart: And y'all sold the crops, like the cotton, to the cotton gin company, or whatever?

McCracklin: Well, he did all that. He carried the cotton to the gin and stuff like that, make the bales of cotton. I was just a farm boy. I don't pretend I'm a city man because I was raised on a farm, you know, in Arkansas.

Stewart: This is interesting. You talk to a lot of blues guys from Arkansas, Mississippi, Alabama and sometimes they'll say, "Well yeah, I had people in the country, but I was raised in the city." [laughter]

McCracklin: No. I was raised in Arkansas, and I feel proud of it.

Stewart: Arkansas here I come, huh? [laughs]

McCracklin: That's right.

Stewart: [laughs] Okay so, did you ever have to, like, wring a chicken's neck and dip it in the hot water and do all that stuff?

McCracklin: Did I ever do what?

Stewart: Have to wring a chicken's neck and pick all the feathers off it, you know? Did you have to do that?

McCracklin: Well, I've never really killed a chicken. That was up to the older kids.

Stewart: You just, what, fed the animals or am I reading into something here?

McCracklin: No, I never plowed mules, my older brother was doing that and my dad. But I picked cotton and chopped corn and picked peas and dug up potatoes.

Stewart: Wow. So, did you have time to go to school?

McCracklin: Oh yeah. We went to school every day. They made sure we went to school, you know.

Stewart: Okay. Now, this is a funny question. Did you ever go bare-feet in the country?

McCracklin: Why do you ask me something like that?

Stewart: You know why I ask you something like that, because my mother, she's from Pine Bluff, and she said, "We never put on shoes until we went to school."

McCracklin: You want to know the answer if I ever went barefeeted? Okay. I'm gonna let you answer this for me: is an elephant heavy?

Stewart: Yeah very! [laughter]

McCracklin: That's the answer right there, if an elephant is heavy. [laughs]

Stewart: Okay, because my mother said that they never really put on shoes until they went to church on Sunday.

McCracklin: Oh, we didn't go to church bare-feeted.

Stewart: No, they put on shoes, she said.

McCracklin: Just round the home, and in the fields–bare-feeted was the thing, you know. At one time, you know, loved to go bare-feeted. A lot of people still go bare-feet.

Stewart: You know, I would love to know, did you have overalls? I'm trying to get a mental picture. Did y'all wear overalls then?

McCracklin: We wore it all: overalls, short pants, and all of it.

Stewart: Well, Jimmy, how was the weather in Arkansas in the summer?

McCracklin: Well, it's just like anywhere else.

Stewart: Was it hot?

McCracklin: It was rough in the summer, that's all. I mean, hot in the summer months.

Stewart: And I presume y'all had outhouses and all that. Did y'all have inside plumbing or outside?

McCracklin: Well, It was outside at that time.

Stewart: Everybody had them.

McCracklin: Yeah, that's right.

Stewart: Well, let me ask you something. Have you ever heard of Hope, Arkansas?

McCracklin: Oh yeah, that's right around the corner of Helena.

Stewart: Okay, now, you know Hope is the watermelon capital, probably, of the world. They grow the biggest watermelons in the world in Hope.

McCracklin: I never recall playing music in Hope, but I know where Hope is.

Stewart: Did you ever go pick watermelons there?

McCracklin: No. I left there when I was about nine. I never lived there after that.

Stewart: Why did you leave your family? I'm not trying to be too nosy, but–you was nine years old!

McCracklin: Well, I had a cousin. He was a lot older than I was, but he wanted to go to the city. I used to fool around in school and hit boys and knock them out, and he said, "You could be a good fighter if you leave." So, I wanted to be a fighter, I thought I did, and inasmuch, I left and went to St. Louis and got started in the boxing game. I won, there, two Golden Gloves championships, actually three Golden Gloves.

Stewart: What weight, Jimmy?

McCracklin: Well, I started as a lightweight, went to welterweight, and up to middleweight.

Stewart: Go on, Jimmy.

McCracklin: I was training under a guy by the name of Pop Slaughter.

Stewart: Pop Slaughter, his name is pretty famous, ain't it?

McCracklin: Oh yeah, he was real famous. Well, of course, his son was the lieutenant governor of Missouri a few years ago.

Stewart: Oh.

McCracklin: I used to work with Pop Slaughter.

Stewart: And who?

McCracklin: Pop Slaughter, and all the fellows round the gym.

Stewart: Pop Slaughter. Now, he was your manager or trainer?

McCracklin: Well, he was a trainer. He owned a gym there in St. Louis on Bell Street. He used to train Sugar Ray Robinson and even Louis used to work out in his gym.

Stewart: Joe Louis?

McCracklin: Joe Louis, yeah.

Stewart: Did Kid Galahad ever [train there]?

McCracklin: I got to know him real good. No, Kid Galahad wasn't around St. Louis.

Stewart: You got to know Joe Louis?

McCracklin: Oh yeah, very well.

Stewart: Oh, okay. Now, you left Arkansas at nine, you wasn't boxing at nine?

McCracklin: I was just a young kid, boxing, you know.

Stewart: How old were you when you had your first amateur fight?

McCracklin: I started boxing when I was about seventeen or sixteen.

Stewart: Wow, Jimmy, you were real young.

McCracklin: Oh yeah, I was a young guy. That's when I met Archie Moore, he used to train there.

Stewart: Now, you and him became real good friends, I think—Archie Moore?

McCracklin: Yeah, we became good friends.

Stewart: Did he live with you at one point, or was that Sugar Ray Robinson?

McCracklin: Well, we lived with each other, Archie did. He used to live with me, and I lived with him. In fact, he the one influenced me in coming to California.

Stewart: Archie Moore?

McCracklin: Yeah, I came to California, and I lived in his place in San Diego.

Stewart: That's during the high point of his career, before he really became famous.

McCracklin: Yeah, that was during the time he was trying to get to the light—heavyweight championship of the world.

Stewart: Wow.

McCracklin: I was living with him then.

Stewart: He was very popular then.

McCracklin: Before that, he got awful sick. And he had a café up there. I used to run his café up there, take care of his home, take care of his family. I learned a lot from him boxing, you know.

Stewart: Jimmy, how many bouts you think you had, how many fights you had?

McCracklin: Oh, I did about close to thirty.

Stewart: Did you ever knock anybody out?

McCracklin: Not really. I only had twenty-one knockouts.

Stewart: [laughs] Oh, man!

McCracklin: It was in the magazines. It was in *Ring* magazine*,* and all of that, you know. I have records of it round here somewhere.

Stewart: You was in *Ring* magazine*?*

McCracklin: Yes, I was. Well, I can show you some records of it, if you want to look at it.

Stewart: We take your word. Wow, I didn't know that.

McCracklin: Oh yeah.

Stewart: You could have just as well become famous in the ring as you did as an entertainer and songwriter.

McCracklin: Well, yeah, well, I could, Ronnie. But I got hurt in a car wreck, accident. I was coming from Los Angeles, I was trying to play music and fight, and I had a head-on collision with a tractor trailer.

Stewart: Wow. Were you by yourself?

McCracklin: No. I had a boy with me. I hate to mention his name, because he died in the front seat, and I was fortunate enough to walk away from the accident. I walked away, and, well, that's what you say when the good Lord's in your corner. His name was Peter Morgan. He has a real famous brother, Joe Morgan, the ballplayer.

Stewart: Yeah!

McCracklin: Almost as young as his brother. Peter was a musician, he was a drummer.

Stewart: What? Jimmy, this is the first time–

McCracklin: Well, this is a big world, you know?

Stewart: Joe Morgan! Yeah, he was raised in Oakland.

McCracklin: Well, Joe Morgan is his brother, and Peter was Joe Morgan's brother. He played drums.

Stewart: I never knew that.

McCracklin: He died in the accident, yeah. Right coming out of Los Angeles in the Grapevine. Just one of them things, you know. I was fortunate enough to walk away.

Stewart: You didn't get hurt at all, hardly?

McCracklin: Not really, no. I got shook up a little bit.

Stewart: And you just decided to stop boxing then?

McCracklin: Well, I didn't decide, you know. My shoulders got hurt, and I was advised by a lot of people, say, "You can sing until you get a hundred, you can't fight that long."

Stewart: [laughs] You know, Jimmy, it's amazing. You're so easygoing. No one would never thought you'd be a boxer.

McCracklin: Well, I don't like talking about it. That's history. That's in the past.

Stewart: You really, excuse the pun, but you're a really dangerous person. You can really hurt somebody.

McCracklin: Well, you know, once you learn, you can always take care of yourself. That's the greatest part. What happened is once I got off into music and starting writing songs and stuff, then I just got away from the fight game. I watch it sometime.

Stewart: When did you start learning the piano, because you're one of the few people who can play after hours. And you have to be a piano player to play after hours. When did you first sit down to the piano?

McCracklin: I did it like you did it, I just picked it up.

Stewart: Oh, okay.

McCracklin: Now, don't tell me you play my music. You play anything just by ear. So I just picked it up. When I was around St. Louis, I was a kid. I used to watch this old guy, Walter Davis, and people like him. There was great blues singers.

Stewart: You got to see Walter Davis?

McCracklin: Oh yeah, my father and him was buddy-buddy. I used to look at him play and listen to him sing the blues. It just got into me, and I said, "Someday I'm gonna do it." So, here I am.

Stewart: Did you ever get to perform at St. Louis when you was young?

McCracklin: No, I didn't perform at St. Louis at that time because I wasn't off into it. I was in the fighting business mostly in St. Louis. But I have performed in St. Louis several times.

Stewart: Yeah, after you made it. So, I would presume that your first professional gig was in L.A.

McCracklin: I would say my first professional gig was in Los Angeles.

Stewart: Did you know Johnny Morris and the Blazers and all them people like that?

McCracklin: Yeah, I met Johnny Morris in Oakland up here. But Johnny Morris wasn't in Los Angeles at that time; him and Bob White and all them folks. I think my first professional gig, if I recall right, was in Los Angeles. I believe that was during either the late fifties or late sixties. We used to play for a guy down there, in a little place called Jack Biscuit. I couldn't hardly carry a tune so good then, but if I remember right...

Stewart: Oh, you was singing then.

McCracklin: Yeah, I was doing singing and playing too. Playing my way the best I could play. It fitted what I was doing, you know. From there on out, that's what I started doing, and Jack Biscuit was my first professional job. I believe that was around 1959 or 1957, it was in that era.

Stewart: I thought it'd be before that, because you had records out.

McCracklin: No. Not playing music. See, a lot of guys get one thing wrong. A lot of people think I've been making records since '45. I was not making records in '45.

Stewart: Yeah, that's when everybody tell me you started.

McCracklin: No, that is wrong. You see what happens is, one guy come along with a pencil, and he uses his own ideas. He runs it, somebody else sees it. they'll take it. She get it, she'll take it. That's what they all can go by. It ain't the facts that I wasn't making records in '45. All I ever did, when I actually started to try and make records was around 1949 or 1950, when I actually started to making records. But what I was doing, I'd make a lot of what they call dubs.

Stewart: Yeah, demos, dubs.

McCracklin: Demos. And Ronnie, and what happened is those demos is with people like Bob Geddins and stuff like that, and Brad Taylor and them folks over in San Francisco, they kept up with those dubs. They'd take it they self. They'd put the dub out and put whatever date they want to put on it. That's just the way all that started.

Stewart: You know, I'm so glad we interviewed you because you're correcting history here. Historians have you, I've seen you in books, Jimmy, recorded first in 1942 and then '45.

McCracklin: No, God, no, not in '42!

Stewart: [laughs] Yes, I seen it! I seen it! I seen a book out of England.

McCracklin: I didn't even know what a studio was back in that time. [laughter] I have to be honest about it. It was about 1948, 1949 when I started making all them dubs. We used to run to the studio, it didn't cost us but two or three dollars. I thought I could sing and play. Me and the fellas would get together. We'd run down to the studio and make a dub. I'd come up to an old man and say, "You want to hear this dub?" "Yeah, leave it here, I'll listen to it." You know anything, you got about twenty-or thirty-five dubs stacked up on there, and they'd take them dubs and sell 'em. They took advantage of it. Who cared about a date, you know?

So, this is the way all that stuff got started. So one guy, he'll write from that. Some other guy, he'll write from that. And then another one will write from it. That's the way it is. So, I just let it be. It can't hurt nothing.

Stewart: So, you didn't even have contracts, there'd just be dubs like you say.

McCracklin: I didn't have nothing!

Stewart: Demos and they would take it and...

McCracklin: And right today, someone has stuff that we was doing in '49 or '50, and all that kind of stuff? It's out on the market! People buying it as a record. Believe it or not, a lot of them like that old stuff. [laughter]

So, this is the way that you get all of that stuff out there in front. And a lot of them say, no, he was born in Oklahoma. You'll write Oklahoma, another one will write Oklahoma. They don't get the real facts about it. They don't care about it, they just want to write on you.

Stewart: Well, see, I found out, as I started chronicle-izing the history and doing what I'm doing now, a lot of people from England, a lot of writers, they tend to make blues like some fairytale life. You sell your soul to the devil and all this Robert Johnson crap. It's kind of like, almost, they try to make some kind of mystery story out of the blues. They don't want to really deal with the truth.

Like Tin Pan Alley, they said that that was a real story. That's just some lyrics.

McCracklin: I've heard that question a lot about the blues. The blues is the originator of jazz, gospel, and all that stuff. It's the blues. That's why I've been fortunate enough to be what you call a writer as well– because the blues is a thing that is a true facts in life. It's not nothing that you guess up on, or create to happen. It's something that's happening or done happened. That's what you write the blues for.

Stewart: Through trials and tribulations of life.

McCracklin: That's right. It's a real part of life. You can take rap, or whatever you might take it, all created from the blues as they called it the blues. And like I said, it's a God-given thing because it's happening in real life. It don't have nothing to do with the color or nothing else. It's the real part of life. So, that's what makes the blues.

Stewart: When did you actually sign your first record contract? Was that with Bob Geddins?

McCracklin: No, no, no. I never signed a record contract with Bob Geddins in my life. [laughter] To be all honest about it, he was a nice fellow, he knew what he was doing. But what happened with Bob Geddins is, Bob Geddins would take your stuff and run the hell away with it. He'd sell it and take your dubs.

Stewart: So, he'd go like to Martin Records.

McCracklin: Any record company because he knew how to contact them and who to contact. But as far as signing a contract with Bob Geddins or Bob Geddins writing this for me, that never happened, Ronnie.

Stewart: So, you never really had a recording contract with Big Town or any of the big labels he had?

McCracklin: Oh, yeah, I had a contract with Mercury Records.

Stewart: No, but Bob had Uptown Records, Big Town. He had the name escapes me of some of his record companies. Art-Tone wasn't that his label?

McCracklin: No, of course, Art-Tone was my label.

Stewart: Oh, I thought that was him?

McCracklin: No, no. I own nine labels myself.

Stewart: I'm glad we could get that straight. One of these writers say that Art-Tone was Bob Geddins' label.

McCracklin: Bob Geddins ain't had nothing to do with Art-Tone. He didn't even know Art-Tone exists. That's Jimmy McCracklin. That's the first label I ever actually owned myself. You go to a recording company on your own, and they wouldn't do it the way they want you to do it. So, you put your own label out.

Stewart: Right.

McCracklin: See? Twenty-five years or thirty-five years ago, you could make your own record label, you go over to the radio station and get it heard.

Stewart: That's changed since then.

Crawford: Am I making you nervous, Ronnie?

Stewart: No.

Crawford: Okay, I just wanted to get him in the video too.

Stewart: Yes, keep rolling.

McCracklin: Yeah, so Art-Tone was Jimmy McCracklin, is still Jimmy McCracklin.

Stewart: Okay, okay, because I have a discography of Bob Geddins, and it had Art-Tone as one of his labels.

McCracklin: No, he had nothing to do with Art-Tone.

Stewart: Maybe because you recorded with him.

McCracklin: I never recorded with him. What happened, Ronnie, I keep telling you. The way Bob got in possession of Jimmy McCracklin's material is I'd go to the studio, on my own, with my musicians, we'd make a dub. The cat at the bar "Man, listen to this." Said, "Aw yeah, leave it here. I want to listen to it." This is the way Bob got in connection with me, and I've told a thousand people this, which is the truth. I don't have no reason to lie, because lying ain't proving anything. Bob didn't write nothing for me– I've been writing my own stuff ever since I got into it.

Stewart: Well, Jimmy, let's talk about the most important record ever out of Oakland, ever. A blues record, there ain't no question, historically speaking with the longevity and the long-life. You know what I'm gonna say, "The Thrill is Gone." "The Thrill is Gone," on the record you see Geddins, Hawkins, and McCracklin. I've seen it Geddins, Hawkins, and McCracklin. I've seen it Geddins, McCracklin. I've seen it Hawkins, McCracklin. I've seen it three or four different ways. Could you tell us the story about the most important record, ever, out of Oakland because that record had two lives. It had B.B. King, and it had M.C. Hammer. B.B. King's used to be "Sweet Sixteen," until he done "The Thrill is Gone," and that's his most popular.

McCracklin: To be all honest with you, I wouldn't lie. Roy Hawkins, Bob Geddins, had nothing to do with the writing of "The Thrill is Gone."

Stewart: What about the music?

McCracklin: Well, the music is always the same thing. All of it was one weight. There's one artist that has something to do with the writing, that's Jimmy McCracklin. I wouldn't lie. Bob Geddins had nothing to do with "The Thrill is Gone." All that Roy Hawkins had to do with it was learning the lyrics and singing it. At that particular time that we did "The Thrill is Gone," we did it at Sierra Sounds right here in Oakland, in Berkeley.

Stewart: Sierra Sounds, I thought that was done in 1949.

McCracklin: That was around '49 or '51. It was definitely between '49 and '55.

Stewart: Okay.

McCracklin: This is where I paid for the section. I and Roy was good partners, you know. Roy was hurt in an accident—he only had one hand. He played with one hand on the piano, and I played the bass part. Roy's left arm got paralyzed in an accident.

Stewart: A car accident.

McCracklin: A car accident. Roy played the lead part on the piano, and I played the bass. I wrote the lyrics, every word that's in there, "The Thrill is Gone." Roy sung it. I paid for the musicians: Ulysses James, Floyd, whoever was on it. I paid them. It wasn't that bad to pay, ten or twelve dollars all we was paid.

Stewart: Can you remember the musicians?

McCracklin: One guy was named Ulysses James. He was a guitar player.

Stewart: Oh, it wasn't Lafayette?

McCracklin: No, it wasn't Lafayette. See, a lot of folks don't know, until you find out exactly what's happening.

Stewart: That's what we're here for, yeah.

McCracklin: And we had another horn player, it was another horn player on it. I can't recall. Those guys have died now.

Stewart: It wasn't Lovey Lovejoy?

McCracklin: Lovejoy? Oh, no, no, no, no. Lovejoy didn't exist. And the bass player was named Floyd Montgomery. Whatever the other guys was, it wasn't more than four or five of us.

I did this thing at Sierra Sounds with Roy Hawkins. He sung it. Why he sung it, why Jimmy McCracklin didn't sing it, at that time, I couldn't sing that type of thing like Roy could have performed it. I even, right there in my player, I got a tape over there to show you the day we cut it. Right in that box, I could show it to you now. I'll show it to you before you leave here. And the way Bob Geddins come into possession, have any kind of name put on "The Thrill is Gone" was, we took him the dub.

Stewart: There you go, here's where it happened, okay.

McCracklin: This is where it happened. What Bob did, we wanted to try to get on a label. We didn't have the knowledge, or the connection, the know–how to go to major labels like Blues Time and deal with folks in there. We go to Bob because he was educated in that business. He was a master when it comes down to making deals and getting yourself in there. I give credit where it's due. Bob took the dub, he goes to Modern Music down in Los Angeles.

Stewart: Modern Music?

McCracklin: The Bihari Brothers.

Stewart: The Bihari Brothers?

McCracklin: The Biharis. He leaves the dub and everything with them. They say, "Yeah, we kinda like this." So, what they did, they put it out, and they didn't get the worldwide exposure or the big sales on it from Roy. They took a shot on it, they put it out.

Bob had his name on there, he didn't have his name, but the way Bob would go down, when he'd get to make a deal "I wrote this, I did." He ain't wrote nothing! But we didn't care. All we cared about was getting our name on the record and getting out there to try to work, make some money.

This is the way it happened, man, you know. So after Modern put out the record later on, I'll say ten or twelve years—see, a lot of folks get the wrong idea about B.B. I didn't actually write that song for B.B. The way B.B. got this song, he heard it on the record that we took to Modern and Modern put into a record. This is the way B.B. came into it. And he'll tell you today, he know I wrote it. He admits that it's myself. [In a documentary film entitled "Jimmy Sings the Blues," a film based on these interviews made by the editor, B.B. King says that McCracklin was the author of the song]

But what happened is, B.B. heard the record, and he kinda switched it around and "This is what I like!" so he puts it out there and all of a sudden, boom!

Stewart: Huge hit. Big hit.

McCracklin: Yeah, it's a platinum for him, you know. The greatest thing he ever did. But what happened is, after B.B. got the record out there, Roy called me from Dallas and told me. I said, "What record?" I couldn't even remember it.

Stewart: What?!

McCracklin: I couldn't remember it.

Stewart: Hold that thought, hold that thought.

McCracklin: I hope it's doing you some good because I'm telling you the truth. Getting back to "The Thrill is Gone," this is the way that B.B. got a hold of "The Thrill is Gone." He got it from the record.

Stewart: So, he somehow heard Roy Hawkins.

McCracklin: He heard the record that I did with Roy, me and Roy did.

Stewart: How did Modern get it from Bob Geddins? How did they steal it? How did they get the rights?

McCracklin: They didn't steal anything. Bob didn't steal it. Let me explain. I go through the same thing.

Stewart: How did they get the publishing then?

McCracklin: They had possession. We knew nothing about copyright and publishing and all that stuff. So, this is the way you gets it back in them days.

Stewart: Forties and fifties.

McCracklin: You don't know how to protect, a writer, or get the writer's credit. In them days, ninety percent of the average Black musician, blues singer trying to get out there and get a name for himself, all he really cared about was getting his name on the label.

Stewart: Right.

McCracklin: And see, people like Bob, and Bihari Brothers, and all them folks already in the business, this is where those folks became multimillionaires. Not only Bihari Brothers, mostly nine out of ten record sales. What they'd do, they'd take the Black guy's stuff, put it out, put their name on theirs, publish it, sell it as in-house publishing, while we didn't know how to do that.

Stewart: And they took all the credit.

McCracklin: They'd take everything!

Stewart: The publishing, the writing. And that's all the economics of the record.

McCracklin: And we be walking up down the street, smoking a cigar, like we done did a great thing. We have, for somebody else. But until you learn, it costs you, you know?

Stewart: Yeah, okay.

McCracklin: See, that's why you said nothing beats experience. So, this is the way Modern got the record. Modern put it on their house, as a publisher. They put their name and Bob's name on there as a writer. But now what happened is some fellow up in Seattle, some older white fellow, I guess he's eighty or ninety years old. But what I want to say is this. He even got credit for "The Thrill is Gone." Ronnie, anybody with common sense would know back in the forties and the fifties or the sixties or the seventies or the eighties, there's no white person out of America could sit down and write a "Thrill is Gone." Now, let's be honest about it.

Stewart: [laughs] I have to laugh.

McCracklin: But what he is a record collector. I don't even know the guy. He's a record collector, and he got credit for it.

Stewart: No, what he is, Jimmy, I found out about that. He's really not a record collector in the sense he's a publishing collector.

McCracklin: That's the same thing, Ronnie–

Stewart: Modern Records, yes, he's a record collector.

McCracklin: Don't cut me off while I'm thinking.

Stewart: Go ahead.

McCracklin: So what he did, he would go out and collect all them old guys'

records and stuff?

Stewart: He'd check the copyright.

McCracklin: He gonna take it. He sends it in to see if he can get a clearance on it, and if you ain't paid by public demand to keep it going, he get a claim that he's a writer!

Stewart: Yes, it's his now.

McCracklin: So, this is the way I'm thinking, this is why we still in court on this. I'm gonna get my song. But, like I'm saying, this is the way that I have a problem with "The Thrill is Gone."

Stewart: So, you found the guy, y'all found him. He's in Oregon?

McCracklin: Yeah. Oh yeah, they're searching over there, because he gonna admit "I didn't write it." All he did was–

Stewart: Re-copyright it.

McCracklin: He got it copyrighted.

Stewart: He re-copied it. When it became public domain.

McCracklin: It was never copyrighted from Modern. They didn't ever take the chance on doing it the right way.

Stewart: You mean, they didn't even copyright it?!

McCracklin: They didn't do nothing. They didn't copyright, they didn't say who wrote it.

Stewart: Oh! See, when a lot of record companies go out of business, somebody [takes over] all the publishing—the whole publishing house of their whole catalog. They might have had, say, fifteen artists. Well, all the publishing on that, they have these sales and people just buy them up. So, it wasn't even that. Man, I mean, I'm more shocked.

McCracklin: Modern Music never even copyrighted it.

Stewart: It went through <u>they</u> hands!

McCracklin: They didn't give Jimmy McCracklin, no Roy Hawkins, nobody credit for nothing.

Stewart: They was stupid to themselves!

McCracklin: This is regardless of what you might think, but this is the way it went down. What they did, they put the song out in a 78. They sent it to the radio station, the song didn't catch on with Roy. They threw it on the shelf, "To heck with it," you know?

Then, twenty years later, here some guy come along, that picks up all that old stuff, he sends in the copies and everything, and if you don't pay my public demand or you ain't got it copyrighted, that's his song! This is the way these people come buy them things. There are people out there like him, that's all they do to survive, you know?

Stewart: Is look for records?

McCracklin: They look for that stuff, where what you call the weakest link have fouled up, and didn't take care of it. But see now, how can you take a song now? Look at the money and the stuff that I've lost and things that I went through to learn all of that. Look what it cost me! It cost me a lifetime almost. I had that same problem with a song called "The Walk." I'm the original [writer], from every note to every verse.

Crawford: Great song.

McCracklin: Oh, thank you. I had that problem with "The Walk" with Chess Records in Chicago.

Stewart: Leonard Chess or Phil Chess?

McCracklin: Both of them, all of them. But what happened is, they took fifty percent from me for about fifteen or twenty years as writer and all of that stuff. They took all the publishing because I didn't have the knowledge of doing it.

Stewart: Did you ever get that back? Get full control?

McCracklin: No. I never will get the publishing back on that.

Stewart: They made a lot of money off that, didn't they?

McCracklin: Oh, Christ, well, "Walk" was a platinum at that time. However, I did get credit for one hundred percent as writer. Yeah, through the people that clears all that stuff up that's working on "The Thrill is Gone." I haven't given up on "The Thrill is Gone." But what I'm saying is, they took twenty percent as writers from Broadcast Music, collectors and everything. I couldn't do nothing about it.

Stewart: God! What snakes! Jimmy, I'm sorry, these are outright crooks. You don't take advantage of people's knowledge, I mean in that sense. They knew they was ripping you off.

McCracklin: Well, if you don't know—I'm just one in a thousand of them. There's thousands of them, the same thing happened to them. You know. If you don't know how to go about protecting yourself, you get hurt.

But see now, the guys coming along now, what they calling these days, they got peoples out there protecting them before they even get started. That don't happen to them. They don't know what we went through, man, you know. So I don't have no grudge against it because I've learned, and I have what you call accomplished an awful lot by learning, by giving away and giving up so much, by not knowing. So, that's just the way the music business was, you know? And it's the same thing in boxing or anything that you got to have other folks doing it for you. If you don't know how to protect yourself, they gonna get you.

Stewart: So, you don't have no ill will against the Biharis—

McCracklin: Why should I?

Stewart: —or Leonard Chess—because they took advantage of you?

McCracklin: No, I don't have no ill will against nobody but Jimmy McCracklin. But I didn't know, so I don't have no ill will against him, really.

Stewart: Yeah, so they say, ignorance of the law is no excuse. That's what a lot of attorneys or establishments would say: "Ignorance of the law is no excuse."

McCracklin: That's true. Well, speaking of attorneys, it's just like one of these big record companies take your stuff, and you want to try and clear it up and get it up back.

At the modern cost of these days, it costs you—if you ain't well off, it costs you so much money to hire peoples to go in there and clear that stuff up. And if you ain't got the money to do it with, then well, them folks going to keep it, because it's just like trying to fight the government, you know? You can't buck the government, and you can't buck them big companies and things.

It's like putting out records these days–I've still got my own label. I got Art-Tone, I still got Voice, I still got Premium, I still got Oak City Records label. That's my stuff.

Stewart: Oak City.

McCracklin: I own two publishers, yeah. But like I'm saying, I could put my own record out tomorrow. But getting it exposed and doing it like it should do, I can't buck these big labels. I don't care how good a record you got, if you don't get it exposed and people don't hear you right, you ain't got nothing. Did you hear my latest CD I did?

Stewart: No.

McCracklin: Everybody here says it's a monster, you know? I got Oak City Records, but I haven't moved with it yet, because I got several people is trying to get it.

Stewart: You got to get a distributor, right?

McCracklin: Distributing ain't the hassle to it. You can get a distributor, and still can't get the exposure, the promotion behind it.

Stewart: Oh yeah, that's what counts, the promotion, the marketing.

McCracklin: Yeah. But the big record companies and the big companies, they've got it sewed up. See, and eventually, you put it out there and get enough action for them to hear, and they'll grab for it.

So that's the name of the game now. You can't buck them folks, you know. It's just fortunate enough, like when B.B. came along and took "The Thrill is Gone," he was fortunate enough to get a guy, the guy picked him up, what they call a hippie guy, picked him up as manager. B.B. had no manager. And you can't do it yourself. He picked him up, and he had money.

He went to all the foxholes he could get into, and got it out there. B.B.'s my buddy, he's a good friend of mine. But like I'm saying, every time he comes to Oakland, he comes here. In fact, he stays overnight with me, and all that stuff. But what happened is this. If he don't get that exposure, he'd a still been in the same position that he was in forty years ago.

But he got that exposure. That don't mean that B.B. is no better guitar player than Ronnie Stewart, or whoever. It's the world who know him and who heard of him. They ain't ever heard of Ronnie Stewart. Ronnie Stewart might could play all around him. But who is Ronnie Stewart?

Stewart: Right.

McCracklin: B.B. don't play no better, maybe not as good. So, this is the idea of exposure, and you cannot take a small record company and buck those big record companies and get exposure because that's the way ninety percent of the DJ's of the TV and the radio stations and all that stuff makes their living is payoff. They'll never stop payoff.

Stewart: Yeah, they claim they did, but they ain't.

McCracklin: Oh yeah, well that's just something to try to calm–

Stewart: Put out there in the news, yeah, to calm the public.

McCracklin: They'll never stop that, man, because if that was the case, it would be just like it used to be. Anybody could play you a record, and you could get your record played. You could go to a radio station now, and in order to get your record promoted and played, you got to pay for it, and if you don't pay for it, you don't get played, you don't get heard.

Stewart: Well, where's that at now, Jimmy? Actually, where are you at with "The Thrill is Gone," as far as the law side. Are you close or are you still where you were at five years ago? Are you still where you were at ten years ago? In other words, the development of you getting your just dues, how far are you from that? Is there a court date and will there be a court date?

McCracklin: On what?

Stewart: On "The Thrill is Gone." Have you been to court about it yet?

McCracklin: Well, it's over a year now that they've been holding it up and waiting to go ahead to make a movement on it. You see, the people out of Chicago, the Cameron Organization, they are the ones handling it.

Stewart: Scott Cameron?

McCracklin: So, you know, and so many of them. They've got thousands of things going on, and you just have to wait until your time come. You can't push it; you can't rush it. So, when he get the right position to make the right move, then he gonna move. Actually, what's happening out there now, Ronnie, I guess you understand it. Money is what running the country. Money used to didn't run the country, the best thing was running the country, but now it's money. It's like a lot of folks say, I don't like rap because rap did me a lot of good royalty wise, you know. About sixteen different guys cut my song on the rap, you know? They've got platinums and stuff off it. But a lot of people don't know that Jimmy McCracklin created and wrote that stuff and did all that. All they know about is who they heard it by.

Stewart: That's it.

McCracklin: See? Just like the Salt-N-Pepa. They biggest record was "Tramp." Lowell Fulson's biggest record was "Tramp." Lowell didn't write one word of it or produce it. I did all of that. But I was just fortunate enough to know how to get my percentage off it, and give Lowell a piece for doing it because Lowell started it. Like I'm saying, look at the money that I lost before I was able to protect myself.

Stewart: God, man, if you could have got the royalties to "The Thrill is Gone," man, you would have had millions.

McCracklin: It's tough, yeah, it's tough.

Stewart: I bet you "Thrill is Gone" has made almost a million in royalties.

McCracklin: Oh, not almost. "The Thrill is Gone," you see, what you look at, you don't look at as one person. Look at the different rap guys, and the different peoples cutting. You know, you don't have to take one guy to sell a million. You can take fifteen or twenty different peoples, then put it out. You sell a million records. A million records ain't a lot of records to sell, when you think how big the world is.

Stewart: Right. That's right.

McCracklin: A million records ain't nothing to sell. You'd sell a million records –it's just like if you pick up the newspaper, look at the television. Ninety-nine percent of the people that you see there getting Grammys and all that kind of stuff is because of the connections and money. It's not that they're that great. And see, what can you do about it. Nothing, but hope that you can get somebody about you to give you a shot like that. It's just like I said. B.B. King might not play no better guitar than you play. You a hell of a guitar player.

Stewart: Thank you.

McCracklin: But who know Ronnie Stewart? He never had the exposure that B.B. King got. But you play just as good or great as he do. So, this is what I'm saying. Until you get to that position that what they call to "get into the clique," you just at a standstill. I'm just fortunate enough to get out there long enough and have so many records out there. They can't hardly deny me, you know?

Stewart: Speaking of that, how did you come up with "The Thrill is Gone?" What inspired you because you know blues is an art form of expression. How did you write it?

McCracklin: No, no it ain't that, Ronnie. It's a true-life thing. It's true, it's just true. Just like folks have questioned me how you come up with "I Just Gotta Know", how you come up with "Think." It's the same thing. Blues is all in life. It's real life happening. Otherwise, you was in love and "Thrill is Gone" is simple. At that time, you could thrill each other, anything was beautiful. Then, you fall out "The Thrill is Gone," ain't nothing there no more.

Stewart: No more love.

McCracklin: That's the whole song.

Stewart: All I can do is wish you well.

McCracklin: Yeah. Wish you well, hope you get back to somebody else.

Stewart: I'm free.

McCracklin: It's all the same thing.

Stewart: I'm free from your spell.

McCracklin: Yeah, you free. You don't have to worry about what they do no more. I'm going out there and getting me something new. It's down man, it's just come alive. It's just like "Think."

Stewart: Did that take you long to write, "Thrill is Gone?"

McCracklin: Oh, no. It don't take me long to write no song. I get my mind made up, I see that my life and other folks' life, I'd write a song within two days. But see, writing a song ain't all of it. The meanings of what you writing and putting the right melody to is what counts.

Stewart: Sure do. The words, but the melody gotta go. "The Thrill is Gone" is very haunting. It's minor, it's in a minor key. It's almost kind of gospely. You talkin' of "Well, I'm free."

McCracklin: But what about "Think?" I just got to doing all them songs. Do you realize how powerful "Think" lyrics is?

Stewart: I know. Yeah, I know. I always think about that.

McCracklin: "I can give up my woman, you can give up your man." Well, that don't make no kinda sense really in the world to take a chance before you think. See, a lot of things would never happen to you if you think in front. You gotta think, see, it's just common sense, see?

Stewart: You better think. What would we do?

McCracklin: Yeah. What we do later on? Down the road, later, you find out both of y'all was wrong, you are in trouble.

Stewart: Yeah, you'd a made a mistake, huh. You'd a made a real big mistake 'cause you didn't think.

McCracklin: That's the way it goes, you know.

Stewart: Well, in them songs that you just thought of, it wasn't just like I want to sit down and write a song. This was something you saw happen to somebody, or happened to you, or happening–

McCracklin: It's just a real life thing. You see life, man, you know? I got a song on this new CD called "Hate." Once I get the exposure on it. I'm supposed to meet tonight with an outfit. They is talking about exposure. You never heard "Hate" did you?

Stewart: No. We get to hear it before the world.

McCracklin: I'm gonna play a little bit for you. Want me to?

Stewart: Yeah.

McCrackin: I want you to hear this. This is the idea that I—right outta my basement. [Plays piano and sings]

Someone in heaven / Please help us on this earth. / Take away that hate / And make a first. / If we don't stop that hate / And our voice is not heard / Hate, oh hate will destroy the world. // There's so many people / That can't get along/ Because that old devil / Is hanging around their homes / If we don't stop that hate/And our voice is not heard/Hate, oh hate. (piano solo).

McCracklin: (laughs) After hours! Here's a song here that was sung by Percy Mayfield. His wife begged me to do it, so here the way I did it. [plays piano]

Stewart: What about legends like you, B.B. and Muddy? You think the people will always relate back to you guys and use your songs to inspire?

Well, I might think that way, you know, but there's always gonna be somebody who will copy some of your stuff, you know. I don't care who it is, how long you're gone, somebody will always have a feeling for what you're doing, and they'll use it because you cannot just ignore that originated stuff.

You asked what other artists covered "The Walk"–Oh Lord, I don't know. Man, it's been covered about between eighteen and twenty times, from different artists. Some of them put an instrumental like the late Freddy King, for instance, he got a song called "Hideaway" which is a transition of "The Walk" and I get credit for it, as a writer. So, You name them. I don't know. Just a lot of people.

Rufus Thomas, he recorded "The Walk." And the Beatles, they recorded "The Walk." I can't name all the guys that have cut "The Walk." I have a list here somewhere I can show you a lot of the guys that recorded "The Walk." Los Lobos, Elvin Bishop, all of them cut my stuff. Bonnie Raitt done "Think." Linda Ronstadt done "Think." Yeah, Rufus Thomas, the Beatles. I had almost a hundred people cover my stuff.

Crawford: Jimmy, can you say something more about what made you start writing, what influenced you?

McCrackin: What influenced me? Supposing I would know a friend and I would see that friend as doing all he can in doing the right thing, and someone maybe he's in love with is using him. That could have been me. It could have happened to you.

So, the ideas I'm writing about there, it's just like a journalist or something, you got to have something to write about. So if it's happening in my life or in somebody else's life, that made me want to write about it

Stewart: The real treasures will always be there.

McCracklin: [plays more piano] I'm gonna show you something. They called me for my next section. They want me to do this thing that Little Milton did. [plays and sings]

Now, my momma told me this morning / She woke me up from a deep sleep / She said, "Jimmy, I just gotta tell ya / That something may hurt you / But won't hurt me" / She said, "I got to leave you, baby."

Listen. Now, hear the tempo. Here it really go. I'm gonna cut this, listen.

Now, my momma told me this morning / She woke me up from a deep sleep / She said, "Jimmy, I got to tell ya something / May not hurt you, but it's gonna hurt me" / She said, "I got to leave you, baby" / Then she began to cry / She said, "Honey, you're not doing your homework. When you try you don't satisfy." That was too much for me / That's why I walked her back straight and cried, "Why you have to hurt me so bad?" / To hear my baby say goodbye / She said, "You ain't giving nothing to me, / You've been good as a man could be / But baby, hugging and just kissing / Don't do a thing for me." She said, "Jimmy, you the judge and jury / And the warrant to decide the case." She said, "You can keep me or let me go, baby" / And I won't be replaced / I gotta tell you that was too much for me / That's why I walked her back straight and cried / "Why you have to hurt me so bad?" / To hear my baby say goodbye.

Crawford: Jimmy, tell me something. How would you describe the blues. We talk about West Coast blues, Delta blues, Chicago, blues. Tell me about the blues.

McCracklin: To be in all honesty to you, there's no West Coast blues, no Arkansas blues, no Southern blues. Blues is a feeling. It's all in what happened in my life or to someone else's life, which is the true facts and a feeling. When you've been mistreated, you're not the onliest one. Someone else in the world has been mistreated that's the blues. It's all in your feeling and the feeling is a true part of life.

[End of Interview]

Interviewer: Joe Mathews

Date: October 5, 1995

Location: Johnny Otis' studio in Sebastopol, California

Johnny Otis
credit Wikipedia

Mathews: I'd like to start at the beginning if we can do that, where it was that you were born and some of your background

Otis: Born in Vallejo, California, 1921. They tell me the fishing was great in Vallejo In those days, but it ain't shit now, because I just went down there day before yesterday [laughing]. We got caught in the mud flats in the Napa River. Born in Vallejo, raised in Berkeley, California. Son of a grocer. My dad was a grocer. In the community of Berkeley, West Berkeley.

Mathews: So, you were born in Vallejo, and grew up in Berkeley.

Otis: That's right.

Mathews: And your parents were both there. What about your grandparents?

Otis: They were all in the old country, I have no idea.

Mathews: So, your folks immigrated.

Otis: Immigrants, yes.

Mathews: When was that?

Otis: I guess in the teens; before that because my dad was in the San Francisco earthquake, which was 1906. So, around the turn of the century, I suppose.

Mathews: So, your mother and dad came over together?

Otis: No, no, my mom came over as a little girl. My dad came as a young man, very young man. But they didn't know each other yet.

Mathews: Where did they meet?

Otis: I don't know.

Mathews: You have no idea?

Otis: I'll ask her, she's still alive. Ninety-five.

Mathews: So how was it that you wound up in Berkeley then? He opened a grocery store?

Otis: I don't know that either. I want to thank him though. Because it was a wonderful place, still is. It's a matter of opinion, of course. If you lean towards the right you'd think it was a hell hole. But it's a lovely place.

Mathews: Your father was Greek. So, was there a Greek community in Berkeley where you guys were?

Otis: No, no. Thank God it was an African-American community.

Mathews: Virtually all African-American at the time?

Otis: Well, there were a few families, like a Portuguese family and a Japanese family and one German family that I remember. The rest was African-American, was Black.

Mathews: And in your family, did you guys, did your mother and father try to embrace Greek cultural traditions and that kind of stuff through church and school?

Otis: They were raised through it. Sure, they were part of the church in Oakland.

Mathews: What was it, Greek Orthodox?

Otis: Yeah, and I was forced to go there for a while, not too long.

Mathews: How did you finally decide to—

Otis: You know, I had to go to the Greek school. And there was this big bearded, Zoro–type character with the cape and everything, and one day somebody was talking in class. And he came right to me, I hadn't uttered a word because I was very inhibited, I wouldn't have done anything like that, not even talked. And he kept telling me, and pretty soon he made me hold my hand out, and he hit me...real hard on the back of my hand with a ruler. Then, it's a wonder that he didn't break my hand. So I jumped up, I went home and told my mother I wasn't going back. She said, "Yes you are!" I said, "No I'm not." And my dad came home, and I told Pop what had happened, he said, "That son of a bitch!" And he went to get his hat and coat to go down there to kick the priest's ass. I thought that was great.

Mathews: So that pretty much—

Otis: That did it.

Mathews: So, you went to school in the public schools in Berkeley then?

Otis: Yes, the grammar school was two blocks away, Longfellow. Then I went to Burbank, which was about a mile away. Then I went to Berkeley High which was another mile, the other way.

Mathews: So where was your house? Is it still there?

Otis: Yeah. My dad and my aunt's husband, my uncle, bought two pieces of property, one on the corner and one next door. And they built on the corner a grocery store-meat market complex and upstairs a house. And next door a house, And that's where we lived, above the grocery store.

Mathews: So, you had the store downstairs.

Otis: Fifty feet from the railroad track. Dohr and Ward.

Mathews: So, when you were kids and so forth, you know, just growing up in Berkeley, what kind of stuff did you do? I mean, you know, was it just a regular city life? Did your dad fish?

Otis: No. My mom did. She took me fishing once on the Berkeley pier. And we were told we could catch "Pogies" there. Pogies. Probably a corruption of Porgy. But they're not even that. They were little surf Perch, or little pile Perch. They were very nice, we'd catch ' em and fry ' em.

Mathews: And then later on as you were growing up and going to school and so forth, at some point you made a decision consciously or unconsciously or a combination of the two to–

Otis: Many writers have stated it as you just did, and it was never like that. There was never a sudden point, like Paul fell off his horse and suddenly became a Christian. I was raised with my little Black neighbors. I just preferred that life. That culture. And I've constantly stayed there, shall always be. I just knew they were who they were. Georgie Boy, and the rest of 'em. And then as we grew older, uh, I was exposed to their, to their lifestyle, from the very beginning, and I just felt it was mine.

Mathews: And claimed it as your own. What about living during the Depression? Was it hard times?

Otis: You call that living? Well, yes it was hard. My dad became ill and coincidentally the store downstairs went bankrupt because the big supermarket thing had started. Piggly Wiggly stores they called 'em. And they would move in a neighborhood and wipe out all the little grocers. Which is symptomatic of what's wrong with us now, the big corporate, fascist state.

It was plenty tough, and then finally we got on...a program where once a week I'd go on my bicycle to a commissary somewhere and pick up bags of this and bags of that and come home and try to subsist on it.

Mathews: Was your dad ever able to get the grocery store going again?

Otis: No. Nor did he try. He leased it out to a Chinese, to a Japanese man and Chinese man, that took the market. And he went to work at Mare Island Navy Yard. And that's where he worked until he retired in the fifties.

Mathews: Well, as far as your early musical influences. Who did you hear that excited you?

Otis: Not much radio in the early days. In the earliest days of my youth radio wouldn't interest me at all. I don't know what the hell was on radio then. Not that I was disinterested in Bing Crosby, I loved that. But that's not what really grabbed me. There was one man in particular, across the street from us, I remember his name as Mr. Moore. And Mr. Moore was a railroad porter. And he ran on the railroads to Chicago, and back to Oakland. And he lived in Berkeley. And he'd bring records, big 78's. I *assumed* that, I never saw these records, but we used to go to the side of his house where he'd have, the window would be open, we could peek in, and see the older brothers dancing with the beautiful young women and, and hear the records. And that's the stuff I heard, those good ol' blues. The one that piqued our fancy was the song that had naughty connotations. It would say things like, "your battery leaks and your condenser ain't right, baby." It was "Terraplane Blues," by Robert Johnson.

And then on Sundays, my neighborhood buddy was Rudy Jordan, and Rudy and I would go to the little sanctified churches, there were two of them. And they would give, hand out graham crackers and chocolate milk to the kids. That was beyond a delicacy. You wouldn't get anything like that during the Depression. And so, Sundays we'd go there and there were other attractions. The next attraction was the cute little girls were there. And finally, the one that became most important to me that was probably third and fourth on my list was, the gospel singing. And the preaching! I would put them in a different order today. The graham crackers and milk would be last. [laughs]

Mathews: In those days that had to be number one, I guess. What about live performances, you know? I mean, as you were growing into your teen years. and were able to maybe get around a little bit more, were there clubs that you and Rudy and your buddies had access to, either go in or hang out the back door?

Otis: We weren't supposed to go in. We would try to get into Slim Jenkins' and on a couple of occasions we slipped in by wearing hats and coats, but they'd throw us out. That was down on West Seventh Street in West Oakland. and there was an upper level jazz ensemble kind of thing going there. Very good, but down the street, when we were thrown out of Slim Jenkins' we had nowhere to go but the buckets of blood and the greasy spoons up and down the street, and three or four of them had music. And sawdust on the floor, they didn't give a shit if we were two years old let alone fifteen. As long as we could buy a beer, go in there and little blues bands would be playing and we'd hear them.

Mathews: All local guys?

Otis: No, these were southern people. George Vann, who later became some prominence, I remember hearing him. Seeing him playing the drums and singing in one of those little dives. He was singing "Goin' Down Slow." Way back in the thirties. And the gospel thing that I heard. That was the music that excited me. There was another music that I loved that had great influence on me. That was the music at home, of the Mid-Eastern, North-African sounds, of Greek, Arabic, Turkish music. Greek Rebetiko and Turkish music. Yeah, folk music, sure.

Years later, I was trying to find that stuff. I had a thirst to hear that good old Greek, Turkish stuff. I couldn't find it anywhere. And finally somebody said, you ought to go down, this was in L.A., said you ought to go down on Pico where the Greek community shops at the Greek stores down there. So, I go down there, and the guy says: "Sure! I get you good Greek music." And he brought me out the Lawrence Welk of Athens, and I played it and I said, "What is, what is that shit?" He said, "That's a Greek music." And I said, "Well yeah it might be Greek music, but it ain't shit." And he was a little miffed and I left. I couldn't find the stuff I was looking for.

I remember as a little kid, three, four, five years old, at the Greek picnics, the old Greek musicians and Turkish musicians from the old country. And they were men in there in their sixties and seventies then! And so, there would be a five- or six-piece Middle Eastern band, and boy they would play that beautiful stuff. And I didn't hear it anywhere. I knew, I knew what I was listening to, looking for. Finally, in the nineteen eighties, I was in Down Home Music, and one of the guys knew I was a Greek, and he said, "Hey, here's something for you, have fun with that." I said, "I don't want that shit." He said "Why?" I said, "I've heard all those Glenn Millers of Greece." And he said, "No, you'll like it." And he put it on, and I said, "Whoa!!" That was it, and since, I've got a few little albums to listen to now when I feel like I'd like to hear some.

Mathews: What kind of instrumentation was used in those bands?

Otis: In a Greek, Turkish band? An oud. There'd be a violin, a clarinet, an oud, a tambura, a drum and the santoor. That thing that they play that looks like a plano keyboard and they beat on it with sticks. Many of them, going a little farther north and a little farther west, the Slavic people play 'em, you know, some Bulgarians and Yugoslavians.

Mathews: Well, as you were growing older then, somehow or another you took an interest in playing music. What led to that?

Otis: A friend who actually lived in West Oakland, but how he and I became friends I don't know. We were buddying around and he told me he was going to form a band. And that I was going to be his drummer. I said, "I can't play no drums." So, somewhere we found a raggedy old drum set, and he got Robert Johnson on bass, himself on piano and vocals, me on the drums, Al Levy on the guitar and Pops somebody, Ed somebody Preston on trumpet, a man with one hand, I remember. And Pops on clarinet, that was the ensemble. And we played barrelhouse. We didn't have any name for it then, there was no name.

Mathews: Did you bring all this stuff into his house, and set up?

Otis: You know, I don't remember. It's too many years ago, I don't know where we did that.

Mathews: Was that Count Otis Mathews?

Otis: Yeah, Count Otis Mathews, and we would play on Saturday nights at a Black gymnasium in West Oakland. Where boxers were. John Henry Louis, the lightweight champion used to, that was his training camp. Again, we got no money for that. But we didn't care, because the little girls were there.

And that was the idea. You know, originally for most people, folk music grows out of a need to be viewed positively by your peers and the community, and to be thought of as a good musician. Not a trained musician, by any means. And that the little girls would flock around. Count Otis had a device where he had little cans, tomato can full of rocks. I don't know what was in ' em, little pebbles and, he'd call the little girls up one by one, pick out the ones he wanted and there'd be about eight girls on stage and he'd do his featured numbered called, "Mama Bought a Chicken." And they'd shake these shakers [makes shaking sound], and while they were up there we got a chance to lean over and talk to them, and pretty soon, you know, maybe—we had ' em, we hoped!

Mathews: So, these were like community functions, sort of?

Otis: No. They were low–class functions. Those little girl's parents would be horrified to know that they were down there, shakin' butt to the blues. That was the *devil's* music in those days. In the funky gymnasium, but there they were. Youth will not be denied, and especially when it comes to things like, like music and dancing, and the kind of clothes they want to wear.

Mathews: So, you would kind of characterize Count Otis—

Otis: Jump band! Boogie blues band. It was really a party band. After hours party. We would play in people's homes on a Sunday at house rent parties, where we'd play and they would sell illegal whiskey in the back room, and they would sell food.

Mathews: For the purpose of getting folks together, paying the rent.

Otis: No, it would be for the purpose of yes, of making some money. Absolutely, house rent parties. There were no bones about it. Everybody understood that family was raising some money, but that the music was going to be a lot of fun. So, they came. And they bought chitlins and they bought ribs and they bought something to drink–a beer or some white lightnin'. And hope that we didn't go blind when we drank that shit. [laughs]

We would get a jug of wine. We were winos. We thought. We'd take a little taste and we all thought we were high. Just adolescent macho sing.

Mathews: Well, how old were you when you started with Count Otis?

Otis: Fifteen, maybe.

Mathews: Fifteen? And how long did you guys stay together?

Otis: A couple years. Until Robert Johnson, our bass player, landed a job in Reno, Nevada, and we went to Reno, yeah. To play in a little joint called the Pea Vine Club, just three of us. Robert Johnson, myself and Count Otis. And there was a man there already, Bruzart, the trumpet player. And we played there for a while.

Mathews: Were you able to make any kind of a living, just stay alive?

Otis: You know, the man had promised us forty-five dollars a week. Well, for God's sake, we almost died from delight. Forty–five dollars–my father was only making twenty–seven dollars a week. To make forty-five dollars a week was a hell of a good job.

Mathews: So, it seemed like a real opportunity at the time.

Otis: When we got there, it turned out it was forty-five for all three of us. Which was still all right, fifteen bucks for kids. But, we had to live in his hotel, and we had to pay him for the hotel and had to eat in his diner. At the end of the week, we didn't have any money. He swore we'd make tips. We never made a tip in that joint. We played from seven in the evening till four in the morning. Seven nights a week. And hardly anyone was ever in there, a few people would wander in. They had a slot machine or two and that was it. Then a game going on in the back room.

Mathews: Well so, how was it that you, that you decided to leave Count Otis' band, did opportunity come knocking?

Otis: We had decided that we'd had enough of that. Robert Johnson said, "Hey, we can go to Denver, Colorado, and my uncle says he'll get us a job as Pullman porters." Well, Otis didn't want that, he went back to West Oakland. By that time I brought my wife in and we got married in Reno.

Mathews: So you and Phyllis had gotten married by this time.

Otis: She was a childhood friend. I sent for her, and we got married in Reno. And from Reno we went to Denver. And in Denver we *almost* got the porter jobs. A couple more days we'd have been doin' it. But I got a job playing music with George Morrision's band in Denver, that saved me. And from that I wound up in Omaha with Lloyd Hunter's band. And from Lloyd Hunter's band we got our own band, Preston Love and myself, the Otis Love Band, and we played at a place called the Barrelhouse. In Omaha.

And from there I came back to Los Angeles on the advice of Nat Cole and Jimmy Witherspoon, who were not big stars then. And they said, "Harlan Leonard and the Kansas City Rockets are in Los Angeles at the Club Alabam and you got a job." Harlan says, "You come there because his drummer, Jesse Price, has been drafted." So, when I got to L.A. I had a job, a top job in town.

Mathews: Wow. Can you talk about what it was like playing with George Morrison's band, was this a swing band, a territory band?

Otis, Yeah, everything was a swing band in those days. Music wasn't his forte, it was entertainment. And the kind of entertainment, it rankled the younger guys in the band. The older guys didn't like it either but they knew that's the side our bread was buttered on. He would, he would Uncle Tom to the white folks. Not flagrantly, but enough to make it very uncomfortable for us. He'd put on a Red Cap's uniform. And of course being a Red Cap was one job that was reserved for Black people. And he'd come out with his violin and he'd sing. "Danny Boy" and he'd cry, actual tears: "Climb up on my knee, sonny boy with" his Red Cap uniform on. That doesn't sound like Uncle Tomming, but it was. And we'd be very pissed off.

He was a sweet guy. I loved George. He was a fine man, but that was his environment, that was the culture he came out of.

Mathews: Your last major recording effort was *The Spirit of the Black Territory Bands.*

Otis: That would have been more like Harlan Leonard's band, and Lloyd Hunter's band. Which were bands that traveled a prescribed territory, and they remained territory bands until they got a hit record. Should they ever gain a hit record, they're suddenly name bands. Then they could travel nationally. Yeah. Well, anywhere in America, because they'd be known everywhere if they really got a hit.

Mathews: So, your Harlan Leonard experience in Omaha was…

Otis: My Lloyd Hunter experience. Because by time I got with Harlan Leonard, he had left the Midwest and he was functioning on the West Coast. He wasn't functioning as a territory band, he was functioning as the house band at the Club Alabam, he was there for a couple of years.

Mathews: Could you characterize any, just in hindsight, any real important lessons, musically. I don't know, as an entertainer. By this time were you kind of looking at this as your chosen profession, you were going to go with playing music.

Otis: Oh, *way before* I left Berkeley. I had seen Count Basie's band at the 1939 World's Fair, and at Sweet's Ballroom, and Jimmy Lunceford's band, and *Duke Ellington's* band and Benny Goodman's band and I thought what we were doing with Count Otis Mathews was really just for fun, not serious. I wanted to be like Joe Jones with Count Basie. However, years later, I came to realize that that was probably the most important experience musically of my life. Playing those blues and boogies, because that's the basis for everything else we have in Black music. But I wanted to be with the big bands.

I'm lucky, because I got to play and make records with *all* those big people— Lester Young, Illinois Jacquet. I got to play with Basie. So my childhood dreams were realized. *Then* I got my own band, and went into the Club Alabam as house band, and that really started me on a career of being a bandleader.

Mathews: When you used to see these bands, the high profile name bands, did you only see them in Oakland, did you ever go into San Francisco?

Otis: They wouldn't be in San Francisco, there was no place for them to play in San Francisco. They had little places like Jack's Tavern where a trio might play, but the big bands played only at Sweet's Ballroom in Oakland. Playing there with my own band years later, it was the strangest feeling. I thought, I used to climb up with friends of mine on the outside of this building. Take our lives in our hands, if we slip, we're dead. And come in through the attic, and if the guy doesn't catch us and run us out we'd slip on down and get in free. We didn't have any money. And here I am, playing in this place, it was very thrilling.

Mathews: I'll bet. Wow, that's amazing. So you went to L.A. from Omaha, and this happened, what sort of chain of events allowed this to happen?

Otis: Preston Love and I had a little band at a place called the Barrelhouse. He was part of Lloyd Hunter's band when I first joined him. And Jimmy Witherspoon, who ran on the railroad as a railroad porter, would come in occasionally, into the Barrelhouse and sing the blues. One day he came in, he said, "Johnny, Lloyd Hunter says if you make your way, not Lloyd, Harlan Leonard says if you come to Los Angeles, you got a job in his band." I said, "Wow, really?" He said, "Yeah."

Not two days later I met Nat Cole, I'd never met him, he was playing in a little joint there, he wasn't a star yet. Yeah, and he told me the same thing. We jammed, played a little bit, and he said," You know what? You ought to contact Harlan Leonard, he sure would give you a job, he needs a drummer." So, I called and I got the job and I went to L.A. and I was in his band for, oh…for over a year. And then Phyllis came to Los Angeles. And then I formed my own band at the Club Alabam.

Los Angeles was a place that was a great magnet for Black people throughout the nation. For a lot of reasons. Number one, there were a lot of jobs then because the war industry was full tilt. And for entertainers it was especially attractive, a lot of clubs, a lot of after-hours joints, and then for Black people in general, it was perceived as a place with a more benign form of racism. It was racist as hell, as it is right now. But more benign say than a Mississippi or an Alabama. And finally, the weather played a part too. Because you're shivering in Des Moines, Iowa, or you're sweltering in Florida, and you say, "Ahh, get to Los Angeles." You know, the perception was that it was *always* seventy degrees, which isn't true, but is much closer to that than anywhere else.

It was 1942. The mood was jubilant! Oh, hell yes. And the people from the South had brought that, their marvelous blues culture with them. And their whole culture of how they cook, because we had a lot of that already. Because Los Angeles was made up of, that part where I lived, was Black folks and they were almost exclusively southern immigrants.

And so, we had the food and we had the way of life. The way the young men walked, the way the young *girls* walked, the way we talked and the humor and the music, it was, and a lot of places to play. And you know, we were striving. It was, one way to describe it, it was our New York Renaissance in the West. So, the idea was to uplift ourselves. Now we had jobs and we had a little money. We thought it was going to be great. Preston Love and I thought, when Truman desegregated the armed forces, oh, great! We're finally going to see the American dream realized. There's gonna be justice, and brotherhood.

Mathews: Was this kind of a mood that pervaded…

Otis: Oh yeah, we all thought that all we had to do was, be on our best, you know, our best behavior and appearance and train ourselves to be excellent. And this was the mood, but you know, racism doesn't care how excellent a human being you are. Either trained or, an innately fine person. Racism cuts all that down. And it wasn't long till we realized we're really not going anywhere, we're going backwards.

These white people did not want Black folks to have an equal share of the pie. And since then, it's been proven over and over again. Oh yes, we had the civil rights laws of the sixties and that was great. And it did help tremendously. Didn't eradicate racism. It didn't take Black people, the mass of Black people, out of that degraded position where they're oppressed and depressed. But a few people made it to the middle class, and we even got a couple of millionaires here and there. A few.

111

But it didn't make a difference. What happens in America now is–the disparity gap between incomes, between white and Black, continue to widen, continues to widen. Black people make less, white people make more. And Black young men, who are not in prison for Christ's sake–almost all our youngsters are in prison, and those who are not in jail or in prison are unemployed.

And if you were Black it just breaks your heart. Now if you are a white person with a heart, it will break your heart. A good statistic that tells us where we are in America is the Infant Mortality Rate. And this is not based on congenital problems. This is not hereditary disorders, it's just everybody as against the infant death syndrome–the young babies that die and don't make it through a year, for whatever reason.

The reasons we know are poverty–it's something like three to one! It's terrible! It's a national *disgrace*, that our Black kids die before they're a year old. It's tragic that little white kids die too, of *course*. But, I'm showing you the effects of racism, yeah. And how the scale is not balanced.

Mathews: I think that getting back to rhythm and blues music in Los Angeles, you've noted that rhythm and blues as a music art form developed in Los Angeles to a large degree, you know. And I wanted to know, what do you mean by that, and how and why did it begin there?

Otis: There were people in L.A., Roy Milton, "T-Bone" Walker, Johnny Moore, Charles Brown, Joe Liggins. That's just a small group of people who have a big band background.

And myself. We always wanted the big band. I was lucky enough to have it for a while, I even got a hit record, "Harlem Nocturne", with it.

But when the war wound down and the jobs, naturally Black people were the first people to be fired–they were the last to be hired too. And then the economy within the community began to suffer, and it was bad news. So when we played somewhere, we couldn't take a big band anymore. We had to go from the big venues, the big Club Alabam and Shep's Playhouse, Joe Morris' Plantation, big places that held a thousand people, we had to go to smaller clubs. And in the smaller clubs you can only take a small group.

So, we all, we didn't sit down and plan this, but common sense told you, you couldn't have five saxophones, you're going to have to have one or two. You can't have four trombones, you have one. You can't have four trumpets, you have one. And when we broke it down like that, it changed the character of the sound. I was disappointed, of course, but then as I listened to that I said, "Shit, I might like this better than the big band." [laughs] And as the years went by, it became established as the rhythm and blues sound. The *Los Angeles* rhythm and blues.

In Chicago we had a country blues tradition that were people transplanted from the Mississippi Delta region, the Howlin' Wolfs and the Muddy Waters and the Jimmy Reeds, who were doing *all* those *marvelous* records. But that was different than ours. They used guitars and drum, piano and harp, harmonica. We used a different configuration altogether.

Mathews: So, the classic R&B configuration of what, seven or eight musicians, like your band has.

Otis: You can trace that to Los Angeles and to New Orleans. And there's *absolutely* no doubt of it. Yes! Every major city in America that had any sizable Black community, they had their nightclubs and their gospel singers and their blues singers and their dancers, yeah. But they all aspired to come to Los Angeles, and they *did* sooner or later.

And then many of them came from New Orleans, with that great tradition of music. And in L.A., the synthesis occurred, and that classic R&B thing was born. *Not* in New York. Not in Chicago because something else, they had other beans to boil in Chicago. And they did what they did all the *way* with that beautiful country thing. But the rhythm and blues, the classic thing that became the folk music of America, during the fifties and sixties had its incubation in Los Angeles, and with a lot of input from New Orleans and other cities. But basically New Orleans and Los Angeles. People want to argue with that, but I know better. That's it. And that's it and that's *it*. And I was there.

Mathews: Some historians believe that the art that's produced during a period, be it music or sculpture or film or whatever, reflects attitudes and a sense of what's going on at the time. Do you think that?

Otis: That was rhythm and blues, it was Black music, it was doing that thing. It was blues based, just hadn't got that name yet.

Mathews: Well, I'm just wondering, did that music speak to the community in some amazing way, and if so, how?

Otis: We talked about this many times. "T-Bone" and Roy Miton and Jo Liggins. We knew when we had the big bands and were out there playing big band jazz swing, Black people loved it. After all, it's their music, they invented it, created it, came out of their community.

But when we played after hours, and those boogie-woogies, they really came to life. Because those southern memories were brought to life. And wherever we were, whether it was as far north as Canada or as far south, if there were Black people around, we played after hours, man. So later, when we broke our bands down, we thought this is what they wanted all the time. It's like in the white world, country and western music. Which is the music of America, white America, that I like. The rest of it you can take it, all of it. But I like country and western, which has an African-American base.

Mathews: The real stuff.

Otis: Yeah, the real stuff. Hillbilly stuff. When they go to calling it "town and country" and they try to *upgrade* that wonderful white, folk music called country and western, it's a form of prostitution. Why do that when you've got a pure thing? Why mess with Hank Williams, you can't improve on that. You know? You can't improve on...who was the man with the band in Texas, the Texas Playboys?

Mathews: Oh, Bob Wills.

Otis: You can't improve on that. Leave it alone. And Bill Monroe with the bluegrass. You can't improve on that, just, that's it. Don't try to upgrade it and update it because it's pure and it's beautiful. You got me on my soap box!

Mathews: That's fine, man, that's what I want to hear! Did you know you had a sound? And when you knew you had it?

Otis: One night at the Barrelhouse Club in Watts in the late forties, we noticed a couple of white guys in the audience, and they usually only came on Fridays, now don't ask me why Friday was white folk's night, isn't that strange? But it was a Saturday and there were a couple of white, youngish white guys and they called us over to the table, my guitar player and I went over and sat down, Pete Lewis.

And during the course of the conversation one of the guys, they were either from Billboard or Cashbox Magazine. Music guys, you know? And they said, "Hey, Johnny, you know what that music is you're playing?" So, I looked at Pete and I said, "What is it?" He said, "Blues and rhythm!" And so, I said thanks when they left. They were innocent, but typical white arrogance.

So, when they left, Pete Lewis he says, "Isn't it wonderful about white people? They define us, they tell us who we are. They tell us what we're playing, and without them we wouldn't even know who we are." We laughed, you know. And about two months later they came back I said, "Oh, shit, Pete, here they are." They did amend it, they said, "No, it's rhythm and blues, not blues and rhythm." I said, "OK, thank you." [laughing]

All our bands were not alike, but they had a common thread, *oh*, yeah. The guitar players were kind of alike, weren't they? And the drummers were playing that afterbeat, [snapping his fingers] and the piano players were boogying. So, what was different was different material. Different material. We were alike, That's what naturally happened when the Black guys from the big band era broke their bands down. They all had a common, cultural, characteristic in the music.

Mathews: And so, this L.A. sound was...

Otis: Louis Jordan. Lionel Hampton. These were, *major* important elements in our music.

Mathews: I guess many have referred to Louis Jordan as sort of the father of the rhythm and blues sound.

Otis: Damn right. Indeed. Well, Louis Jordan didn't do what we did. He didn't have the four horns and that guitar, the blues guitar. He didn't do that, *we* did that. But he did something else. He gave us the *spirit* of that thing. With the *fun* and the blues, based songs, and that form of singing, and that *joyous* solos and things in his band. And Lionel Hampton didn't have that either, he had a big band. But he gave us a lot of things.

Mathews: Including the vibes in the format?

Otis: Not the vibes. I'm the only one who played the vibes in those days in the R&B. But if you ever went to see Lionel, that electricity, that *marvelous* showmanship, and his *love* of playing, you could see it, and feel it. It went out to the audience, he'd *march* through the crowd with his band, and he'd be doin' this [lightly stomps foot in slow rhythmic beat], and the after beat would be going–Count Basie. Was blues drenched. Of course, it was more than that, of course. He played *everything*. When Jimmy Rushing got up and sang the blues, that's when the people really, you know, loved it.

Mathews: Did Count Basie ever move in the R&B direction at all, away from the big band sound?

Otis: Well, he had a small band for a couple of years. And it was a beautiful small band, but it was a small Kansas City ensemble.

Mathews: Who do you believe were the greatest and or most impressive of the R&B musicians or bands?

Otis: Just mentioned 'em. [laughs] Count Basie, Duke Ellington, Lionel Hampton, Louis Jordan.

Mathews: What about Lester Young?

Otis: I don't think I'm unique in my reverence for Lester Young. Musicians who really have a receiver of Black music, Black culture, they know. They know who the master is, he's the guiding spirit of modern jazz music. Lester Young. From him, other people grew, like Charlie Parker. But, Lester's just a marvelous man. With that mournful but at the same time, exuberant, joyous sound, and sometimes very melancholy but *powerful* at all times. Lester Young, there's nothing like him.

Mathews: What about Big Joe Turner. How did Big Joe Turner fit into all of this?

Otis: You know, Joe Turner cuts across so many lines, he started out as a kind of a country blues singer and became a *rhythm* and blues singer, and he also was highly thought of in the early days in the jazz field–it shows you how it overlaps. Art Tatum and he did things together, then later Pete Johnson on the piano.

Another, singular character–Joe, Big Joe Turner, nothing, nothing else like him. With that big, rich baritone voice and his unassuming manner. No ego, just a great singer.

Mathews: Big, powerful singer.

Otis: Powerful singer. And then on the other hand, you've got Charles Brown, Fay Terrell, Brook Benton, Roy Hamilton, all those *marvelous, beautiful* singers. Joe Turner and them were *shoutin'*. The others were crooning.

Mathews: I remember once you played a record on your show, and I'd never heard it before. I was a version of "Every Day I Have the Blues," the one that Joe Williams made a big hit...

Otis: Did I play it?

Mathews: *You* played it,

Otis: I don't remember.

Mathews: I just remember it, maybe this will spark your memory of this. He sang it and it was great, it was great. But I remember you were speaking to the idea that perhaps that wasn't Joe Turner's niche. Where Joe Turner really excelled was out of that context.

Otis: I would have to hear it, and I would probably have the same reaction.

Mathews: But talking about Central Avenue, I'm kind of unfamiliar with the way Los Angeles is laid out. What would you say about that scene?

Otis: Before my time. When I got there in the forties, it was at its height. The greats didn't necessarily play Central Ave. They might be playing at the big hotels, not the hotels, but the theaters and things in town, you know? Or a one-nighter somewhere, but they came to Central Avenue to party. There were three big clubs. Club Alabam, Forty-Second and Central. Joe Morris's Plantation out in Watts, Plantation Club. And Shep's Playhouse, which was at about Fifth and Central.

Shep's Playhouse had four or five floors. And there would be a combo on one floor and a big band. Gerald Wilson's band or Bardu Ali's big bands. And smaller bands. Eddie Haywood's band and Roy Milton's band. At the Club Alabam there was only one big room.

Mathews: Who would play there if the big names didn't play?

Otis: I will always thank God for the fact that I played there! That's who played there. [laughter]

Mathews: Did you have a, did they cut you a good deal, was it a good relationship?

Otis: Sure, it was OK. Yeah. The man at the Club Alabam–there was a union scale, he paid it, he was a good man. Curtis Moseby. He was certainly good to me, he allowed me to build a big band there, and become the house band and as a result, move on.

JOHNNY OTIS: Interview 2

Interviewer: Joe Mathews Interview date: October 12, 1995

[Location: Otis' home in Sebastopol]

Johnny Otis
Credit Wikipedia

Mathews: Good morning Johnny. We're going to pick up where we left off from last week, but I'd like to first ask Johnny about a couple of things that came to light from last week's interview session. And, I'm wondering, it just came to mind, were you a self-taught musician?

Otis: Yeah. I didn't have any instruction of any kind, at any time, and it *shows*. [laughter]

Mathews: So, when you picked up the drums you just figured it out and just started doing it?

Otis: Yeah, I did it, yeah. For what it was, that's the way I did it.

Mathews: And the piano, same thing? And the vibes?

Otis: Yes.

Mathews: Just learned them on your own? There was a mention last time about Count Otis' featured number called, "Mama Bought a Chicken." And you mentioned that he'd bring the little girls up on the stage with the shaker cans, and, was this the heavy beat rhythm that you used in "Hand Jive"?

Otis: Yes, it's the same thing.

Mathews: Where did that come from, do you know?

Otis: West Africa. All Black music came from West Africa, with other influences, but *basically* it's African music.

Mathews: And so this was the beat that Bo Diddley used.

Otis: Well, and before Bo Diddley, Hambone. And then, "Hey Little Girl With the High School Sweater." There's so many things. The best known is Bo Diddley, but he was not first by any means.

Mathews: I notice that you still incorporate the "Mama Bought a Chicken." Was that sort of a folksy kind of a thing? I mean, was that sort of one of those phrasings that everybody knew?

Otis: Everybody didn't know it but many people knew it within the Black community because it was a cultural thing. It was a little folk poem. "Mama bought a chicken, thought it was a duck...stick him on the table with his legs stuck up. Here comes baby sister with a spoon and a glass, trying to stir the gravy from his yes, yes, yes." It was very naughty in those days.

Mathews: You mentioned that you started with Count Otis when you were about fifteen years old, Johnny. What did your parents think about all this? You're playing in a band?.

Otis: They don't know what I'm doing. We'd go down on Saturdays and play that gig, if there was one. Either a house rent party or go play at the Black gymnasium in West Oakland and that was it. We didn't practice or anything like that.

Mathews: Was Count Otis a fairly accomplished musician?

Otis: He was not technically adept by any means but he could play what he played. He could do the boogie-woogies and the barrelhouse jump blues, that he could do. And he had a lot of good songs that he would do.

Mathews: Well, I'd like to ask you about your early experiences hearing the great big band stars, like Count Basie and Duke Ellington, that came through Oakland. And I asked you whether or not any of these guys played in San Francisco.

Otis: Not that I know of. Where would you play in San Francisco in those days?

Mathews: I don't know, the hotels?

Otis: What, a white hotel? They didn't play Black bands. The Fillmore might have been there but it was all white and I don't know what it was, at that point. I don't know. Basie, Duke, Lunceford and the rest of 'em, Andy Kirk, they played at Sweets Ballroom in Oakland for one night and kept on going. Now they *might* have, they did play *theaters*. No, no auditoriums, no ballrooms in San Francisco, but theaters in Oakland and theaters in San Francisco perhaps.

Mathews: A lot of racism.

Otis: It was the time when we were very naive and we thought that we should clean up our act, there was nothing wrong with our act, but we were told we'd have to get a lot of education and be on our toes in every way, and then we would get equality. That was bullshit. Racism doesn't care about how excellent you are. They are concerned with your color and they immediately, you're either– or not just color– Jewish or Black or gay and you're in trouble in America. Then and *now*.

Mathews: And this was apparent as time went on for you folks down there.

Otis: It's our bigoted heritage here in America. The Europeans who brought that poison with them have never relinquished it, and they continue to apply it to Hispanic people, to African-American people, to people who have a different sexual persuasion, gay people, to women in general. I mean, you know, you hear all this stuff all the time now, and it almost sounds like clichés, but it's true, and it is tragic and it is a bad situation and we are saddled with it in America, and whether we'll ever get rid of it, I don't know.

Mathews: I don't either, but you are so right, it's definitely part of our existence. I asked you about your first experiences or what you first heard about Central Avenue. When you arrived out there in Los Angeles from the Midwest, did it really seem like the "Promised Land" so to speak?

Otis: Well, sure, from a musician's standpoint. There were night clubs and little joints *everywhere*, after hours spots and there were places to work and I was lucky. I was lucky to move into a premium spot in L.A., for Black musicians the Club Alabam. With Harlan Leonard's band. That was a great stroke of luck on my part, and the fact that the war had taken some of the great drummers out of the market and gave me a chance to move in, I hadn't been drafted yet. I was like, eighteen, nineteen at the time.

Mathews: Right. And so, this was 1941. What about the clubs on Central Avenue and the places. Was the clientele mostly from the Black community?

Otis: Yes.

Mathews: Were there mixed audiences?

Otis: There were. White people would come occasionally, but they were not mixed in that sense, no. It was a Black audience.

Mathews: You mentioned last time that a lot of the big band stars would maybe play downtown in Los Angeles, but they would come to Central Avenue to party and hang out. So, you would see celebrities down there.

Otis: Oh sure. Lena Horne, Lionel Hampton, Count Basie, Duke Ellington—of course.

Mathews: And they would be sitting in the audience?

Otis: Yes.

Mathews: Did they ever jam with those bands?

Otis: No, I don't remember that. You see, the shows were absolutely programmed, and we all knew that when a celebrity comes out, he or she does *not* want to be called up do a goddamn jam. And you make them uncomfortable and they won't come, and there was a kind of a standing rule. Acknowledge them but don't bother them.

Mathews: They were fortunate to have so and so in the audience this evening.

Otis: I have a photograph that I saw recently of me sitting on the drums, I used to have my drums in the front row, and Lionel Hampton at the mike talking to Babe Wallace who was the emcee that night. But he didn't come back and play, and we didn't do that to him. If anybody would do it he would. He's great about that, yeah.

Mathews: I wanted to ask you about the structure of those evening programs. How did they work, you had comics, or dancers?

Otis: We would come to work and I think we would start at nine o'clock and we'd play for an hour. Then we'd take an intermission and come back and do a show.

Mathews: What kind of a show?

Otis: A stage show, which I'll describe to you. Then we'd take another intermission and come back and do I think another dance, short dance set and *then* a *show*, another show. And then after the show, just play another maybe half hour up to—we'd play to two o'clock for Christ's sake. I don't remember exactly what the schedule was, it was something like that.

Mathews: So, three sets of band music.

Otis: Yes, three sets of band music and two shows. And the shows consisted of whoever was on the bill. Well, first of all we'd have six or eight show girls, chorus girls, which was part of why that was a premium gig. [laughs]

Mathews: Did you guys have to back them up, the music?

Otis: Well, we played everything, everything musical came off of the bandstand and the stage where the show was done was also the stage where the dancing was, where people danced on that stage. And then when the show came on, nobody danced, they sat down, and they watched the show. And there would be a comedy team perhaps.

Mathews: Who were some of the guys that you remember?

Otis: Moke and Poke, I'm not going to think of their names. The High Hatters, Moke and Poke. There were, you know, a lot of comedy teams.

Mathews: Redd Foxx?

Otis: No, not yet, Redd Foxx, never heard of him in those days. He hadn't got out there yet.

Mathews: Did dance teams come in and perform too?

Otis: Yes. Coles and Atkins, all kinds of great tap dancers and interpretive dancers and solo women dancers, interpretive women dancers, fire dancers. And then there would be a star, Faye Terrell, or a Moms Mabley, or the Peters Sisters, and that would be the featured attraction on the show. And of course, the band would play two or three numbers during the show.

Mathews: Did you ever have an opportunity to rehearse during the daytime?

Otis: We didn't rehearse. Nah, we rehearsed every two weeks for the floor show, it would change every two weeks. And at that rehearsal, if we had a new song, a new arrangement, the band, we'd run it down right quick. My guys were so adept. We'd run it down once or twice, we had it, and it was in the book.

Mathews: So, when someone came in, a star performer or something.

Otis: We had to rehearse all that.

Mathews: Oh, you did.

Otis: Oh, sure. Every two weeks there was a rehearsal. That was very organized, and the music was quite demanding, yeah.

Mathews: You'd get stars in and they'd give you, they'd say we're going to do these numbers.

Otis: Wynonie Harris and the rest of the people.

Mathews: What about the transformation between the daytime setup in these clubs and their opening in the evening performances. The owners and, were there people in there working, what was it like in the daytime?

Otis: I don't know. You know, I don't know. I remember there might have been somebody in the back cleaning the bar or something. And somebody cleaning the kitchen out or working or beginning to cook, I don't know. I don't remember that well.

Mathews: Was there ever an occasion where you would be in those clubs before you went to work, you know, like you'd be in there...

Otis: Not if I could help it. We would sleep to the last minute.

Mathews: What about the daily course of life in the community? You were a resident, and all of you and your neighbors and other residents. What about the bonds between the residents that defined the community, like the restaurants, places like Father Divine's and Ivy's Chicken Shack and the barber shops and other merchants and other interactions that would–the regular life.

Otis: What about it?

Mathews: What do you remember about hanging around in town?

Otis: I don't remember hanging around in town–if I had to get a haircut I'd go down to Central Avenue and get a haircut. If I, for some reason, was not going to eat at home that night, I don't know what that reason might be. Occasionally we'd go to one of those beautiful restaurants and have something to eat.

Mathews: Were there any places in particular that you remember?

Otis: Oh, there were so many, Ivy's was surely one. Ivy's, I don't think that Ivy's opened early in the day but there were places that were open. With *hearty* soul food. You know, from early in the morning on.

Mathews: I remember in your book you mentioned that the local barber shop was a place where guys would go.

Otis: Not the local barber shop, there were many barber shops, up and down the road there were quite a few.

Mathews: Was there one in particular that you frequented more often?

Otis: At first, and I've forgotten the name of it. It was right near the Los Angeles Sentinel office, on Central Avenue, and I've forgotten the man who cut my hair, but one of his daughters was a featured chorus girl at the Club Alabam. And I remember him, then later, I would go into Broulet's down a little farther, and he was a bookie.

Mathews: So, it was just a place where people used to go to hang out and shoot the breeze and catch up on what's going on in the neighborhood.

Otis: There were regulars who hung out in those places, it was not the musicians. We had other fish to fry. We'd go in and get a haircut or maybe one of the guys would get his hair processed and keep going. But there were regulars who hung around, it was a little social club, the barber shop.

Mathews: And the topics of conversation would range...

Otis: You can't tell what it might be – it might be about nuclear physics, it might be about the ass on the chick that's walking by the window.

Mathews: Anything that came up.

Otis: Yes, and if that's sexist, well, that's the way it was. That's the way it *still* is. [laughs]

Mathews: I wanted to ask you, once you became firmly entrenched in the scene there and as the big band era came to a close, and a lot of the Black bandleaders were breaking their bands down to a smaller size, things that you talked about last week. And you were playing on a regular basis and started to develop your own band, how and when did your traveling road show begin? Was that "The Johnny Otis Show," is that when it all started?

Otis: I was out on the road. My first hit record, "Harlem Nocturne," got me out on the road. I was lucky to land the annual Ink Spots tour, the *real* Ink Spots, in 1947, and that took us all over the country. So I got a real taste of one whole year of touring throughout the United States and Canada. It was great, it was mostly theaters and big ballrooms. And then when I got back home, and I opened the Barrelhouse club, when the big band thing went down hill.

Mathews: When was that?

Otis: 1948. And I had a thought: lets go to San Diego there's a club down there, I don't know the name of it anymore. And I'll make a placard, very much like the placard I saw back in the forties, for minstrel shows and other entertainment. It was an oversized placard and it was printed in black and yellow, orange. Well, it was twice as big as a regular placard, you know, not too big. But those colors, yellow, orange and black, you could see it a long ways. And I thought, this is 1948. I made a placard and I took all the people who were singing with me.

Mathews: Who was with you then?

Otis: Little Esther Phillips, no she wasn't with me yet, she wasn't singing yet. But I had Pete Lewis on the guitar, Lady Dee on the piano, and I don't remember who the singers were now, some blues singers from around that were working at the club. And I made it look like a *road* show. Actually, it was the people that worked in the Barrelhouse. And I even added a name that was fictitious, Washboard Willie, we needed one more name.

And you know, wouldn't you know it, a few years later I found out there was a Washboard Willie [laughs]. But when we did that and we did such *tremendous* business in San Diego that night, you couldn't get in that show, and I said, "Wow!"

We had eight songs on the hit parade that year. And so, our placards read, "The Johnny Otis Rhythm and Blues Caravan," with all my regular singers and musicians listed as separate artists, and it was impressive. It looked like the carnival was coming to town. When I got to Capitol we decided to call it the

"Johnny Otis Show." And it's been that ever since.

Mathews: Where would you stay, was that always a hassle?

Otis: Yes, it was a hassle, depending on, in the South since we played in so many cities, getting a place to stay. Well, you know, staying in a white hotel *was* out, they would not allow us.

And in the North, many of those were taboo too, they just wouldn't give us a room. And in the South, there was nowhere for us to eat, and also in much of the North, the same thing. Nowhere to go eat. And so we wound up eating cold cuts, *or*, if it was a big enough city where there was a Black community, we'd find a Black restaurant. And if it was big enough there might be a little Black hotel where we could stay too.

Mathews: Did any of the local folks ever have you in?

Otis: Open their houses? They did. Yeah, the promoters would set that up for us, and nice people they would let us stay there for the night. Very often. And then when we couldn't get a place either with a private family or with a Black hotel or if they were nonexistent, then we slept in the goddam bus. And it wasn't a sleeper bus. But that was the way it was.

Mathews: In your first book you wrote of an experience at a woman's house, Mama Lou's?

Otis: We were there for a good week or more. Oh, she ran a house of prostitution, and that was an example, I think it was Iowa or Ohio. Those two states get crossed up in my mind. And it was a railroad center, at least there were a lot of railroad guys there. And she had a big old-time mansion, Victorian, you know, furniture and what not. She had a big place in the back where– it was nice enough, where the girls stayed. And she had white girls, Asian girls and African-American girls. So she had room– where did she put us?

Mathews: In the garage or something.

Otis: We *could not* go where the girls were. She absolutely wasn't going to let us get near 'em. But you know, she'd get drunk every night, and as soon as she got drunk and passed out, then we'd party with the girls. By that time all the Johns were gone. She was Black but she would not allow a Black to come in there as a customer, only whites. They were a bunch of funky honkys that worked on the railroads, and they were prejudiced, and if they saw Black men in there there'd be a problem.

Mathews: Well how in the heck did you wind up in there?

Otis: I don't know how we got that, I think the promoter got it for us. And we stayed there and she wanted my piano player to come in, Lee Wesley, and play after hours. For money, she was great, she was generous. As soon as we'd get through at the theater about eleven-thirty, for him to run down there about midnight. That's when her business really started. And this great big, *beautiful* piano she had. And she always referred to her Bill, and she'd start crying as she got drunk, because Bill died and he was her pimp. And they owned this whorehouse together.

Bill was a boogie-woogie and blues piano player, and so Lee Wesley sat down once and played the blues and she made a deal with him, but he couldn't stay sober. By midnight he was drunk, so you know, I sat down once and played a little bit, she said, "You got the job!" So, I'd go in there every night and play.

Mathews: And you got paid.

Otis: Yes. And quickly, you can't wait for those white guys to leave so we could put her to bed and we could run in the back and get the girls. Hey! [laughs]

Mathews: Well, you know you've been given and assigned a lot of credit for the discovery of some great talent in the music business. I wondering whether or not you could tell us about some of the folks and the circumstances that surrounded your finding them, so to speak. I remember hearing Etta James in an interview once talk about how she was just a little girl that came up to your hotel room, scared to death.

Otis: She with two other little girls. Yeah, and my manager. And I tried to tell her, "Tonight." And she said, "No, I've got to sing" or something.

Hank Ballard and the Midnighters were driving down the street in their stretch-out van. We were going down the street too and I said, "Oh look there, it's the Royals." They weren't the Royals. They called themselves the Royales. They were playing on that name because these other guys had hit records. So when I realized it was kind of a sham, I invited them to come to the club, to the ballroom that night. And I put them on and they were great. And I got them, you know, recorded. That's how that happened.

Mathews: So, the Royales, did they continue on as the Royales?

Otis: No, they became Hank Ballard and the Midnighters.

Mathews: And Little Esther, she was just a neighborhood kid?

Otis: Yeah, a little kid in the neighborhood. Didn't I tell you that story last week?

One night I went to the Largo Theater, in Watts on 103rd Street. There was the Linda Theater for Hispanic people, Latinos, and the Largo Theater where Black people went. And on Wednesday nights they had talent shows. So, I went in on a talent show and sat down, my bass player Mario and I. And this little girl was part of the talent show, and she sang, and I was *blown* away, and I said, "God,

I wish I knew that kid." And a girl sitting in front of me said, "That's my sister!" and I said, "Well, go get her." And that's how I found Esther.

And years later we were doing an interview, much as you and I are doing now, and Esther was in on it and the man asked me, "When did you first meet Esther?" And I recounted that story, and she said, "*No*, you met me before that. Out in your chicken ranch, we used to catch the chickens for you." She says, "One day, we were out there and Phyllis had brought us some cookies and some Kool-Aid, and we had finished catching the chickens and I sang and you heard me." I said, "Was that you?" I remembered it like it was yesterday. Oh yeah, a little girl about seven or eight years old, and I said, "Good lord, I knew you way back then." And who else? Big Mama Thornton and Marie Adams I found down South in Houston. She was out of Alabama, I think. But she was living around Houston.

Everywhere I went after I discovered Esther Phillips, who became the big child star in the African-American community nationally, stage mothers and fathers would bring me their kids, and that's how that happened. We played in Houston, and Don Robey told me, "Hey, here's a chick wants to sing with you." So, I brought her up and she sang, and it was great. So, we started recording her. We recorded in Los Angeles. I took her with me. She became my singer, and we recorded in Los Angeles.

Mathews: Speaking of the recording industry, I'd like to just ask you some of your impressions about that. I guess as the Los Angeles R&B movement really started to take off after the end of the war, so emerged all of these independent record labels. And I read somewhere that between 1945 and 1952, nine of the significant R&B labels were located in L.A. Can you tell us about these early years of the independent labels and who started them?

Otis: The Renee brothers, Otis and Leon were the first. They said, "Hey, there's no license required. No special permit to have a record company, you just make records." If you can find shellac, because it was during the war, and you know, because it was in short supply, you put the records out. And that's how it started. Then other people followed them. And that's exactly how the independent labels started out. Two Black men started it, later, white guys the Messners and the guys at Modern Records, the Biharis, they followed. Jack Lauderdale was real early with Swing Time Records. Early forties.

Mathews: And this was pretty fertile ground, I guess. I mean there were a lot of great musicians who didn't have contracts.

Otis: Yes... None of us had contracts. You were either Duke Ellington, at that level, or you were Bill Broonzy, you know, a country blues singer. In between was that thing that was later to become known as R&B, that the people really wanted to hear. And was just sitting there in those little clubs where we played.

And finally, somebody said, "Let's record that," and at that point all hell broke loose. You just got a couple of musicians, go down to a studio, pay the time, maybe a hundred bucks, and walk out of there and go to the place where they make the masters and then go to the pressing plant. Then maybe for two, three hundred dollars you get your five hundred records and you're in the record business.

Mathews: And that's it. What about distribution, what did you have to do?

Otis: You know, these guys were resourceful people. The Biharis. They realized they had to go around the country. Sometimes country and western little distributors, or whatever they could find. Yeah.

Mathews: I read where jukebox companies were a good sale, I mean that was a big deal to sell a thousand records back then.

Otis: Yes. [Whispers, "I haven't got much time."]

Mathews: I just wanted to ask you, I know that a lot of us have heard so much about how many of the great Black men and women of the time lost out on the financial benefits of recording.

Otis: Because you're dealing with unscrupulous people. The Sid Nathans and the Herman Lubinskis and the Leibers and Stollers. Leiber and Stoller, we had a deal, a handshake, an *agreement*. And they found out they could disaffirm the contract, because I was twenty-one and they were under twenty-one. And they did and they beat me out of "Hound Dog." Which was, you know, millions. And I had really thought through the years, oh, one day they'll say, "We ought to give Johnny–" but they've never done it and I guess they never will. There's just, you know, no integrity. Thieves! I could have put my kids. through college, that was a big score. But, be that as it may. They found they could cut me out and they didn't hesitate, they did. Mostly we would record for companies and they would never pay us, even though we had contracts.

If you had a hit record on Savoy Records, he had about thirty-five distributors around the country. So, when "Double-Crossin' Blues" hit, I got an attorney, and the distributor told me, "He has sold two hundred thousand records." Just for that area. And my company is telling me I've only sold forty thousand records, *nationally*. So the attorney said, "I'm going to have to have a big retainer because I've got to go to every one of those cities and requisition the books." So, we couldn't do it.

Mathews: And, what eventually was able to turn that around?

Otis: Once we got wise. Because, you know, we weren't going to stay ignorant forever. Once we got wise we found out about publishing, songwriting, song royalties. And then we made sure we had attorneys and whatnot to check the contracts. And we went to major labels. And there we weren't screwed as bad as we were on the, you know. I went to Mercury, Capital. There I got a fair shake.

Mathews: But little ones, like Black and White Records.

Otis: I don't know about Black and White. All I know is about Modern. They were absolutely, you know– they were thieves.

Mathews: The last thing I wanted to ask you about, Johnny as we wrap this thing up, I wanted to ask you about the emergence of radio, Black radio in particular. I guess airplay had to be a part of the modern production equation, didn't it? I remember last week asking you about whether or not you heard music on the radio when you were a kid, and you said, "Nah, radio wasn't much." I have to think that popular radio shows that would play music and had disc jockeys.

Otis: In the forties we got nothing. In the fifties we began to get some shows, you know, I'm talking Los Angeles. I don't know about the rest of the country. Because Los Angeles was a very racist place and there was an unwritten rule, "Don't play Black music." They didn't do it. And if it weren't for Al Jarvis, a white man with a heart, and with some guts– he began to play Black music. He was a hero to us because he was jeopardizing himself doing that. Because the racists who ran the industry, then, as against the racists who run the industry *now*, you know, they didn't fire him because he was strong. Make believe ballroom. Strong guy, he began to play Black music and pretty soon–

Mathews: Was there a station then, that the Black community eventually became to identify with in those times?

Otis: Well, before there was any "alleged" Black ownership, there was Hunter Hancock with "Harlem Matinee." This was in the late forties. And then KGFJ came along and we were told it was a Black station, I never believed that. But, it had Black disc jockeys and they played Black music and that was great.

Mathews: I've read sometimes where the disc jockeys really pretty much defined the relationship between the station and the listener, regardless of who owned it. Were there any special personalities? You mentioned Hunter Hancock.

Otis: Joe Adams, Hunter Hancock, Charles Tramell, Lonnie Johnson. Oh, there were a lot.

Mathews: Were there any that stood out that had real flair?

Otis: They *all* had flair. All these I'm telling you were good. Later, Huggy Boy. They were all good or they wouldn't be on the air two minutes.

Mathews: What made them really good?

Otis: First of all they had a taste for the music, they understood what to play for the audience. And they did it with a little wit and a little flair, all of them.

Mathews: So their playlists were always stuff that they wanted to play?

Otis: No. [laughter] It wasn't very often things they wanted to play because they liked them, but things they'd been *paid* to play. It's payola.

Mathews: Was that payola thing working then?

Otis: Yes, it was.

Mathews: And that means that somebody would have to pay you. Say if you wanted a record played you'd have to pay the disc jockey to play it?

Otis: Yeah. Yes, it was legal then.

Mathews: When did it become illegal?

Otis: After the payola probe, then the laws changed.

Mathews: You eventually got into radio, right?

Otis: Yes. I came home and I was tired of traveling and having to have a hit record immediately in order to draw crowds, and I called a radio station and told them I wanted to be a disc jockey, and it turned out to be a guy who knew me, of me, and he put me on at KFOX, Long Beach. And that's how I got my station. 1954.

Mathews: Was Black music being played on a fairly regular basis?

Otis: A little bit. Hunter Hancock.

Mathews: Well Johnny, I guess in closing I just wanted to ask you one thing-

Otis: Are you a republican?

Mathews: I think I know the answer to that.

Otis: It's the same answer I'd give you if you asked me if I was a democrat. [laughter] Anyhow, what is it?

Mathews: The Monterey Jazz Festival in 1970 when you assembled that great lineup of people who had played during this time, and I just wanted to ask you, just from the crowd response, you know how you can feel that sometime, what was that day like? That must have been one magnificent day.

Otis: Oh, it was. It was sunny and nice and mild. It was absolutely capacity packed. And the audience was equally men, women, Black, white, and Hispanics, and young and old. It was great, it was great. That's twenty-five years ago, there were still people, relatively young with a flavor and an understanding of quality African–American artistry. That has almost disappeared now, unfortunately.

But the bible says what goes around comes around and maybe we'll see a change someday. Where our young artists, our young Black artists, there'll be some budding Aretha Franklins and Ray Charleses there and they'll carry on the tradition. I hope so, because this crap they're playing now, you know, it's entertaining and it's shocking, but it's not artistic. It's not African–American artistry, it's something else altogether.

Mathews: Are there any young artists out there that you've heard?

Otis: Not that I've heard that I know of. Could be, I don't listen and I don't go anywhere so I don't know.

Mathews: Well Johnny, thank you very much.

Otis: If you need something, call me on the phone.

(End of interview]

Interviewer: Caroline Crawford

Date: January 15, 1993

Location: The Sadler home in Livermore, California and a "Blues in the Schools" performance in Oakland

Haskell "Cool Papa" Sadler

Credit. The Bancroft Library, University of California, Berkeley

Sadler: My name is Cool Papa and I reside in Livermore.

Crawford: You have been called the last of the down home bluesmen. What does that mean?

Sadler: Down home means rotgut blues or straight blues.

Crawford: When you say Oakland blues, what do you mean?

Sadler: It's the sound. You got Chicago blues, Texas blues. It's come a long way. Oakland blues has its own sound.

Crawford: What is the Oakland sound?

Sadler: My sound comes from Texas, and I have been here so long, Oakland blues is derived from all the other blues.

Crawford: When did you come here?

Sadler: '56. I came from Los Angeles. I was born in Butte, Colorado. I was born in 1935, April 6. I left in '49. Haskell and Mildred Sadler. My father was from Tennessee and my mother was from Dallas, Texas. Why did they come from Colorado? I don't know.

Crawford: How about your grandparents?

Sadler: I never knew them.

Crawford: How about brothers and sisters?

Sadler: They died before I was born.

Crawford: What did your parents do?

Sadler: Mother did housekeeping. My dad did laundry at the end. He was a porter. In Seattle.

Crawford: Was there any music in the family? When did you become musical?

Sadler: Yes, m'am. Oh, a long time ago. In the '40s.

Crawford: You were pretty young in the '40s.

Sadler: I started playing in the 1940s. I left for Los Angeles in 1953.

Crawford: We want details here! You can give me details.

Sadler: I started in the school dance band. That was '49 and I graduated in '52. Then I had a teacher, Lark Charles, he taught me the blues. Lark was from my town. I read a little but mostly I played by ear. I read a little. I played in the dance band, just chords, and that is when I learned that the guitar was a living instrument and not a lead instrument.

Crawford: What was the band like?

Sadler: The band in school? It was an orchestra, really. I played guitar, I played rhythm. We played at all the various schools in the city. It was the only dance band in the whole system.

Crawford: Was it a big band?

Sadler: Yes! It was a full orchestra. We played dance music, "Stardust" and things like that.

Crawford: And you played blues?

Sadler: Yes, Lark was a blues performer.

Crawford: "Lark" like a bird? Who was most important–who influenced you?

Sadler: In my music? "T-Bone" Walker and Lowell Fulson. Those two was my roots, that was the records I had. Lightning Hopkins and Muddy Waters.

Crawford: When did you come?

Sadler: In '53. By Greyhound Bus. That's where the breaks was. That's why I left. There wasn't much happening careerwise in Denver, and I thought I'd take a chance and go. I was free to go. There were more clubs and more record companies in Los Angeles in them days. I had a hard time in Los Angeles police-wise. You know about my domestic problem. I didn't like Los Angeles.

Crawford: Were you married at the time?

Sadler: Yes, but I did a lot of work at the time. Johnny Otis. I was recording at his studio, my first recording. "Do Right Mind," "Gone for Good." [sings]

Crawford: Oh, you recorded in Denver as well. Talk about that.

Sadler: Well, I met a guy who wanted to do some recording, we did it at his house. Gary Johnson? And another guitar player. I forgot his name. I just cut it. They found it in Europe and I didn't even know it had been released. He also released the other record I did in Los Angeles. On tv-rainbow in Japan. Those were my first.

Crawford: How much did you do in Denver?

Sadler: Just nightclubs. A lot of little clubs around there. No progress, nowhere to go back then; it's changed now. Grotto clubs and saddle clubs, Elks, Legion. Yeah. All in them various air force bases, officers clubs. Late '40s and early '50s. I played a lot of lodges. I stayed in L.A. till '56.

Crawford: Who was playing there?

Sadler: It's easier to say who wasn't playing. Fulson was there; "T-Bone" was there. Big Jay McNeely. Bo Jackson was there. The blues community was all over L.A. You had downtown, 5th street, Center Street, you had Watts, West Los Angeles, Club Four and all these places. That's where the guys and the babes went, like Club Four, and all.

Crawford: Who were the audiences?

Sadler: Middle-aged people, kids too, see, you didn't have that other music to contend with. Didn't have rock and roll, didn't have soul, either you go to the blues or standard jazz, one of the two. You had a rounded audience; they appreciated the music. Mostly clubs.

Crawford: Did you do some writing?

Sadler: Yeah. All my music I write. I been doing that all along.

Crawford: Do you have the original scores of all your music?

Sadler: No. I sure don't. Yeah. I left L.A. and came to Oakland in the last part of '57. Then I went home back to Denver and played with the band. Barefoot Miller and Robert Johnson, saxophone player. We left and went to Wyoming and Omaha.

Then I went south and when I got there a friend in Omaha happened to walk by the club where we played and said that "Papa's in there." I said, "OH yeah! Let him in!" C.B. Malone, my piano player in L.A. You all go back Sunday I'll go back with you to Alabama, so I did. He just happened to be walkin out there that night, a sailor on furlough. He hadn't been there before, hadn't played there.

So, I went to Tennessee and on to Mobile, Alabama. We played there. That's where I met my wife. I went back to Mobile and hooked up with the jazz band. They hired me to play blues, all over Alabama, legions and nightclubs and I hooked up with George Walton at a white club called the Stardust. In downtown Mobile. Stardust, I mean Paradise.

Crawford: Would you talk about meeting your wife. Maybe you'd like Jane to tell it.

Jane Sadler: I had just met my first husband, got a divorce and came down to the Mobile Airport down there. Went into this club, the Paradise with my girlfriend. Dancing is my second nature. Right, and this band was up there, and he did his act, and he looked at me and I looked at him, that was that! And so I had a car. At that time, I was working in a clothing store in Pritchard, Dixie Shop, and so I got a card with my telephone number and threw it on the stage.

Crawford: That was forward, wasn't it [laughter]

Sadler: If they had caught me at it, I would have been hung. Literally hung. I mean, a white girl come on! They had that at the time.

Crawford: Well, what did you think when she put out her card so prominently?

Sadler: With my friend Percy, I'd seen her out in the yard, and said that's going to be my wife. Never gave it another thought and she walked in [laughs]!

Jane Sadler: I never knew anything about prejudice–never gave it a thought. And so when I went down there I had to fight with everyone. They said, "Don't bring your Yankee ideas down here and I just had to fight with everyone because I'd never been brought up that way.

Crawford: So then what happened after that night?

Sadler: Well, we got together. We got together after that, when they almost caught me. I was leaving the house one morning and I got in my car and they flashed their lights. They'd been watching us but they wasn't sure and they found me going to her house. I got in my car, they flashed the lights, I took off, they chased me and I got to Davis Avenue. That's a dangerous Black area so they cut me loose. So the next night when I came to work I never brought my car in front of the club. Never. So I told Jane I said we've got to get rid of that car.

So what I did was I traded the car. I had a green Ford and I got me a blue and white Mercury. You get your license plate when you buy the car. So what I did I took the car up in the woods, that red dirt, that car was a mess when I came to work. I parked it just a few doors from the club and when I came in the club Mayor Posten said, "What you think about this segregation thing?" They was ready to start marchin' down there.

I said, "You know, I'm not from here. Way I feel you don't like the way they live In the North, come South, and you don't like they live here go North. That's the way I feel. That's what I feel. How you feel about it? Then he said he wanted a drink. I said I got one in my car. I'll get it. So I went to my car, I went to the door, I left, he saw this dirty car, and I had a drink, and saw six of them. When I got back to the club, they were sitting at the table and said, "Naw, it ain't him, this guy had a green car, this guy got a blue and white car and I know he ain't just get it, cuz its it's dirty as hell. If it's one things Blacks are known for when they first get it, they could buy a total wreck and clean and shiny, they automatically do that, keep it clean and shiny, and same thing about the car, they could buy a 30-year-old car and all beat up and keep it clean and shiny at least for a few days."

They were so sure. Then I left the house and they passed me on the stairs, and them days I had something that was new to them, a Black man with straight, wavy hair. So they'd speak to me on the stairs. And I'd keep going. And that was what was so funny. The Cubans, and Africans, long as they got papers, they're not American negroes—they can go anywhere.

Crawford: And they don't get bothered.

Sadler: No.

Crawford: So, you performed at the club, and Jane went to see you perform. Then what happened?

Sadler: We stayed there until that happened and then I said we gotta get out of here. Go on back to Denver. So she got on the bus and I drove the band. There was Percy, Washington, Johnny Davis and Marcel. Davis' piano, Percy's drums, and Marcel drums. Just a trio and we picked up a bass where we were. That was something else, we got screwed outa our bass. I think about that all the time. I was here with Earl "Good Rockin'" Brown.

That's when I came here. I got to Oakland with Earl Brown, used to be with Charles Brown, saxophone player. I stayed with him four years, and then he played all the little towns like Merrifield and he'd go to Reno in winter, and Las Vegas in the summer. Stockton, that's where he lived. Still lives there. Marysville, Vallejo, all the little towns we did.

Crawford: When you left Mobile how long did you stay in Denver?

Sadler: Our son was born February, '62. His name is Pasco. We call him the blues robot, cuz he goes on some of my jobs, he's like a robot–a dance machine. He's at home.

Crawford: Oh, that's great. You left Denver when he was an infant.

Sadler: He was eight weeks old. We went to Phoenix, Arizona, for three months. Played in a little dive. Out there on Lorry Road...or something.

Crawford: That a blues scene?

Sadler: They had little clubs all over. We got the money and after we left.

Crawford: Did you get a house where you played short term?

Sadler: Oh, yeah, house or hotels. Then we left there and went to Las Vegas. Talking about '62. Oh, that town!

Crawford: You liked it?

Sadler: Yes. Went there and bought a home, Mercury Grove. That's the missile place. That was the lifeline of the city. No industry outside and the gambling. That's why Vegas doesn't look like Reno with the snow. On the west side, the Chinese closed the club down. They owned the clubs on the west side.

Crawford: Had you decided to live there?

Sadler: Yeah, we bought our home there. We had musicians like Della Reese, Count Basie. All them. That's the reason we bought. So, then we left Las Vegas and went to Reno, Tahoe. I played Tahoe for about nine months, a place called Grass Clutch. And we stayed up there until the winter, things got bad, we were living off Jane's jackpots.

Crawford: Jane, are you a good gambler?

Sadler: I don't know, I'm just lucky.

Crawford: Is that it? Well, I know you are lucky in love. Are you a gambler too?

Sadler: Not really. I got two gamblers. Jane and Marcel. I gotta keep [straight].

Crawford: So then what happened after you left Las Vegas?

Sadler: We went to Reno and stayed there a couple years and then everything got bad there, and the wintertime came and there was no work. Savoy Club and Minnie Lou's, and I always had a standing job there from then on, so I came on back to Oakland, and Grannie passed so that went out the window, but I put a little band together for a little club on Seventh Street, you know the House of Joy? In '57, Slim's, he was gone, he'd moved to Broadway.

Crawford: You knew Slim. What was he like?

Sadler: Quiet guy, nice to work for, I never had no problem with him. At the time he made the move he didn't have the support.

Crawford: Didn't he lose the lease and the property got sold?

Sadler: Yes, he closed it down but it's still there. It wasn't open. Nobody picked it up and kept it going like Esther's across the street.

Crawford: What was the community like?

Sadler: It was great for blues. Slim Jenkins and House of Joy, Manhattan, you had the Morocco, you had Club RumBoogie, which is Continental Club now, Three Sisters, you had the Triangle Club, in Berkeley on the corner; it's closed.

Crawford: How about recording?

Sadler: I did mine in L.A. I didn't do too much.

Crawford: Did you know Bob Geddins?

Sadler: Yes, he was my buddy. He was a wonderful old man. He helped a lot of musicians.

Crawford: At one time he had several labels, didn't he?

Sadler: He had quite a few. I never recorded for him. In the early days I did these for Flash label and first thing I know it was sold. Clifford Chenier had it... his sons got it after he died. Next thing I know it was sold. He took me out there and we dubbed it in Johnny Otis' studio. I didn't get nothing for that. The way they used to get you they still get you same way.

Crawford: I know. Others have complained about that too. They would sell the masters and then distribute them all over.

Sadler: They used to get you. First thing they'd, they'd bait you with a new car. Nice apartment. Figured you came from working class of people or something of the sort. Apartment in your lap. You can't say no to that and there aren't no ties you think, but they keep a bookkeeper. At the end of the year they'd come to you for x amount of thousands of dollars for their services.

Oh, they'd taken care of the apartment, bought you new clothes, new Cadillac, and all that kind of stuff, Buick, something, and then they'd say, "Do you like that?" and you'd say, "Yeah," and they'd cut the song you wanted to cut and that song could make a million dollars. "Tell you what we'll do, we'll go back in the studios." I had the song he liked, "and we'll do it again and call it even." The Platters. The Coasters. "You get the gigs out of it." In them days that's the way they did it.

Crawford: They'd record your music to pay them back and you'd get nothing.

Sadler: You'd get nothing and you were so glad to get out of debt.

Crawford: You got out of that business early. What labels did you record for?

Sadler: Just Flash. And for Galaxy. That was Ray Schacklin. Fantasy Galaxy got connections in England but no money for the records that they did. I thought they'd make a master for me, but they refused. I recorded "Should Have Known." "That Was Yesterday." Back in the '60s.

Crawford: Where were you living in Oakland?

Sadler: West Oakland, on Myrtle. Then we left Oakland. We toured a lot in the northwest. I broke the rules up there. They didn't have B.B. King or nobody. It was strange, brand new to them. Portland, Seattle, Yakima... I opened up for people like the Mother Lode.

We played armories. That's what we did. We opened for The Mother Lode. The Rink, Allas Glacier. People like that. They kept us on quite a while. We were all right. We went to Canada, Alaska. We went to Juneau, Alaska, Ketchican, we went to Prince Rupert.

Crawford: How were you received?

Sadler: They just wanted to dance. Just like now.

Crawford: Let me ask Jane how life was when you were on the road.

Jane Sadler: It was great. Who cares, whatever? We always lived in nice places, we never lived in no dumps, because I wasn't about to. The people were so nice in Salem, really, just great! We used to go out in the street lined with English walnut trees. You got all the walnuts you wanted, apples, cherry. You just walked along and got it. We enjoyed it. We was there three years. I hated to come back to Oakland. I didn't like Oakland and never did. Part of the band came back. Zack was like our son, eighteen when we picked him up in Reno. Practically adopted him.

Crawford: Well, where did the name Cool Papa come from?

Sadler: I was named by a policeman. [laughter]

Crawford: I wouldn't have guessed that!

Sadler: He was a mean policeman! But he took to me and the way I got the name he used to pick me up at the canteen on Friday night and take me to Blue Grotto nightclub, he'd take me and I'd play, played there and supposed to be twenty-one. I was fifteen! You know you're too young to go in there and have a shot.

He started calling me Cool Papa. And I been holding on to that name ever since. Policeman Moore gave me that name—blues for a Haskell Sadler. No blues in Colorado then. Outside the guys I told you played, we didn't have a strong bass, so the name came just in time. And that's what I been going by. He used to come every Friday and pick me up. He took to me. My dad met him.

Crawford: How did your mother and father like that you were a musician?

Sadler: On, they loved it. They backed me 100 percent. Yeah.

Crawford: Did you have musician friends back then?

Sadler: Lark, Larry. Spoon is in New York somewhere, haven't seen him in years.

Crawford: Did you ever want to live in New York?

Sadler: I had no desire to go to New York. When I was on my way to Europe spent a day in New York. It's too busy. I'm too slow.

Crawford: Could you describe your style?

Sadler: I don't know. I play funky blues to get the attention of the kids. Blues sounds old-fashioned to them.

Crawford: Let's go back to Oakland.

Sadler: That was '71. I brought a band with me. It was great in Frisco. All the blues clubs. The real blues. Like the Blue Mirror. Hard jazz. You had Bop City and Rocco's Bandstand, mainly more blues, then soul came in and blues and soul. Rock has always been there and then you have that devil heaven thing— that was over to the clubs like they are now. I played in the Holiness Church for four years and I caught a lot of hell from the preachers.

Crawford: Well, that's because the blues came straight from the Devil, isn't that right?

Sadler: Straight from the Devil, that's right, and they tried to hit me with that all the time. They hit me with "you can't serve two gods," and I hit them with "seek ye first the glory of god, take care of the evil of today, because tomorrow isn't promised to you." I let them ride with that for a while.

Crawford: Were you churchgoers?

Sadler: I'm Baptist, but I played the guitar in the Holiness Church. I denied the fact that I'm going to work tonight, at church on Sunday. All the church work was charity. I got the gift and I give that to the church, and then I go out and make my living. I say that I'm out of this world and then I'm in the world. You have to do what's going on in the world and to live in the world. I haven't been in the church for years.

Crawford: When you were in the church was there a choir and did you play and sing gospel?

Sadler: Gospel choir and the whole shop. I went to the Holiness Convention in Chicago in '59. Holiness, holy ghost, Pentecostal. Yeah.

Crawford: Is there a close relationship between gospel and the blues?

Sadler: No. Also, there wasn't a close relationship with going to the moon. We hadn't got there yet. All these things they throw at you that haven't happened yet. Because this belongs there and that belongs there and they throwed that out now. The music I chose was concert, blues and country and they were closely related, as to where they go. Country is all kinds of music, still country but not to the same free change as it used to be. I've got a couple of gospel songs, a couple of country tunes.

Crawford: You said your music was mostly in your head. In what form did you write?

Jane Sadler: I studied classical music for nine years, so I wrote it down. None of his music has been published. That's what we are thinking of making a book. A regular book with just his music in it. A songbook. They've been after him to do that for at least five years. We've got to get it together—I've got it everywhere! I have no idea how many songs—a lot of them he doesn't play anymore because a lot of musicians can't play it the way he wrote it. They just don't know how, even the good bands, but some of the songs they cannot do.

Crawford: How would you describe your music?

Sadler: You know, I don't know.

Jane Sadler: Just papa that's all. Wake up in the middle of the night and start writing.

Crawford: How does it come?

Sadler: I write about things happening around me. My blues don't say a lot about losing my woman, or losing my money. I sit around and write like "Resource Blues." They are building in the country, like the San Joaquin Valley. That's a source of food for the whole world. Right there in the San Joaquin Valley.

Now you go out there you see building complexes—that's a resource stolen from the people. "I'm going to sit and have a concrete meal." I got an award for that, a grant from Sacramento State. They gave me ten grand—from the blues archives, from the state, from the congress, [Barbara Boxer]. Six of them sent me placards and congratulations.

Crawford: When did you write this?

Sadler: 1976. Going from Stockton to the Bay Area. People didn't pay much attention to that song. People don't realize what's happening. I did it but they didn't pay much attention. They did finally. The song was too early when I first did it.

Crawford: How do you go about writing a song? Do you think about it for a long time?

Sadler: It just comes out of nowhere. I wrote about my leg being gone, onstage-I sang it before it was written. "I ain't got no kidneys but I still got balls!" [laughter]

Crawford: That's made you famous, Cool Papal! What other subjects are on your mind?

Sadler: About how the world is changing, about the homeless, and their going to the moon in the spaceship like they did yesterday, leaving things here in the condition it's in. Poor man, about as far as you can go, what can you do? You tried and tried and tried and nothing has... every time you think you're going to do something, the bottom falls out, you know. "The world is changing. nowhere else to go." I'm crying 'cause I'm glad you're gone."

I'm going to write about the president [Obama]. I hope he's going to do something. I'm skeptical because you don't just go and do it. I believe he'd like to do it, but it don't work like that, Congress doesn't work with you, can't get too much done.

Crawford: He loves the blues.

Sadler: Yeah, he does. That's a good sign, a darn good sign. [Someone's] wife is friends with [Hillary] and was going to take tapes down to the inauguration—"If I Were President."

Crawford: What songs are special to you?

Sadler: "Poor man." "I'm Going to Move to a Place Somewhere." "I don't need no problems, I've got enough of my own."

Jane Sadler: He wrote one in the hospital. I got a call at 3:30 a.m. and they said they couldn't get him out of it. I stood by that bed till 3:30 in the afternoon, talking, touching, and finally brought him out of it, He wrote a song "My Sweet Lady Jane" but he couldn't think of the music. So, I asked James to write the music. He's supposed to have it tonight.

Crawford: That's great! We'll hear it tonight?

Jane Sadler: Cool Papa wrote the words, but he couldn't really get what he wanted. If James doesn't get it right, Papa will do it.

Sadler: I can't think of the words. I wrote that in a crisis. Most time when I write a song, the melody is in my head, I know what I want to do with it right now! It takes a few minutes, but I already got it, what I want to say. A song like "Cryin' Out Loud," that song was about getting sick.

Crawford: Do you have a favorite key?

Sadler: A, G, C and E. A is my best.

Crawford: Do you think we are going to hear "Lady Jane" tonight?

Sadler: I have no idea. I have no idea.

Crawford: Do you want to take a rest before you go on?

Sadler: I'm all right. Yeah.

Crawford: In the early '80s what was it like?

Sadler: Little Willie John used to come there. Harry, James Wilson. Bob Geddins. We was doing the thing at the college. I knew Sonny Rhodes like my brother. Frankie Lee, Mississippi Johny Waters, Ted Butler, Johnny B. Goode.

Crawford: Who among them influenced you?

Jane Sadler: Papa's his own man. He influenced THEM!

Sadler: I mostly am.

Crawford: How about "T-Bone" Walker?

Sadler: That's my favorite. I backed him several times.

Lowell Fulson: those two are my always favorites. "T-Bone" is the best at the ninth, he's so smooth, dominant, you know, but laid back.

Crawford: He used the ninth–

Sadler: Yeah, he used the ninth.

Crawford: His "monster chord"–

Sadler: Yeah. It was his "monster chord", I like Gatemouth Brown and I liked Albert King. He died three weeks ago.

Crawford: How did you relate with other musicians? Did you hang out with them?

Sadler: No. I don't hang out with them, never have. All my friends are straight, regular people, just go to a job, caring heart, going out and work all day in that hot sun, and at night all night long listening to music. That's remarkable to me.

I used to get tired, depressed, discouraged and I'd make me a box lunch and go to construction site. I'd sit all day long and eat my lunch and go home when they got off at 5 o'clock, and I'd feel pretty good about playing the guitar. I felt damn good about playing the guitar.

Crawford: Have you written about this?

Sadler: I haven't. It's just been a thought. It's been a good life for me, and I never made it real big, but I made it, you know what I mean. It's taken care of me, and I've been places I wouldn't have been able to go—don't have that kind of money.

Crawford: Would you talk about Europe?

Sadler: I was astonished by Europe, I really was. The places that you play at, big old auditoriums, amusement, marble stairs, brass rails, teakwood, ivory all over the place, and what I like about Europe they came to see you! I don't care if B.B. King was next door, the people who came to see you! Here they come to judge you. They is critical, and don't know what they talking about to start with. There is constructive criticism and bullshit criticism. The stuff they write [here] is bullshit, bullshit criticism. I'm talking about the people. They sit around, mainly the Blacks, all smug trying to...scared to clap their hands or tap their foot. I don't care if they are Black brothers...all of them, all of them. Eli's, he's a Black brother, it's a blues club, you see what I'm saying. You take the same music and I usually just walk in the club, and they say....no blues in here.

When I first came in here, I said to myself, "Aw shit." When I first came in here because I thought it wasn't the real thing, that they wouldn't accept the blues like they did.

Crawford: What do you think about white audiences?

Sadler: That's great! I love it! That's another criticism that it will ruin the blues. You say white boys couldn't play the blues. Used to tell when it was a white or Black playing you could tell by the flavor of the guitar or the horn. You know what I mean? But now, you can't tell who it is on that record. You have no idea. You see Charlie Pryce for the first time—you see him, you'd swear he was Black. That's his soul.

Crawford: How did you happen to go to Europe?

Sadler: That was with T.J. Records, Tom Boyce. I made that album in '82 and he took the album over there. He does business over there, and that's how I ended up going over there. I went to Copenhagen, Amsterdam, all over Norway and Sweden, went to Germany and ended up in Iceland before coming home. Couple weeks. I'm telling you they'd have a line around the block. And the way they'd treat you they'd bring flowers in a crystal glass, you know, and that goes a long way–cause you play your heart out all night long, and sometimes you'd.... thank you. A lot of people told me I made their day. That's my million dollars. That means I'm doing my job and I've done something. I don't know why. Sometime musicians are arrogant, walk around like they're holier than thou. I like to have people know that I love them, that I'm concerned. I'm not going to say that I'm generally sorry, can I help you? You need somebody to talk to sometime, don't hesitate to let me know and I'll listen. I went there and I made people part of what I'm doing. A lot of musicians don't know how to do that, give the cold shoulder and you're going to get the cold shoulder. John Lee Hooker is cold and he's arrogant. I love the man, but he's arrogant and he's cold. Yeah. He's a son of a gun, see. During the days of "T-Bone" and Lowell Fulson, and he's a cross between them. He's a cross between Muddy Waters and Lightnin' Hopkins, and it's his turn now. He's making money.

Interview 2 with Haskell "Cool Papa" Sadler

Date: February 09, 1993

Location: A high school in downtown Oakland

Haskell "Cool Papa" Sadler
Credit Wikipedia

Crawford: Well, hi, Papa.

Sadler: Hi.

Crawford: What do you want the kids to learn about the blues today?

Sadler: Just that it's not a depressing music, as they're led to believe. There's all kinds of blues expressed, every kind of mood there is.

Crawford: Do you try to tell them about the history, about different kinds of blues in Texas and Chicago and all?

Sadler: Well, I just tell them I'm playing a variation of the blues, different changes, different moods. And it's something that they can understand, before we lose them. A lot of them think it's old-fashioned music. That's how come I do my funk blues, to get the kids, to get them dancing and listening. That's how come I write those styles.

Crawford: Are they going to be dancing?

Sadler: No, but they'll get up. And when my son do the rap thing, that wraps them up. They usually get into that.

Crawford: They get into that. I know from this young man, who wants to be a drummer, that he remembers you from last year.

Sadler: He's a good one. He's a good little drummer.

Crawford: He was waiting for this all year. He came last year and he said he's coming again. How many schools do you play in?

Sadler: Well, I'm only doing two. If I get to the eighteenth, that'll be two. But up till then, I was doing five, six of them. See, but I don't know what happened to the program or what. Maybe they got more people.

Crawford: That you're doing less shows than you used to.

Sadler: See, the first year, I did teaching in the classroom. See? And I took Ronnie Stewart in there and we taught the history. I know the history, so needed somebody that could answer the questions, so I brought Ronnie Stewart.

Crawford: He was going with you to answer the questions?

Sadler: Ronnie Stewart, from the Blues Society. And [a bass player]. And that was enough for us to play and explain, see? So I did it that way for a couple years. Then since I lost my leg, I've been touring [the school] assemblies.

Crawford: And all the kids come; all the kids in the school come.

Sadler: Yes, because I can't get around and get to the classrooms, see?

Crawford: Well, this is better, in a way, isn't it, because it's a bigger audience?

Sadler: It'd rather do this. I'd rather do this.

Crawford: What kind of response do you get from the kids?

Sadler: I've been getting real positive [response). I've been lucky there.

Crawford: Any of them turn up at the clubs?

Sadler: No.

Crawford: Or call you at home?

Sadler: No. No. No, they don't show up at [laughs] them clubs.

Crawford: Well, if you were to try to explain the blues style, what would you say about it? The Texas school.

Sadler: I came from Colorado.

Crawford: From Colorado, right. But say Lightnin' Hopkins, you would talk about his style, because I know he influenced you.

Sadler: I like Lightnin' Hopkins. That's one of the people I've learned off of records. And Muddy Waters, those folks, and "T-Bone".

Crawford: And "T-Bone". What would you say about their style?

Sadler: I don't know. It's unique in what they do. Each of them has their own distinctive style.

Crawford: And they influenced you. Are you aware of taking certain things from their style?

Sadler: Yes, when I first started playing. And then I started to develop my own. They have a lot of short cutbacks. So I had to play different styles. I learned not to take off; that's what I saw right there.

Crawford: What are you going to play for the kids today?

Sadler: I don't know.

Crawford: You don't know?

Sadler: I never know what I'm going to do.

Crawford: Just what strikes you?

Sadler: Mm-hm.

Crawford: But will you do "Resource Blues?"

Sadler: Yes.

Crawford: That's good awareness music for them, isn't it?

Sadler: Yes. Basically, that's how come I don't worry about no set group. Like a lot of bands, you see they've got all their songs written down, what they're going to do, and they go straight down the list. Well, I don't do that because I feel different every night. You see? And my music's got to come from my soul.

[introduction at assembly:]

Teacher: I've had to tell you four times to get quiet. Don't let that happen again. Last year we were fortunate enough to have Cool Papa Sadler and his friends come and perform for us. And we were so excited about them that we invited them back again this year. Please be as wonderful as you can be and enjoy yourselves. I present to you Cool Papa Sadler and his friends. Give them a nice warm welcome. [applause]

[music]

Interview 3:

Date: February 24, 1993

Location: The Sadler home in Livermore, California

Crawford: Okay. We're out here in Livermore with Cool Papa and Jane, a brand new house. I wanted to ask you some questions to kind of fill in our last session, about your life.

Sadler: All right.

Crawford: We came to the Blues in the School. Was that your normal performing style out there? Did you change it in any way for the kids?

Sadler: No.

Crawford: No. Do you always play amplified, or do you sometimes play acoustic?

Sadler: No, I always play amplified.

Crawford: You never did play acoustic guitar.

Sadler: Yes. I started out.

Crawford: Sure. Just a different sound. But you like electric.

Sadler: Yeah.

Crawford: I saw the lyrics for "I Were President." Could you sing that one?

Sadler: *"If I Was President"? [sings] "If I was president, the first thing I would do. If I was president, the first thing I would do. You wouldn't have to go hungry, there'd be plenty enough of food. If I was president, there's one thing for sure. Say if I was president, there's one thing for sure. You'd have a roof over your head, wouldn't be forced to sleep outdoors. If I was president, there'd be plenty of good-paying jobs. If I was president, there'd be plenty of good-paying jobs. And the honest people of this country wouldn't have to steal, beg and rob. If I was president, I could guarantee you this. If I was president, I would guarantee you this. Blues be something to listen to and not the way to live." [end of singing] That's if I was president.*

Crawford: I wish you were president.

Sadler: Hey, I was trying. [they laugh]

Crawford: How were you trying?

Sadler: I running. I've been running for the last time, four years ago, and the time before that.

Crawford: I believe you're going to make it.

Sadler: Third World, I was going.

Crawford: You've got a good program.

Sadler: Yeah, I got a platform.

Crawford: You mentioned your teacher in Denver. That was Lark Trout?

Sadler: Lark Trout.

Crawford: What was he like and what else did he do? Was he a teacher?

Sadler: He was a musician. No, no, he wasn't a teacher, he was just a blues player. I was sent down from his niece in school. She said, "My uncle plays." Took me over there, introduced me to her family and her uncle. I met him and he started working with me.

Crawford: What were your memories of him?

Sadler: He was a relaxed, laid-back person, in the "T-Bone" style, Texas style of guitar. Very pleasant.

Crawford: And did you stay in touch with him?

Sadler: Oh, yes. He died. It was the year before the last we went home. So it's been at least seven years or better, he just passed. But every time I go home, I go by and see him.

Crawford: I just saw a picture of you with your guitar up. I can't imagine how you played the guitar in those positions, but he had that kind of style, too.

Sadler: Yes. [laughs]

Crawford: I wanted to ask you about the scene in Oakland, what you remember. Do you remember Slim's [Slim Jenkins]?

Sadler: Yes, Slim's. The Hi Hat, the Manhattan, Esther's [Esther's Orbit Room]. Slim Jenkins, Jenkin's Barbeque.

Crawford: These were all different places? Jenkin's Barbeque?

Sadler: Yes.

Crawford: And they all had music?

Sadler: Not Jenkin's Barbeque.

Crawford: Was there dancing?

Sadler: The House of Joy. Oh, yeah, there was dancing. All kind of juke joints. was up and down 7th Street, before they put the post office there. On both sides of the street. There was plenty juke joints to play and have fun. I think all that's left down there now is Esther's. They don't have music.

Crawford: Pat and I went into Esther's. Do you ever go there and check in with Esther?

Sadler: I played there. I played there for the grand opening of the kitchen. Anniversaries, things like that, I've been in there. It's so small.

Crawford: It's so small. Has a little stage. But we were in there at noon, before we saw you, and it was lively. It has a nice feeling about it. In those days, Seventh Street was a center for the blues, wasn't it?

Sadler: That was the center. At least one of them. Then you had East Oakland, you had the House of Joy, the Bowling Alley. I'm trying to think. They had all kinds of little clubs out there. They had Tiki Jacks, in Berkeley; they had the Triangle Club. Oh, heck. They had the RumBoogie, which was the Continental Club now. Then you go way out to the North Richmond, you had Minnie Lou's and the Savoy Club. And Winchester, I think it was. That's the little area way out in North Richmond.

Crawford: I wanted to ask something more about the other day at the school.

Sadler: I just did it the other day, too, since I talked to you. At Lowes Junior High.

Crawford: Some of the kids got up to dance and they liked that.

Sadler: They had a ball.

Crawford: The young drummer. I thought he was good.

Sadler: He's good, he's good.

Crawford: I thought he made your drummer nervous.

Sadler: Yeah. [they laugh] He got nervous cause of being nervous, that youngster keep it up.

Crawford: Do you often get that at the schools, where you have musicians come up and play?

Sadler: Not too much, but I get them on the dance. And the little girls came down the aisle dancing. Yeah. They was onto it, wasn't they? Yes, indeed.

Crawford: Does your son go with you all the time?

Sadler: Most of the time when I do Blues in the Schools. He used to come to the Marriott all the time and I use him on a lot of my places that I play.

Crawford: Will he do the same kind of thing, the robot dance?

Sadler: Yes. That was the idea, to show that you could do your modern dance to the blues. See, people down the blues so that it's old-fashioned and out of date and you can't do the modern dances to it; and I just knock it out with him doing it. I don't argue with them, nothing like; I show them. And *then* I tell them, evidently, you can't dance, because your man has got done doing what you said couldn't be done. See, and that eliminates all arguing, because he dances to the blues.

Crawford: You were talking about when you played and sang in the church, in Holiness Church, right? What was the format of that church?

Sadler: Just preaching the good news. Just the basic.

Crawford: Sippie Wallace said that the blues and the gospel are the same. If you just take a blues song and you put in the Lord, then you have a gospel song. What do you think about that? [laughter]

Sadler: It's pretty much the same. Pretty much the same.

Crawford: Are you preaching when you're singing? Are you sending a message?

Sadler: I'm sending a message; I'm not exactly preaching. A lot of my songs, you could do in church because they have nothing to do with "baby" and all. Like "Resource Blues," for example, see, it has to do with issues that could be talked about in the church, as well as out of the church. Things like life-story things, where mostly, it deals with more than losing your money or your lady or your man or whatever.

Sadler: I could try. I'll do a thing. "Resource Blues." [sings]

They're filling our farmlands up with buildings. I'm going to sit down and have me a concrete meal. They're fillings our farmlands up with buildings. I'm going to sit down and have me a concrete meal. For bread, I'll chew on bricks and for meat, I'll eat on steel. A year ago, I took a ride off in the country. You know the fields was full of corn. A year ago, I took a ride off in the country. You know the fields was full of corn. All I see out there now is brand-new houses. Lord, all the vegetables have gone. Now there's one thing that connects to me. They talk about a population explosion, say they ain't going to be enough to eat. They don't stop messing with the natural resources, you know that's a low down dirty shame. Because when everything is gone, you just got the greedy man to blame. Concrete don't taste like no potatoes. And you know bricks don't taste like bread. It's almost too late to help anybody because most of the land is already dead

And that's what you see around here; all this was farmland.

Crawford: That's powerful.

Sadler: Yes, all this was farmland. Pop-up lab over there, business parks all up and down there. All that was grazing land. I mean vegetables. All that. See, we used to supply a third of the world's food, right out of this valley, and it's all gone. Mainly, it's almost all gone. With houses and business parks and malls and so forth. You can't bring that land back. It takes years. Once you build on it and man move in, it takes years of bringing it back.

Crawford: We are coming to realize that. That recognition, for you, came well after you wrote it, didn't it? The award was in 1991.

Sadler: When I first wrote it, they didn't understand it. It was too far ahead. See, I wrote that back in '76. Willie Nelson came out with one. That was in the nineties or the eighties. Mine was already out, but got nowhere. But Jay Johnson is trying to get together and make a video of that song. It hasn't been produced. It hasn't been distributed, except personal sales.

Crawford: You wrote about the moon, the fact that they said you can't go to the moon. And here we are, we've been on it, walked on it.

Sadler: We've been on it. The world is changing.

Crawford: Do kids have a harder time today than we did in our time?

Sadler: I think they do now. I think they do. I wouldn't want to be a kid today. They almost have no choice, on account of the drugs, because of the way it's laid out to them and come to them. That's how come all of them got hooked. It used to be if anybody was hooked in schools during our days, it'd be somebody across the track. Some real poor family. And they wouldn't be hooked on drugs; they'd be hooked on alcohol. Then they finally slipped into marijuana. Back then, if you was on drugs, you was a entertainer of some kind. See, if you was a entertainer, they'd bust you in a minute, just for being a entertainer. I got busted a lot of times, just for being a entertainer. I never used drugs. Just for being a musician.

Crawford: Did you go to prison?

Sadler: A couple times. They'd hold you for suspicion. Just something to hassle you with. They didn't find nothing, because wasn't nothing to find. Just like they used to pick you up in Los Angeles a lot for suspicion of robbery, suspicion of this. That's just a way to bust you, hold you seventy-two hours. and let you go. They didn't have no proof; they just said they did and you were suspicion. They'd bring you through the lineup and all that kind of mess. They got me for that a couple times. That's how it was.

Crawford: Did you write about it?

Sadler: No. I don't think I did.

Crawford: Anything more about racism in California?

Sadler: I had trouble in Los Angeles. Because I mix-married then, too. Back in the early fifties, they just wasn't ready. You really got a lot of slack. Snatched me off the bus, made me take off my shirt, like they was looking for drugs. Just messing with me. See, she wasn't a prostitute and I shouldn't have had her. That's how they figure. You see? Too good for you. You deserve a night lady. You all deserve one another, so to speak. Because that's what it was in them days. If you see a Black and white couple, most times it was a hassle.

Crawford: That wouldn't happen any place now, would it? Would it?

Sadler: It happened all over the place then.

Crawford: But now?

Sadler: That don't happen now, there's just too many interracial marriages.

Crawford: When you got to the coast, was there trouble?

Sadler: No, Jane and I never had no trouble.

Jane: Well, a few people would look and say something. Of course, I'm always the type of person to just tell them off. That's the way I am.

Crawford: You haven't talked about the children.

Sadler: My children. Now, my daughter, that's the one I haven't seen in thirty-seven years. I don't know where she's at. She's down in Los Angeles somewhere and I have no ways or means of trying to find her. But her mother's still alive and still in Los Angeles. She's there; that's how close they was. The last time I seen her she was two. She's thirty-six now. So, I've got three kids the same age. I've got my son, teaches karate. He's the oldest of all of them, but by a month or so. Otherwise, for one short period, they're all the same age. And then next year, he'll change, in October.

Crawford: He's the oldest one.

Sadler: He's the oldest one. I know where he is; he's in Denver. I write him and call him and see him. And my other daughter that's in Denver, I write her and call her and see her. But Bonnie, I lost contact, period. I don't know if she's married, have kids or anything.

Crawford: You'd like to know.

Sadler: I would like to see her. I would like to find her, if I ever got the money together where I could spend some time down in Los Angeles. Which I'm sort of leery of Los Angeles now–all the districts and gangs, you got the right colors on and all that kind of carrying on. So, I'm leery. But I would sure like to find her, just to say hi.

Crawford: She'd like to find you, too, you can be sure.

Sadler: I'd hope so.

Sadler: When I left Los Angeles, I left it, because I had a lot of trouble in Los Angeles, with the law. See, they railroaded me for a whole year, behind my wife. When I left, I left. That was in '56. That's when I came this way.

Crawford: How did they railroad you?

Sadler: They framed me. I was supposed to wife beating, and I didn't do it. I was working. I was out there trying to make a living.

Crawford: Where were you singing and where were you playing?

Sadler: Bunch of juke joints.

Crawford: Central Avenue?

Sadler: Central Avenue, Hole in the Wall. Oh, I can't remember all them places.

Crawford: Was there more down there than there was in Oakland?

Sadler: Oh, yeah! Because you had 5th Street. I worked 5th Street, I worked Central, I worked West Los Angeles. Then I worked San Bernardino, little towns around. Victorville.

Crawford: Nice town.

Sadler: And Barstow. Barstow. That club's still there, Fred's Place.

Crawford: Still going strong? Do you ever play those clubs now?

Sadler: I haven't been back there. Every time I got to Las Vegas, I've been thinking about running up and see if it's still open. I heard it's still going. I would like to see Fred. It's still the same old Barstow, just has gotten bigger.

Crawford: That was where you did your first recording.

Sadler: Yeah. With B.B. Brown's Blues Band. We recorded for Mr. Phil Philbright. He's the one that had Clifton Chenier, back in the fifties, did "Bump the Rock." He was having him in Louisiana, when he got me. And then he sold me to Flash Records and I did my recordings over again, in Johnny Otis' studio.

Crawford: What was the connection with Johnny Otis? You mentioned that before.

Sadler: No, that was just doing the record. And then on one of my records, "Do Right Mind," I've got a place where he'd cry while I'm doing the solo. He's crying on that record. Because I sound like I had pneumonia.

Crawford: He provided the sound effects?

Sadler: He devised this crying part, because it sounded like I had pneumonia.

He said, "No, I'll cry for you."

Crawford: I heard it on the recording.

Sadler: That's the way I sound. [laughs]

Crawford: Do you have copies of those? Do you have those recordings?

Sadler: No, I don't have one copy of "Do Right Mind." They redid these songs on that P.V. label in Japan. They redid them. They got a California blues legends record album out. That's supposed to be on there.

Crawford: Did you get something for that?

Sadler: No.

Jane: Is it available around here, do you think?

Sadler: I don't know. You might get it at that place in El Cerrito, Down Home Blues. Or you might could order it. He had it, at one time. I think they call it *California Legends.*

Jane: So, they didn't pay you anything for that?

Sadler: I haven't gotten nothing from none of them records. I didn't get nothing for "Buick 59," and it was a hit with the Medallions. I don't know what label they was on.

Crawford: I wanted to ask you more about Europe because you mentioned how well you were received in Europe. You mentioned you went to Iceland.

Sadler: Yes, Iceland.

Crawford: What was the best reception that you got over there? You mentioned the king of Denmark greeting you.

Sadler: I don't know, they all was good. It really was. Just astonishing. To see all them people there for you. No matter if B.B. King was next door, they'd still be there for you. They'd go to whoever they want to see. It's not like in America, the competition. If somebody like B.B. King was next door and I was the following door, oh, they'd miss me that night. Mostly. See? But there, they go to who they want to see and you get the right reception. They really show the affection for the American music and musicians over there.

Crawford: Why do they like the blues and jazz particularly?

Sadler: I don't know. But they really do. They're into the music.

Crawford: I think so. Because when the blues began to diminish here in the sixties and seventies.

Sadler: Yeah, it was blooming. A lot of those musicians moved over there.

Crawford: Oh, is that right? Did you ever consider that?

Sadler: No. No. Have to learn the language.

Crawford: That's right. What do you remember about Charles Brown as a person, about his music?

Sadler: I like what he does. He's a great person.

Crawford: Do you ever see him? He lives here in Oakland, as well. He loves the track.

Sadler: Yeah, he loves the track. Him and Jimmy McCracklin, you could find them at the track. I don't see them. See, I never went out. I rarely go anywhere with a lot of musicians.

Jane: Never has. When he wasn't playing–

Sadler: I'm really misinformed about the musicians.

Crawford: You were an unusual musician.

Sadler: Yeah. Well, the musicians generally have the same thing, talk about music, music, music, music. So I had other friends, so I could talk about something else. I do the music.

Crawford: You told me that you liked to go and take your lunch out to the construction sites. Then go home and play the guitar.

Sadler: When I used to get just tired, wanting to quit, I'd just pack me a little box lunch and go out to a construction site and stay there all day. Then I'd be happy when they get off. [laughs]

Crawford: What happened then? Did you go someplace and have a beer?

Sadler: Yeah, I'd do that and then I'd come on home, and I was all right.

Crawford: Well, how about "Take your hands up off your hips."

Sadler: *I say draw in your lips, take your hands up off your hips. I say draw in your lips, take your hands up off your hips. You know damn good and well/ ain't about to live like this. Well, you always raising sand, fill my life with misery. You know you always raising sand, filling my life with misery. You got to hurry up and change. I'm just about to set you free. I done told you once and I ain't about to tell you twice. I done told you once. I ain't about to tell you twice. You got to learn how to smile and bring some happiness in our lives. I say draw in your lips and take your hands up off your hips. I say draw in your lip, and take your hands up off your hips. You know damn good and well I ain't about to live like this.*

I wrote that.

Crawford: Thank you.

Sadler: Average guy, wake up in the morning, the woman's mouth all stuck out and hands on her hip and raising sand. He come in from a hard day's work and she meet him at the door.

Crawford: Raising sand?

Sadler: Raising sand. Raising hell.

Crawford: That's a great song.

Sadler: It is, at that. That's what I write.

Crawford: That wasn't about Jane, of course.

Sadler: No, it wasn't Jane.

Jane: Well, Jane does things like that.

Sadler: Yeah, every once in a while.

Jane: Oh, yeah. I'm no angel.

Sadler: No.

Crawford: How many years have you been married?

Jane: Thirty-eight.

Crawford: Well, congratulations, and it's been a pleasure talking to you.

Thank you both.

[End of interview]

Interviewer: Joe Mathews

Date: May 7, 1996

Location: Brown's home in Stockton, California

Earl "Good Rockin'" Brown
Credit: The Bancroft Library, University of California, Berkeley

Mathews: Today's date is May 7, 1996, and we're at the home of Earl "Good Rockin'" Brown in Stockton, California. This interview session is for the Regional Oral History Project at the University of California at Berkeley and the National Endowment for the Humanities as well. Well, good morning Earl. I'd like to first thank you for having me into your lovely home today and to say that it is surely an honor and privilege for me to be sitting with you talking about your life and career in music. So, thank you very much.

Brown: Good morning and thank you.

Mathews: I guess I'd like to start with the early part of your life. I know you were born in Arkansas.

Brown: El Dorado, Arkansas.

Mathews: When was this?

Brown: Oh, my goodness [laughs]. So they tell me that I was born right across the street from the local school. The old-fashioned way, real primitive way, alright? Not at the hospital, right at the home. Yeah, September the fifth, 1931.

Mathews: And you stayed in Arkansas for a while?

Brown: We lived in El Dorado, Arkansas up until I was roundabout seven years old. Then my folks moved to Dallas, Texas.

Mathews: Is your birth place still there, the home where you were born?

Brown: Oh, no way, no way. Oh, my goodness. You're talking about Arkansas, right? Oh my, no. If I go back there now I would be like a total stranger in the twilight zone. Because even the place where I was raised up in Dallas, Texas, it's a graveyard there now. I was there last year and went to the street corner, the sign is there but, my goodness, the houses and stuff, everything just have *changed*. My wife and I, we stood there, and I tried to see if there was anything that looked like it did when I was a kid, a teenager, you know. Nothing. My goodness, freeways run through there.

Mathews: Well, did you attend grammar school in Dallas?

Brown: Yes. Let me see. I didn't come to California until 1943.

Mathews: We'll get to those California years, to be sure. So you were there from about age seven to about fifteen. You lived in Dallas?

Brown: Up until around about fourteen years old.

Mathews: What was it like growing up in the South in your early years?

Brown: Oh, my goodness. Well, growing up, I knew I had a lot of fun in Arkansas as a kid. Kids are kids, and we don't know any better, you know. We don't know what's going on other than our neighborhood. So, it was fun times being a kid, and I can remember, my other relatives, they all went to the *cotton fields,* see? And they would get on this big old wagon, and I thought that was a lot of *fun.* [laughs] And I remember, I wanted to go with them and they said, "No, you're too small, you're too little. You'll be on the way, you stay home." And I was *crying.*

And so, when I got older and realized what they was doing, I said, "Thank God.... thank God I didn't have to go to the cotton fields." [laughs] Oh my goodness, that's what I remember, that really do stands out, in Arkansas. And before we moved to Dallas Texas, I remember riding the trains...I think it was about three hundred miles, I don't know. But that was an adventure in itself. I had never been on a train before and as a kid, to ride the train, you know what I mean... I didn't even have an idea about segregation, you know. I was just having *fun* on the train, and running up and down the aisle, you know. And I didn't know at that time that my goodness, we had a certain section to sit in and all that, you know.

So, when we moved to Dallas, Texas, for the first three years, every year we would go back to Arkansas to visit the family, and we had to ride the train, OK? And so I really did enjoy riding the train, it was really fun for me. But, in Dallas, Texas, at the age of twelve...I never will forget it. In Dallas, Texas, that's when I started noticing about the different races. And so, they had a theater there, this is where all the Blacks *went,* OK? And this was in North Dallas. And so, at this theater, well, back in those days after they showed the main feature film, they always showed a short type of film on entertainment or something. Last round about fifteen or twenty minutes or something. And so this one particular time they were showing a film, Louis Jordan. And he was a great saxophone player and singer, you know, entertainer.

Mathews: It was a short with just Louis Jordan?

Brown: Yeah, yeah. And so, this was the beginning. Up to that time I didn't know what I wanted to be, you know, what I wanted to do in life. And so, sitting in that theater and I saw Louis Jordan up on that screen, I said, "That's what I want. I want to be like that man up there." And so, I couldn't wait to get back home to ask my mama, "Mama, *please, please,* Mama buy me a saxophone, because I got to play like Louis Jordan."

Mathews: Did she know who Louis Jordan was?

Brown: Yeah, she knew, she knew. Because he had records out at that time. And so after bugging her for about three or four months, she finally gave in. My first saxophone cost my mother about a hundred and twenty-five dollars. And so, she found a person who could give me music lessons, OK? So my music lessons lasted about three months.

Mathews: Did you go to someone's house?

Brown: I went to this guy's house; I can't remember his name anyway. But I didn't learn on the regular cane reeds that most saxophone players use. At an early age my teacher saw that I was too rough, so he put me on *plastic* reeds. So right today, if I was to use a cane reed to play on, I would sound like an amateur.

Mathews: Is that right, so you're still using them?

Brown: I still use them today. They're very expensive, but that's what I have to play on is plastic reeds. So, I started after only three months of lessons, I started listening to phonograph records and have my horn out and I learned to develop an *ear*. What I could hear. I see if I could duplicate it, I'd try to find it, you know. And so, I got pretty good at that. Play right along with the records.

Mathews: Who were some of the guys you used to play along with?

Brown: Oh, my goodness. Earl Bostic. And Louis Jordan was my inspiration, and that's what motivated me, see? And so that's all I've ever had is three months of music lessons out of my whole life.

Mathews: And otherwise, you were self-taught?

Brown: Yeah.

Mathews: I'd like to ask you about what your folks did. What did your dad do back in those days back in Dallas? Why did you move to Dallas?

Brown: Well, before we moved to Dallas, my mother and father was divorced. See, so even as a baby, I didn't know my father real well. I'm glad you asked about that because I thought about how much money people was making back in those days and I tell my children today and they just can't *believe* it, you know? A person making four and five and six dollars a week, you know. They just can't hardly *believe* that.

I knew my father, I know he didn't have the education that he should have had. And I knew that he was one of those kind of persons who was a hard-working man but was making probably five or six dollars a *week*. And so being a kid, we never thought about how much stuff cost, but I can remember my mother giving me fifty cents and going to the store and buying fifteen cents worth of pork chops, and a loaf of bread and ten cents worth of bologna. And my *goodness*, I never thought about it.

And when we'd go to carnivals and stuff of that nature, I know that, my goodness, five cents would get me a double scoop of ice cream, a *nickel*. So being a kid we would always ask for a nickel. Yeah, a dime or something, but that would be about it. So I was just amazed, but my mother raised my brother and I.

Mathews: There were two boys?

Brown: Yes, two boys, no sisters. My brother, he passed away in the middle seventies. And so, it's now just myself and my mother. Yes, she's in a convalescent home now, she's eighty-four. She'll be eighty-five in December.

Mathews: So, what took you to Dallas, then?

Brown: My mother, bless her heart, you know what I mean? She did not get a full education herself. But she wanted to be a beautician. That's what brought us to Dallas, Texas, because she went to the beautician school in Dallas, Texas. She learned how to do hair, and she also was very aggressive and smart to want to own her own shop. So, she accomplished that. I remember in Dallas, Texas, my goodness, she used to send us places to get our clothes tailor-made, you know what I mean. So, we were one of the few kids in school, going to school with tailor-made slacks and shirts and suits, you know. And so, hey...she did all right. She had other people working for her, and my goodness, she kind of spoiled me and my brother, you know, yeah.

Mathews: Mothers have a tendency to do that.

Brown: But I want to tell you this. Because I tell this to my children. In Dallas, Texas, in the early forties, the house we was living in was a three-bedroom house. Real *nice-lookin'* house. This was before my mother got her own beauty shop, see? And I guess, like all families, you go through hard times, you know. And as a young boy, the landlord came by for the *rent*. OK? And unknown to me, my mother didn't have the rent to pay him at that time. And so, she told me to go answer the door and tell him that she wasn't there, you know. And she told me, "I'll be hiding in the closet." And so, I didn't know how to lie. The man come to the door, and he says, "Son, where's your mother?" I say, "My mother, she's in the closet and she told me to tell you that she wasn't here." [laughter]

Mathews: Did she hear all this?

Brown: And so, he burst out laughing...he burst out laughing, and my mother, she came out of the closet and she was laughing. See, unknown to me....well, they became very friendly, you know what I mean, because she rented from him, you know. So, they both had a big laugh. And so, he said, "Zola, when can you pay the twelve dollars?" Twelve dollars a month. Twelve dollars a month.

Mathews: For the whole house?

Brown: *Yeah*!! Yeah. And I tell my kids about these things, how things have really changed. A dollar was a dollar back in those days, I'm telling you, my god. My uncle, my uncle Pious in Los Angeles, Pious Brown, in Arkansas, he had a two-story home. He worked for a trucking firm and I'm pretty sure he didn't make no more than ten dollars a week, you know what I mean? But he owned a two-story house, and he had another house and then when they moved to California, to Los Angeles, he bought two homes in L. A. So, this was back in the fifties. OK? So, I just don't see how they did it, you know? But the property was very cheap, and it was more easy to get into, I guess, whatever.

My relatives who didn't have the education...and knowing how much a Black man would make back in those days, I'm just really *proud*–my heart, you know, I really appreciate what they went through. Because I knew as I started playing music and started touring the South in the early fifties and hit every southern state and I know what *I* went through. Man, I can imagine what *they* must have went through. So, I really do admire them... working hard and trying to make something of themselves.

Mathews: That really is admirable. It's nice that you are able to have that kind of a perspective, you know? Because it was terrible in a lot of ways, and it wasn't going to get a whole lot better for a while. That's all right. What about your grandparents, Earl, did you know them at all?

Brown: Yes, I knew my grandmother, on my mother's side. And I have one aunt that, I knew something was wrong. You know as a kid everybody else is dark skinned, and then up comes a person in the family who is very light skinned... her hair just straight and curled and she, my *aunt*, you know? So, being a kid, we just took it as it came, you know? Until you get grown, then you look back and see where, my goodness, well, that's when I knew that my grandmother evidently, all the kids that she had, had different daddies. You know what I mean. Lo and behold, there was one. Yeah.

Mathews: I'd like to ask you about what you remember about the music you heard as a kid that got you excited. Now you mentioned going to the theater on that fateful day seeing Louis Jordan up on the screen and that was it. But were there others?

Brown: All that I was exposed to before then were Louis Jordan records, Count Basie, Tommy Dorsey. Tommy Dorsey was where I learned how to dance. My young aunt taught me how to dance to boogie woogie, whatever it was... Tommy Dorsey "Boogie Woogle..." something. But at parties we used to have when I was growing up, we used to dance to Tommy Dorsey records and big band sounds, Count Basie's and all of them.

Mathews: So, all the records would be spinning and...

Brown: Yeah, well the big 78s. Those were the kind of records that we had, you know? And so I didn't get exposed to the *blues* until I came to California.

Mathews: So, you were hearing the big bands and all. Were you involved in the church at all with your family?

Brown: Oh yeah, I'm glad you asked about that. Yeah, I was raised up in the church. Oh, my goodness, it started in Arkansas. I can remember going to church every day. Yeah, we went to church *every day*. We would go to church *every day*. They would have something going on every evening, know what I mean? And back in those days we would have to walk to school, we would walk everywhere, OK? So it was just a normal thing and my goodness, and it never dawned on me why we would go to church every day. Because we had *fun*, you know, being a kid, it was a fun thing. And they would have me to come up and sing along with the choir, you know, and lead some of the songs off. I thought that was *great*.

Mathews: Was your mother in the choir?

Brown: Yeah, My mother and her sisters, they had a gospel group together and my goodness, they was good *singers*, you know. And so, all the old people, they thought sure I was going to grow up to be a preacher.

Mathews: Is that right? You seemed like a real natural.

Brown: Yeah. And that's really kind of funny the way things turned out. But my mother raised me really right. At an early age I knew that hey, I didn't want to get involved with drinkin' and smokin' and drugs type of things, you know.

Mathews: And so, the church upbringing was really important in your young life.

Brown: Yeah. I figured that it had to be a gift from the man upstairs for me to learn so quickly and I knew that music was going to be my way of life. That was the way I was going to make my living. You know, I don't care how much education I would have received, I knew that music was going to be my livelihood, was going to be my profession.

Mathews: So, I guess the real turning point was the day you went to the theater and you saw Louis Jordan up on the screen and that's when you knew that this was going to be it.

Brown: That was the turning point.

Mathews: And you got after your mother to get you a sax.

Brown: That's it. And I learned how to play that thing and when we moved to Richmond, California in 1943...can you imagine a kid?

Mathews: So, you were already playing for three years before you moved to Richmond?

Brown: No, let me see. I think two years, almost two years, just fooling around learning different songs and stuff. I never played with a band before. And so now when we moved to Richmond I was around about fourteen, almost fifteen years old. And here's a kid...I never seen mountains before. I never saw an ocean before. And my goodness, as soon as we reached Richmond, California...

Mathews: How did you get there?

Brown: On the *train*. On the *train*. [laughs]

Mathews: Must have been quite a ride.

Brown: Oh, *what a ride*! My eyes was this big. I was just taking in everything. and you know what I mean? Just letting it all soak in. And I just couldn't *wait* to get to California because my parents had told me about, well, in California, all races of people mixed together, you know? They go to school together, you know what I mean? Because all I seen was one side of things in Dallas, Texas. In Dallas, Texas, once a year, that was the only time that Blacks could go to the county fair. They had one day during the *whole* twenty days of the county fair going on...one day they would let Blacks go, all right? That was our day. That was it, man.

And the neighborhood we were living in, two blocks down the street, well I see other white families. And we *played* together. We played, we'd roller-skate, hockey, you know? And we would play together, no problem, all right? But we didn't go to school together. And that was only two blocks from where we were living and like I said, no name calling...we just had great fun, all right? Teenagers, we were playing. So getting ready to go to the theater, like I tell my kids, I said when you all get ready to go to the movies now you just pick up the paper and pick out which one to go to. When I was coming up, my goodness, I didn't have no *choice*. I had to go to that one.

Mathews: What was the name of that theater, you remember?

Brown: Was it the State Theater? I think it was the State, because it was located on State and something. But we finally hit California.

Mathews: So what was it that brought your folks out there, what lured you mother out of Dallas?

Brown: Better-paying profession, and the shipyards in Richmond. Back in those days the shipyards was hiring people like you wouldn't believe, and the money was *good*.

Mathews: So you moved out there when the war was still on, right? So, there was a very large African-American community by the time you got there.

Brown: Oh yeah, that was a big migration of Blacks come into California during that time and they was making money like you wouldn't believe. And they was able to buy cars and buy homes and better their lives. See, what brought my mother out to California was that the rest of the family had already gone and they was writing and calling saying, "Child, you better come on. You better come on."

Mathews: So, you had heard a lot about that California was quite a place.

Brown: Oh yeah, oh dear. So, my mother worked in the shipyards. And my uncle and his wife, my Aunt Hannah, they was living in Berkeley. They had a nice place in Berkeley. At that time, driving a new car, you know? So right there in Richmond, this is where my music career started.

Mathews: Yes, I was going to ask you, once you got out there did you find there was a lot going on musically that you started to hear? Who were some of the guys that you remember out there as a teenager?

Brown: As a teenager in Richmond, I started to hear about Jimmy McCracklin, Lowell Fulson and LC. "Good Rockin" something [Robinson]...oh my goodness. So anyway, they had a recreation facility where teenagers could go and play ping-pong and other things, in Richmond. And so every week they would have dances. And so, there was a little group, a band, you know. And so I decided to hang around with them, and then it seemed like I was the best one out of all of them. [laughs] And so on the Sunday afternoons, and I'm sixteen years old now, almost sixteen.

Mathews: So, this would have been 1945 or thereabouts?

Brown: Yeah. I would say forty-six. 1946. In north Richmond they had a club called the Savoy. And back in those days, I guess, the laws wasn't as strict as they are now, because on Sunday afternoons they had jam sessions. And people like Lowell Fulson, Jimmy McCracklin was playing at this club. So I was almost sixteen when I went into that club and started sitting in with the musicians and stuff. This was where Lowell Fulson heard me play.

Mathews: For the first time? Was at the Savoy?

Brown: For the first time. At the Savoy at a Sunday afternoon jam.

Mathews: Was he a pretty established player by that time around there?

Mathews: Yeah, he was just getting noticed, in other words, he was recording at that time. No hit, no hits of anything, but people knew him as a recording artist.

Brown: So, that was through Bob Geddins outfit?

Brown: Yeah, Bob Geddins. And then he had just got on with Jack Lauderdale in Los Angeles, but he was living in Vallejo, California. And so, he would drive from Vallejo to Richmond and play these engagements. Big Joe Turner was playing in north Richmond at the time. He came a few years later. Because Big Joe Turner, he made hit records first before Lowell. But anyway, Lowell wanted me to join his group. He had a piano player, drummer and bass player. That was it.

Mathews: And so, you sat in on this one session and right then he knew that he wanted Earl Brown to be in the band. Wow. You must have knocked him over that day.

Brown: Yeah. Well, see, I had a lot of energy. I just couldn't stay still when I played, know what I mean? I had to be jumpin' all over the place, you know. Back in those days you saw saxophone players that just stood up there like a statue... just cool, you know what I mean? Here I am, I'm just jumping all over the place, jumpin' up on the tables, walkin' the bar and playing the saxophone. So, Lowell say, "I want this kind of guy in my band." So, he had to come to my house and talk to my mother and convince her to let me, you know... I was almost sixteen.

Mathews: So, he came over to the house and sat down with your mother.

Brown: Yeah, to beg to let me, you know. I was still in school, yeah, shoot, my goodness.

Mathews: Well, what did she think about that?

Brown: She had to think *hard* and *long* about that. So finally she gave in. Not right away, it took about six months, before I started playing with him. So I knew I was about sixteen-and-a-half years old when I started playing with Lowell.

Mathews: I'll bet your classmates must have just...

Brown: Oh, my goodness. You know, it was played low key. He promised my mother that he would watch me and he wouldn't let me around any drinkin'. That he would look out for me and that he wouldn't let any harm come to me. Because those night clubs, where adults came, and people dancing and gettin' drunk and you know. And so ninety-nine percent of the audience was all Black back in those days.

Mathews: So, this was at the Savoy and the other local clubs?

Brown: Yeah.

Mathews: Did you play only at the Savoy at first?

Brown: No, at first only at the Savoy. Then, in Vallejo and Oakland, Sim Jenkins' Place.

Mathews: You played at Slim Jenkins'? I was going to ask you about what the club scene in Oakland and around it was like at that time. Was it really thriving?

Brown: It was thriving. I also tell my kids that back in the forties in fifties, Blacks owned a lot of businesses and clubs and stuff. And you know, it was nice. But today you don't see that. You just don't see it. And so, the hard thing was that I was sixteen years old, in the twelfth grade. And I knew that I was going to be graduating, and before I had a chance to graduate, Jack Lauderdale sent for us to come to Los Angeles to Universal Studios to do a recording session. So, this was my first chance to be on record, for the first time, you know.

And so, my god, by the time that date took place I was seventeen years old. And my goodness, we went to Los Angeles to Universal Studios and that's when I met Lloyd Glenn and Bob Hadley and the drummer Eddy Piper, OK? And so, Lloyd Glenn had been playing in movies, been in a few movies, you know. He was playing the piano on the screen. And so, I was just all in awe, being in that kind of company, you know. So I had never been nowhere before, a country boy.

Mathews: And next thing you know you're in Los Angeles. How did you get down there?

Brown: We drove. Just me and Lowell, me and Lowell.

Mathews: And you tied in with the other men down there?

Brown: And so unknown to us, one of the songs...we recorded four songs, one of the songs was "Every Day I Have the Blues." And even before we went to L.A., when I started playing with Lowell, that's when I got the feel for the blues. When he was singing, I would play in-between his singin'. And we started a trend, see? We are the ones who started this. And then we had a lot of other people copy that style after we got it going. And so, I would listen to him sing and I would play in between his singing and "Every Day I Have the Blues" became a hit. It hit *big*. I went from rags to riches, I'm telling you. Just like that. And we went back after we did the session, and we didn't know it was going to be a hit, so we came back to Richmond.

Mathews: How long did the session take, did you do it in a day?

Brown: We did it in a day. Jack Lauderdale took us out to Universal Studios. We went in there and this is where a lot of other big-name movie stars recorded in that building, OK? And so, we went back to Richmond and two or three weeks after we came back to Richmond, they had already released the record and my goodness, we received a phone call from Jack Lauderdale say, "Looky here. Seem like the record's gonna go. It's gonna *go*. And we need to get y'all back here because we got to put a group together. And we got to get you fitted for uniforms and got to get you a bus."

Mathews: So they could get you out on the road.

Brown: There you go. Get out on the road and make *more* money. And Lowell had to talk to my mother. He said, "Looky here, we need him in the band, he's on this record." Well, my mother say, "Well, he's got to graduate." And I really wanted to go. I begged my mom. I say, "Look here, mama. Even if I graduate, this is what I want to play. I want to be an entertainer. I want to make my life playing music. Mama, *please*, *please* let me go. Let me *go*." And I think I told my mother a lie. I think I told her that I could finish school at a later date. I *think* I told her that, but I don't know. But, during that time I was so excited and so happy that I was in my first recording session and that I was going to be playing music and making money. Making *money*.

Mathews: What year was this, Earl?

Brown: 1949.

Mathews: 1949 is when "Every Day I Have the Blues" hit?

Brown: There you go. And I'm going to tell you it hit *big* time. In Billboard it stayed up on the top number one position on Billboard for about fifteen weeks or something. Number one across the board everywhere.

Mathews: So, you guys mobilized the band and hit the road...

Brown: Hey! When we got back to LA., *that's* when I found out that Jack Lauderdale had sent for Ray Charles out of Seattle, Washington.

Mathews: Had you heard of Ray Charles at that time?

Brown: Yeah, I had heard of Ray Charles and he had a trio. See, Ray Charles, when he first started off, he was trying to find himself. He was just like myself... imitated Louis Jordan. I could do Louis Jordan to a tee. Note for note. And in later years, when I was traveling with Lowell, I met Louis Jordan face to face and I was able to show him that I could copy his style, see? And he just, oh my goodness....we'll get to that further on down the road.

Mathews: So anyway, Jack Lauderdale asked Ray Charles to come down.

Brown: Yes. Jack Lauderdale wanted to put Lowell Fulson and Ray Charles together as an added attraction type of thing. In other words, Lowell had the biggest hit out, so Ray Charles was going to be an added attraction to Lowell.

Mathews: So, Ray was actually in the band then?

Brown: Yeah, he was in the band. Oh yeah. That's when we all got together, in 1949. And that's when.... (takes a moment to remember the name of a player) a great saxophone player.

Mathews: Stanley Turrentine?

Brown: Stanley Turrentine! Thank you, thank you! I'm sorry, Stanley! [laughter] My goodness. Yeah, we was all together, OK?

Mathews: Was Stanley Turrentine a musician in Los Angeles at the time?

Brown: *Yeah*, yeah. And he was the tenor saxophone player, and then Billy Brooks, the trumpet player, all right? Out of Ohio....Dayton, Ohio, I think it is. So that was the band that was formed and Ray Charles became the musical director for the band. See, because he had more musical ability than Lowell, all right? Because Ray was into arranging big band sounds and stuff, he had the *ability*, you know. And so that was the group. We had Ray on piano, Lowell on guitar, bass player, drummer, Eddie Piper on the drums and then we had three horns. I was on the alto, Stanley Turrentine on tenor and Billy Brooks on trumpet. And we got suited and booted and they got us a bus, and Jack Lauderdale had a 1949 convertible Buick. *Beautiful*, beautiful automobile and Lowell say, "I want that automobile." And he gave him the keys. "Go on and take it."

Mathews: So, did you take the bus and the Buick on the road?

Brown: Oh *yeah*, oh yeah. Yes.

Mathews: So where did you go?

Brown: We left L. A. and do you know? It was a whole year before we came back to LA. We hit every state, city, in the United States. This happened for three years in a row.

Mathews: So, you'd come back and go back out again?

Brown: There you go. That's right. When we came back we went back into the studio, did another session and from that session, "Blue Shadows," that became a hit. "Low Society Blues", that became a hit. "Guitar Shuffle" became a hit. "Lonesome Christmas" became a hit. See, so we just makin' all these *hits*. And touring. And in the South, my goodness, when we hit Texas we had to play thirty one-nighters. We didn't have time to get our clothes cleaned. We would have to buy a *whole* bunch of shirts, see what I mean? Because, hey, we didn't have time to get the shirts laundered.

It was an experience for me because that's when I noticed drugs, using and all of this type of thing was going on. And as a youngster, you know what I mean, I had never been exposed to any stuff like that. And I had to constantly say, "No man. Hey, I don't use this stuff. I don't need it. I'm on a natural high." See what I mean? I didn't even smoke a cigarette. And I saw families at these different clubs and stuff, and people at the beginning, they was nice and friendly, but when they get to drinkin' they used to all fight one another. I say, "That's what they do to you? No, I don't want no part of *that*." See?

Mathews: So did Lowell sort of follow through and watch out for you?

Brown: Well, at the beginning he was there looking out for me but once he saw that I had a mind of my own and that I wasn't going to be influenced by these other characters in the group, you know what I mean? Everybody knew Ray's problem, see? So I just never let that affect me, you know?

Mathews: Well, when you guys were on that first tour in particular, and you were out on the road for an entire year, it would be from one date to the next?

Brown: That's right. There you go. Check into the hotel and just overnight. Boom, the next morning we all on our way to the next place. We get there that evening, three or four hours before it's time to play and then we played and then stayed and that was *it*.

Mathews: Did you notice by any chance that scoring drugs was a real hassle? Did you notice that Ray's addiction, for example, caused problems, being able to get the stuff to keep him? Because you can't go without it.

Brown: No. See, it wasn't no problem for Ray to get what he needed. We had a manager, a road manager. I don't know who in the group looked out for Ray to get what he had to have, but he got it. It wasn't no issue, and the whole time in the full years of being in that environment with Ray, I never saw him be arrested or the law come into play. Only after that period of time that he had a run-in, you know. The higher up you go the more they protect you.

Mathews: So, was this the same core band, for how long? Three, four years?

Brown: Yes, that's right, that's right. That's when I got the chance to meet B.B. King, in Memphis, Tennessee, for the first time.

Mathews: Was he on the radio then?

Brown: Yeah! He was a DJ. He was playing but he as a DJ. And Fats Domino, see.

Mathews: So, you went through New Orleans.

Brown: Yeah, lord. Meeting all these people for the first time. And then another thing, playing engagements in Mississippi and Louisiana and Arkansas. A lot of the places we couldn't even stay at a hotel. So, people had to let us stay at their *homes*.

Mathews: So, people would invite you in.

Brown: Yeah. Our manager would have already arranged before we got there, got people who would say, "Yeah, we'd be happy to let the band stay at our house." For overnight, you know? So that's the way it went.

Mathews: Particularly in the South you found that it was real inconvenient and a hassle?

Brown: I could write a book on the incidents that took place in the South.

Mathews: Such as...

Brown: One of the things that I like to share with my kids—and you can tell in this interview that I like to share a lot of things with my kids. I've nine kids altogether. One by my first wife and eight by my second wife. But anyway, this one incident took place in Little Rock, Arkansas, maybe a little town outside of Little Rock, Arkansas. We were travelling, passing through, and so we wanted to stop to get something to eat. Alongside the road there, it's a little small town, there. And there was a restaurant, cafe. Big sign.

So, we pull up, and see, like I tell my kids, back in those days, out in the public, if you want a drink of water, it looked so *stupid* and funny now when we look back on it, but then, it was the normal thing, that's the way it was. You wanted a drink of water, instead of one fountain, they would have *two* water fountains. And hanging over one of the fountains there would be "white only," "colored only." See? And people was trained like robots. As I look back on it, what's stopping a person, wasn't nothing to stop me from drinkin' from the "white" fountain, you know? But being trained and programmed, hey... "colored." So, I drink on this side, OK? So, this restaurant, what was so funny about this was they had *two* doors, entrance doors. Now, on the left side the sign said "colored." On the right, "white," all right? So now, you walk in this door, they got a partition straight down the middle of this restaurant, just like this. And when you stand up and walk in, well then you can look over on the other side and see the people on the other side. See what I mean? See each other.

And that was so funny to me, know what I mean? This partition was straight down the middle of the room. On the left, all the Black folks. On the right, all the white folks, OK? And that's the way it was. And boy, we *laughed*. And from time to time when we was eating, we would stand up and look over, Oh, my god. So that was the funny part. The sad part...one of the most *frightening* incidents that took place in my life. When I was nineteen years old, right out of Macon, Georgia. That's when we came face to face with the Ku Klux Klan. In a lot of the southern towns, they had places to set up eight or nine or ten miles from town where bands would play. And so, this particular place was about ten or twelve miles on the outskirts of Macon, Georgia. And we had finished playing an engagement, and loaded up on the bus, and our manager was a Third Degree Mason. I didn't know what Masons was, I knew little of the organization, what it represented. But he would tell us little bits and pieces on the tour. And so he was the manager of the group, and he took care of business.

And so, on the way back headed towards Macon, after finishing that engagement, must have been around about two o'clock in the morning, and we wasn't going fast.

All of a sudden, I had just kicked back ready to doze off, getting ready for the next town, you know what I mean? And so, I could feel the bus *swaying*, you know? That got our attention. On the side of the bus was a white couple, young, in a convertible, holding up a fifth of liquor. You could tell he was drunk; the guy was drunk. And he want to have some fun, and he was trying to run onto the side of the bus. And that's why the bus was swaying, trying to slow down. And he got in front of the bus and wouldn't let us pass.

And by this time everybody on the bus was awake, wide awake now. "Well, what's going on?" And so, we're looking out the window and this guy, our manager, got fed up with this. And so, he waited till the guy got on the side of the bus where the driver was. And so, he opened up his briefcase and he pulled out his pistol and stuck it out the window. And the guy saw this in the convertible, and he *took off*. He took off.

And so, we thought that this was the end of it, OK? *Man*, surely about fifteen. minutes after that we was coming into Macon. Off in the way distance we could see the lights flashing and the torches...fire, you know. And so, as we get closer, we can see exactly that they had the road blocked off. So, we said to ourselves, you know what I mean. I was scared to death, I'm nineteen. I had *heard* about these kinds of things but the older ones, the other members of the band, they say, "Well, we're not gonna let nobody beat on us. We ain't did nothing wrong and if we're gonna have to die we're go down *fighting*." We geared up for, you know, hey. We ain't going to let nobody beat on us.

And so we had to stop, they had it blocked off. So as soon as we stopped and the bus driver opened the door, and the manager said, "Let me try to talk to 'em." So a few of the Ku Klux Klan people came on the bus hollering obscene names to us, rustling us and the police mixed in with them, rustling us off the bus. And had us stand outside the bus with our hands [on the bus].

Mathews: So, the cops were there too.

Brown: *Yeah*. The *cops*, yeah, they was there too. And some of the local people that wanted to see what was happening. So, everybody was whooping and hollering, saying hey, this was going to be a thrashing. And so, Ray Charles was standing on the other side of me. We all had our hands up against the bus. And so, by that time, all the shouting and stuff, I could see from the side, saw our manager go to the head police guy that seemed to be in charge, and he *shook* that man's hand.

And I never will forget this. He shook this man's hand... that guy, he just *froze*. The policeman *froze*, he was just *shocked*. It just happened for a few seconds. And I saw that and in my mind, I said, "What is going on?" As soon as he shook that policeman's hand, that policeman holler out to everybody, "Hey, hey! I want everybody to be quiet. Stop! I don't want nobody to say *nothing*!"

And he said. "These people haven't done anything. There's a big misunderstanding here. I want everybody to go home and we're gonna see that these people get back on the bus and we're going to escort them on their way."

Mathews: Were there guys in the white sheets and the whole thing?

Brown: Yeah, *yeah*. Our manager, he was a Third Degree Mason. He shook this man's hand, and after he shook his hand, then he embraced him with his other hand, and then he whispered something into his ear. And after that, this man, he say, "Hey. Everybody...we got the wrong information here. These people haven't done anything, and we want everybody to just go on home. Go about your business, because these people here haven't done anything wrong and we're going to escort them on through the town." Ku Klux Klan and all the other folks were whooping and hollering, they turned around, they put out their torches and they turned off the lights and all this stuff and we got back on the bus and our manager stood there talking with the police for about three or four minutes, as people start to fan out. Because the Ku Klux Klan, see, I know *now* after years of experience, the Ku Klux Klan was the top local officials type people, probably some of them was the policemen *themselves*. See what I mean? So, but anyway, the guy that was in charge, they respected him to obey his words. And we got back on the bus, and we was escorted through Macon, Georgia, and on our way.

Mathews: Have you any idea what it was that the manager was able to say to this guy.

Brown: I learned that the Mason organization is *powerful*. See, that's an organization where, I don't care what color your skin is.

Mathews: Did he have the ring?

Brown: Yeah, he had a ring. And I know that if you're a Mason, I don't care no matter where you are at...if you are in trouble, if you're standing on the side of the highway and if you know how to give the *signs*...if another Mason see you, that Mason gonna *stop*, and *help* you. No matter...I don't care how he personally feel or whatever. But if he's a Mason, he's gonna stop and *help* you.

Mathews: So, the Mason's bond is above everything else.

Brown: There you go. His bond is very... that's when I first realized that the organization is that powerful.

Mathews: That's something I'm sure you'll never forget. Everybody that is still around will never forget that.

Brown: Never will forget that.

Mathews: Lowell recounts in an interview about playing in an auditorium, I think in Atlanta. And he said that in this auditorium that the Black kids and the white kids were divided by a rope. Do you remember that?

Brown: Yeah! Yeah, I remember...oh, it's crazy. *All* through the South. All through the South. See, rhythm and blues records was bought by white kids... and they would *hide* them from their parents, see what I mean? And see, they would only play them when the parents weren't around. [laughs] And see, all through the South they would have the white folks, the ones that really loved blues, rhythm and blues, they would be in a different section. They would be roped *off*.

But when the music started playing, they jumped over the rope. They'd be boogying down, I'll tell you. It was so funny, I said, "My god." You know, it really was stupid, I'm telling you. To look back on it. They were just ignorant. That's right. That's what it is. All the prejudice and stuff is just ignorance. *Ignorance.* Yes sir, that's what it is. That's right. You can't blame the folks because they was *raised* that way. From babies they was raised that way, so hey, they living in an environment, right? In that era, and that's the way they was raised. Like we was raised up on certain foods. And we get grown and we love those neck bones and collard greens, cornbread and black-eyed peas and candied yams, you know? And *chittlins*.

Mathews: God man, you're making me hungry. [laughter] Let's eat!

Brown: Yeah, I say so!

Mathews: Well, you're giving everybody a pretty nice benefit of the doubt, I think, but there is a lot of truth in what you say on that idea. You know, I'd just like to ask about some of the most memorable or most exciting places that you men played on the road, like the Apollo Theater or places in Chicago or the Howard in D. C. Did you guys play all those places? What was it like playing at the Apollo for example?

Brown: Oh, my goodness, I never will forget that. That was the first time I saw, playing in the theater. They showed a movie and then we'd have to do the show. Then they'd show a movie and then we'd have to do a show. You do about four or five shows in a day. You'd start around noon time or something. And that's the way it were, and they had the dressing room upstairs. I can remember women trying to get into the dressing room from the fire escape.

Mathews: So, what year would that have been? 1949, 1950?

Brown: 1950, 51. I think we played the Apollo in 1951, I think.

Mathews: Were there other acts in addition to yours that would play these dates?

Brown: Oh, yeah. Moms Mabley. Oh, she traveled with us too.

Mathews: That must have had the bus going.

Brown: Oh, my god. That woman. I just look at her and I just laugh. She was a *natural*. A great, great, fine lady, I'm telling you. I never will forget the old man that worked at the Apollo. The stagehand. He gave me some advice that sustained me to this day. My goodness. He said, "Son, always be yourself." See, he saw in me what I probably didn't see in my own self. Out of all, the whole group, he saw that I was the youngest and that I did not drink or smoke. I wasn't into the lifestyle of the others. And he say, "Always be yourself. Never outsmart yourself. Never try to be what you are not." You see?

I didn't quite understand that at that *time*, but it always stayed with me. And another thing that he told me, he always said, "Never showboat." And what that meant was that, if you know how to do something, just go on and do it. Don't get out there and try to do something you ain't used to doing. Because if you do, you gonna fall *flat* on your face. You see what I mean? Stick to what you know and do it the best you can. Don't try to do something that you ain't used to doing. Don't put on airs or whatever. Just be yourself.

And he also told me, and this is what I really do appreciate, because growing up without a father, he said, "Son, every paycheck, every dollar you make, you pay yourself first." At that time, I say, "What you mean by that?" He said, "You'll understand. Every dollar you earn, learn to pay *yourself* first, before you pay all of them other people."

Mathews: Yeah, well, particularly in the entertainment business, everybody wants a piece.

Brown: Yeah, He was telling me to sit down with pen and paper and see how many of those dollars could I put aside, for myself for that rainy day, and for the *lean* days that might pop up in the future. See what I mean? And so, months after that, because, hey man, I was having a good time. I was learning things that I never *knew* existed. Homosexuals, or playing in clubs that was just all males. With men's dancing with men's and women dancing with women. You know, my eyes was seeing all this and I never *knew* things like this was going on. And so, after all of that, that stuck in my mind, and so I started thinking about, I'd better save some of this money I'm making. I got to thinking about the material things I'd like out of life I would like to have. Other than just buying clothes, you know.

And so, I started sitting down with pen and paper and I said, "I'm making all this money every night, my goodness." And I started saving this here, you know. And I started counting the years and thought that if I keep doing this, I say, "Oh, I'll be all right." [laughs] And so, I started *doing* that.

Mathews: And this was a man that worked at the Apollo? Do you remember his name?

Brown: *Yeah*, he was a stagehand. No, I don't [remember his name]. He was an old man; he'd been there for years. He's seen James Brown, he's seen *everybody* come through the Apollo. Everybody that was somebody played at the Apollo. I'm telling you. And so, it was amazing, they had the stage where you push a button, and it goes forward, back and forth. They had a microphone that would scoot up right out of the stage. And I had to really watch out for that because I was very active. So, when I was playing my saxophone and I was jumping up and down, the guy would put the microphone up there and I would lay down on the stage and he would lower the microphone down. And one thing I really appreciate about Lowell and Ray. When we played the Apollo Theater and the Howard Theater, we had to bring in other musicians because we had to be like a house band to back up all the other acts. I only had three months of music lessons, see? I wasn't the best music reader around. But I was blessed because I was on all the hit records. So, they had to bring in another saxophone player to play the parts because I couldn't read the music. By that time I was strictly an ear musician, know what I mean? I could hear and duplicate it, but I couldn't sit there and read no chart. So, they had to bring in another musician and they had to pay him to play the set.

Mathews: And that never jeopardized your position.

Brown: No, that never jeopardized my position, so I got lucky. So I would sit there beside him and when it was my time to blow, the solo, I would throw a solo on, see?

Mathews: Oh, I see. So, you were still playing. You know, I remember reading something that Lowell mentioned, I think it was at the Apollo, somebody challenged Ray Charles on something like that. That because he was blind, he wouldn't be able to do these arrangements for the other performers? So, he typed it out in Braille and then someone would draw up a chart.

Brown: Throughout our whole tour there was a whole lot of incidents, that people didn't believe that Ray Charles was blind.

Mathews: People didn't believe it?

Brown: Yeah. A *lot* of people didn't believe it. See, Ray Charles didn't use a cane. He didn't use a seeing-eye dog. And Ray was just *Ray*. And we would walk right beside him, and he would just hold our arm, know what I mean? And that's the way we got *around*, OK? And see, this is why Ray Charles could play cards with us, Ray Charles could drive a car on the road while I was sitting beside him.

And the way I do it, I just have my hand right behind his neck there, you know. Right between his shoulder blades, and he'd be driving. And this is at night, no traffic, hardly any traffic. And so we let him *drive*, see? And I'd be talking to him the whole time. "OK Ray, you're going straight, just keep going straight. OK, go to the right, just a little bit to the right. Come on back over to the left a little bit. Now hold it steady right there, you're doing good, you're doing about forty-five or fifty, and just hold it right there. I want you to slow up..." and I'd kind of pinch him a little bit. "Put your foot on the brake, kind of slow up now, we're coming to a little curve, gonna go to the left," you know. [laughter]

Mathews: So, you'd just talk him right through it.

Brown: Yeah, just talk to him. And he could feel the hand on his back, see? And no problem. Only time he got in a wreck, we let him drive in Los Angeles. He run all up on the sidewalk and hit a garbage can. [laughter]

Mathews: Was Lowell letting him drive the Buick?

Brown: No, Ray had his own car. Oh, my goodness. Ray would do things, silly little things, like you would be onstage, and people take his picture. Somehow he could feel the flash...he'd turn around and, "Thank you."

Mathews: Really. Maybe he could hear the camera click, you think?

Brown: Could be, because his hearing is perfect. And I tell everybody that it's amazing how he could pick women.

Mathews: Yeah. How did he do that?

Brown: I'm telling you...we'd try to fool him sometimes, know what I mean? Put an ugly girl on him and he'd, "Oh, no." He'd know. Yeah, he'd run his fingers, he can tell if she's all *right*.

Mathews: That's amazing, because you guys literally lived together for four years?

Brown: Yeah. Every day, every night. I'm telling you.

Mathews: How was the Howard Theater? Was that exciting going into D.C.?

Brown: Yeah, and I was trying to think of the lady singer's name; not Sarah Vaughn. Ella Fitzgerald. That's where one of the times we played at the Howard

Theater, we played there with Ella Fitzgerald. 1950. Oh, my god, I'm telling you. It was Washington, D.C. I was really during those early years, I was really disappointed in Washington, D.C.

Mathews: In what way Earl?

Brown: Seeing so many people...I had always put Washington, D.C. up on a pedestal. And to come to find out that it was really, it was bad. It was ghetto, *ghetto!* The masses of people that was living *bad.* I thought that since that was the capital of the United States, you know...I'm young, you know. I'm still a country boy, you know what I mean? And then seeing it. I thought it would be better than the rest of the United States. I thought it would be better than the rest of the country. But it wasn't. I have so many stories about so many entertainers, some things I don't want to say.

Mathews: Save it for the book.

Brown: Yeah, save it for the book, yeah.

Mathews: But that was pretty exciting when Ella was on the same bill?

Brown: Yeah, yeah, oh my goodness. I got a chance to, you know, to be around her. When you are around people, you get a chance to know them for what they are. Billy Eckstine and just all of them. All the great ones.

Mathews: And there you are, right in the middle of them.

Brown: Right in the middle of them. Oh, my god, I'm telling you.

Mathews: Well, at some point you decide to go out on your own. What happened that made you decide that you didn't want to do what you were doing anymore?

Brown: *1953.* The words of the old man at the Apollo Theater spoke to me, really took hold. I began to start thinking, I say, "I can't keep wanting to play like Louis Jordan. I got to have my *own* identity. Who am *I?*" Ray Charles went through the same thing, because when Ray joined up with us in Los Angeles, Ray started out playing like Charles Brown, trying to sound like Charles Brown, and Nat King Cole. And later on, Ray Charles came into *his* own identity, and that's when he started making them hits, when he started to sound like his own *self.*

And so, in 1953, I said, "My goodness, I've got to stop imitating Louis Jordan. I want people to know me for who *I* am." And so, in my plan I start changing up things, and doing things where, I ain't heard nobody else play like that, see? And so slowly but surely, I started to develop, make the transition, and start a different sound. It's not a smooth sound, it's a more rugged, *growling* type of sound that other saxophone players don't play like that.

And so, I started playing like that and I started thinking, well my goodness, I'd like to have my own band. I'd like to be my own boss, you know. That meant, well, I'm going to have to leave Lowell and the band. And I said now, "Where should I do this?" By this time, I am about twenty-one years old. And so, in Detroit, I made up my mind in Detroit that I'm going to leave the band and go back to California and try to start my own group. And so, I came back to Richmond, left the tour, and I'm telling you, that was *hard*.

That was hard to do because, hey, the money stopped. And the traveling stopped. And I could see how a person can get wrapped up, and their head get *big* as a watermelon. You know what I mean? If you let it get to you. So, I was happy that I didn't let that happen to me. I always just stay humble, people gave me compliments, I always said, "thank you," you know. I never told anybody that I was great, and being at that age, and everywhere I went, my goodness... practically every day, no matter where you went, you would hear your own self on the radio. And in restaurants, people playing the records, you know what I mean? And then a lot of the time, other people didn't know that it was you sitting in that restaurant, and on that record. But I just stayed humble and didn't get the big head about the whole thing. I had a plan of action, saving my money and I knew that it was time for me to be my own boss.

Mathews: Were you able to leave on good terms?

Brown: Yeah. We left on good terms...and I went out on the road with Muddy Waters for three months.

Mathews: Really. How did that happen?

Brown: Well, after I came back to Richmond, then I lived in Oakland. Chess Records got in touch with me. Wanted me to record for them.

Mathews: Weren't there two brothers?

Brown: Yeah, Leonard and his other brother, the Chess brothers. And so, I signed a contract and started recording for Chess Records out of Chicago. And so that's how I met Muddy Waters. And so, I went out on a tour with Muddy Waters for three months.

Mathews: And you were part of his band? That must have been neat.

Brown: Yeah, Part of his band. Little Walter couldn't make it, so he got another harmonica player, just as good. But Little Walter back then in those days, he was *supreme*. On the harmonica, nobody could touch him. Nobody could *touch* him. So he was the *man*. Yeah, I toured with Muddy for three months down through the South. Yeah, lord. I tell you, Muddy didn't really want me to leave him, I'm telling you. Yeah, see, but I was still trying to be my own boss. I had learned from just being quiet, watching what goes on behind the scenes and who was handling the money and who was getting paid what and all this.

Well, I said, "My goodness, I want to be my own boss. I want to have my own band." And so, I left Muddy, and Muddy really took it hard. He really became attached to me, you know. We had a good working relationship, and he just wanted me to solo, know what I mean? He liked the way I played them blues, you know. Back in those days, you just didn't hear a saxophone player that could play the blues. And even *today*, that's why I think I have a monopoly going when I get out on the blues circuit, you know what I mean? Because all you hear is guitars and harmonica players. You don't hear no really genuine cat steppin' out there that can play some blues on the saxophone, you see?

Mathews: So, you're going to have work for as long as you want it.

Brown: Oh, my god, it's going to be a *great time*. Even now as I play around, my goodness, I just don't run up on no other saxophone players that *really can play the blues*. And get that *feeling* in there like it supposed to be, see? So after I left Muddy I came on back to Oakland.

Mathews: So what year was this, 1953?

Brown: No, no, no, no. No. When I went out with Muddy, it was in 1954 or '55, when I went out on the tour with Muddy, OK? And after that I came on back to Oakland and I ran into Lawrence Busby. He lives in Oakland right now. He's a plano player. And Little Red was the drummer. Little Red had the group, and that's how I formed my band.

Mathews: That band sort of became your band?

Brown: Yeah.

Mathews: How did that happen?

Brown: Well, Lawrence Busby, at that time I think he was round about twenty— eight or twenty-nine years old. Here's a guy that had been in the military, was married and had a couple of kids, and he took a liking to me because I had a *style* of my own. And playing, I had all this energy, you know what I mean? And I had a *good ear*. Jazz, blues, whatever, I could play it, see? And so, I guess he liked that, me being young. And he wanted to make this extra money on weekends or whatever playing, because you know, he's got a family. And so, he said, "Well hey, it's your *group*." Let me see, who did we have on bass? We had a bass player. And a guitar player.

Mathews: So, piano, bass, drums and a guitar and your horn.

Brown: Yeah. And so, we started playing with the local clubs and the word started spreading, you know. And the way I got the name "Good Rockin'" Brown was, a lot of the ladies in the club, you know what I mean? I usually *rock* from side to side when I play and they would holler out, "Go Good Rockin'! You a good rockin' man! There's a good rockin' man!" So, when it got to the point where I had to put out flyers and stuff I said, "Well, how am I going to advertise myself?" So, I thought about what all the people was hollering out. I said, "Well I'm going to call myself "Earl 'Good Rockin'" Brown."

Mathews: And that's how it got started and that's what it's been ever since.

Brown: Yeah, that's it. That's what it's been ever since.

Mathews: So, this must have been 1955, 56, right in there.

Brown: Yeah, right in there.

Mathews: So, you came back to Oakland, and you got the band going, and basically you kept your home base in Oakland?

Brown: Yeah. Kept my home in Oakland. Then I would start branching out to places like Stockton.

Mathews: Did you play any places in San Francisco? Did you ever play the Fillmore?

Brown: Yeah, we played in all those places. I can't even *recall* the clubs in San Francisco back in those days. Lots of clubs.

Mathews: Jimmy's Chicken Shack? There was a man who passed away not too long ago, and there was a tribute to him, and it was quite a place.

Brown: It was in San Francisco where I broke my *horn* over a guy's head. You know, back in those days, and even still today, women will chase after entertainers, OK? And so, it just so happened that we were on a break and went outside. It was the first time that I ever kept my horn around my neck, I don't know why, it was hot that night. And I just run off the bandstand and we ran out to the front door, standing beside the car. And so, this jealous guy, his girlfriend all night long had been making out, just emotionally, over the band.

And so, he thought she had eyes for *me* or something. So, he comes outside, and we're standing out there beside the *car*. And he was *serious*, this guy, he wanted to jump on me. And so, I could see him reaching for his gun, you know? And so, I saw the butt of the gun and so, and just natural instinct, I just had my horn, that's the only thing I had to defend with, and I just.... Wham! I hit him with my horn and knocked that fool out, and broke my horn. I couldn't play, we had one more set to do and I didn't have two horns back in those days, I only had the one. And I just had to sing for the rest of the set.

But that same guy, after he woke up, I went to him and talked. I say, "Hey, I'm sorry for hitting you, but you been drinkin' and you was *wrong*. I don't even *know* your lady. You are getting ready to jump on me. I'm just here doing a job, I'm entertaining people, I cannot snub ladies, you know? I have to show like I'm being friendly with them. I'm doing a *job*, man." A lot of people don't understand that you know. And so, he was all right. I didn't want to leave him with that impression. See, because I'm out there in public and I don't know the next time that fool is going to show *up*. [laughs]

Mathews: Planning ahead of time.

Brown: Yeah, that's right!

Mathews: Did you record while you were out in Oakland?

Brown: Yeah. Like I say, I was recording for Chess Records. "Dust my Broom," I recorded that, and "Turn Back the Time."

Mathews: So, you didn't have to go back to Chicago.

Brown: No, I did it in Oakland and shipped the masters out there. I only did one session in Chicago.

Mathews: What about Bob Geddins? Did you ever have any contact with him. at all?

Brown: Yeah. Yeah, I knew Bob, know what I mean? Naturally being with Lowell, but I never did record for him. He was a local recording person and from what I gather, his distribution wasn't as wide as the rest of them.

Mathews: Well, he really was sort of a one-man operation.

Brown: But he was like a *pioneer*. Yeah, Bob, because he gave a lot of the local entertainers a *shot*. Through Bob Geddins I guess, the rest was able to move on, see? Like Motown, a lot of the artists, they left Motown and went on.

Mathews: Did you have any other relationship with Jack Lauderdale or Swing Time?

Brown: *Yeah*, yeah. I made a big mistake, I never will forget. Jack Lauderdale took me under his wing, and was going to let me go out as a solo. And unknown to me, see, I didn't know. All I knew was I'm in the studio recording and I'm not thinking about all the advertisement stuff being printed up and all of this stuff. Right at that same time, a rival studio company in Los Angeles, I don't even remember the name of the other record company. But I let them talk me into signing a contract with *them*. I hadn't signed a contract with Jack Lauderdale. All this happened in one week, one week. In other words, I went into the studio for Jack's Swing Time Records to record, and I knew Jack was going to get around to sitting me down to sign a contract.

But at this particular time I made a mistake and lost sight of myself, whereas I shouldn't have let this other person talk me into, you know—he *conned* me into coming over to the other studio, filling my head with a lot of big dreams and stuff, what they going to do for me and all of this. And so I quickly signed a contract that said that I would be with them, you know.

And I go back to Swing Time Records, and being green and inexperienced and I told Jack Lauderdale what I had did. And then Jack said, "You did *what*?" He said, "Look here, this is what we got." He took me into the studio, into the back room where he had artists and stuff, people working for him. And he showed me all the layout stuff, the promotion stuff that he was getting ready to do for me for the session that I had just got through doing for him. And I felt this small, you know what I mean?

Mathews: So there was no way you could get out of it?

Brown: No. When he saw that I was that stupid, and did a stupid thing, he tore up all that stuff. Gone!

Mathews: Did you spend much time in Los Angeles? Was Central Avenue still going?

Brown: Oh yeah, yeah. Every time we would come off the road we were staying in Los Angeles and naturally we would visit the local sets and clubs, and what have you.

Mathews: What do you remember about Central Avenue and the clubs? Was it still a happening place?

Brown: It was the main drag, the *main* drag.

Mathews: Was the Club Alabam still going, and Joe Morrison's?

Brown: Hey, all the clubs—everybody that was somebody winded up on Central Avenue. That was the main strip. That was the *strip*, no doubt about it. That's where everybody *went*.

Mathews: Did you guys play the clubs down there?

Brown: Yeah, we played a few. A few. Like I said, we was big stars then, you see? And so, we would just go in, and a one-night thing, you know. And that's it.

Mathews: Did you ever socialize down there when you weren't playing and hear other artists?

Brown: Once, once in a great while, because once you come off a tour—see, our main thing was for socializing, we would go up in Beverly Hills at them *parties*. See, we'd get invited to go up on a higher *level*, see what I mean? So, when you talk about going out socializing, are you going to go back down on the strip or are you going to go on up to where the big boys are, where some of the movie stars hang out? So that's where we spent a lot of time when we were back.

Mathews: Who would have parties up there?

Brown: Oh, my goodness. I wouldn't want to say on tape. All I can tell you is that these was successful, rich individuals who was in the entertainment industry and they gave parties, and everybody that *was* somebody was at these parties. It was a *different world*. And it gave me an opportunity to see peoples' lifestyle on different levels, so I could know what I want out of life.

And I was thankful to have the opportunity to be able, number one, for God to give me that kind of talent. Because I come up on horn blowers that could run me up under the *table*. Play a *circle* around me. But I had a special type of a talent that was *different*, see? And so I just felt blessed that I was able to travel all over the United States and see people that the average person just don't get a chance to just sit down in the same room with.

Mathews: I remember asking Bill Doggett about this when I was sitting down with him. He mentioned there were folks giving parties up in Beverly Hills, but there was some kind of political, communist party type stuff. Do you remember anything about that?

Brown: No, no, no.

Mathews: This was earlier, what he was talking about was around 1945.

Brown: No, but maybe the kind of parties he went to, maybe those kinds of things was going on.

Mathews: He was saying that people would come down and recruit Blacks, for example, in this communist political context.

Brown: But you know, in my life, I just know that nobody ever approached me. And I didn't see nobody else being approached in that type of fashion. But hey, I'm not going to be naive and say that those kinds of things didn't take place. Yeah, I knew they took place, yeah.

Mathews: But once you became a celebrity of sorts, then you made the "list," so to speak, and were invited to these things up there? I'd like to ask you about some of your ideas and insights about rhythm and blues as an art form, as its own particular musical genre. Bandleader Johnny Otis is on the record as saying that because of a multitude of factors, including the musicians who went there, like Roy Milton and Charles Brown and Joe Liggins and "T-Bone" Walker and Lowell, etc., that the classic R&B configuration and the resulting sound took off in Los Angeles. What are your thoughts on that? Was there a West Coast R&B sound, something that was unique to this area, that grew out here, because of a lot of the folks who were coming in?

Brown: That is a hard one, because when I look back on it, when you grow up in the Bay Area, and you are in the mix of a group that is playing rhythm and blues... I'm going to say this. When Bill Haley and Elvis Presley started playing the same music we was playing, they called it rock and roll. They changed it. And that always *bothered* me, you know? They *changed* it. They put it in a different category. I mean, hey, it's *rhythm and blues*. Because the way Elvis played, the way Bill Haley played, we were playing like that for years. Yeah, they said. Well, they're not playing rhythm and blues, they're playing rock and roll. See? But to get back to your question, you *could* say it was a West Coast thing but in traveling all down through the South, they were playing like we were playing on the West *Coast*. You know? I don't know who started it.

Mathews: The seven or eight musicians. After the swing era came to an end and the bandleaders broke their bands down and they got small.

Brown: Well, see, you take Louis Jordan. Earl Bostic. They had the R&B band that was sounding like that, OK? So, everybody who had a band was doing R&B.

Mathews: Everybody that was playing then. Well, I'd like to ask you about Louis Jordan in that context for a minute, if I could. People who write about music and the development of rhythm and blues into its own distinct genre, unique music form, say that the impact of Louis Jordan was enormous. Certainly, he was important to you. Can you tell us why in your mind you think Louis' work was so important for what was going to become rhythm and blues?

Brown: He had that small band and the *sound* that he got from that small band. The *tempo* of the different songs...it just made you want to get up and dance. He had that sound that make you want to get up and dance and he was a good singer, a great saxophone player, and you could just tell he played with *feeling*. See?

So, he was able to *transmit* all of that to the masses of people. And you couldn't help but enjoy, *looking* at him. Because, he wasn't your typical, sophisticated, stand-up saxophone player, all right? See? He was like certain movie stars that we have today that you see on screen. When you see them, your eyes just stay on them, because you don't want to miss a *thing*. And that's the way Louis Jordan came across to people.

Mathews: Yeah, he connected so well.

Brown: Yeah, he connected.

Mathews: There was a music critic by the name of Ralph Gleason. He wrote for newspapers in the Bay Area. Anyway, he was quoted as saying that much of Louis Jordan's greatness was due to the fact that Louis Jordan "sang Black and he sang proud." There are a lot of social analysts and historians that embrace the idea that the art that is produced in a place and during a time is a direct reference to the attitudes that were present during that time. I'm curious to know that in your mind, did rhythm and blues, the classic thing that all of you men and women were playing and singing, did that possess certain qualities or have a certain creative energy like Louis Jordan was able to express during these years that spoke to and reflected the mood and attitudes of the Black community?

Brown: Yes, yes, yes. It was a special talent that a person has to have. The reason why Louis Jordan and the others who was able to duplicate it and become a success, was because Louis Jordan–the songs he sang was *everyday* about *living*. See, the masses of people, whether you was white, Black or whatever. You could identify with his lyrics, see what I mean? And if you had any ounce of dance in your body, [chuckles] you would want to pat your feet or jump up and down, all right? See, that type of energy and that feeling that he brought to it.

But rhythm and blues is something that you cannot fake. You can't fake that. You got to have it here. [pats hand over heart] And see, when you got it here, then the masses of people, you can please the masses of people. That's what gets those applause, that gets that great *response* when you see an artist onstage and doing his or her thing. When they are doing it from here, that's when you are going to hear that great response. And if they are not doing it from here, then you ain't going to hear that great response. [laughs]

And I'm going to tell you. Other kinds of music you can learn it and kind of halfway duplicate it. But to *sell* it, it got to come from here. And it doesn't make any difference what color you are, see? But if you can't do it from here, then you ain't going to be able to sell it. That's how come we have hits out.

You can imagine all the records that people record. And only a handful, few, become hits. Why is that? That is why. Michael Bolton. This brother, lord have mercy. Anybody watch this man sing, you have to get emotional inside. You see, this brother, he's singin' from here. And you can feel it when that guy sings. You see? Barbra Streisand. All the greats. When these people do what they do, it comes from *here*. They ain't putting on no airs, it's the way they feel. And that's the way when I perform, people know it's coming from here, because I feel *everything* that I do when I'm onstage. I give a hundred and ten percent, see?

Mathews: That's how it was when I saw you at the Paramount. That was a great performance. It wasn't long enough, you know?

Brown: Oh, my goodness. The kind of money they paid me to do that little bit, I felt bad. [laughs]

Mathews: I'm wondering if you see this connection today, from what is coming from contemporary Black artists.

Brown: No. And it's sad. It is very sad that the music industry now, and the image that it portrays—I feel sad for my grandchildren. We don't have people coming up today that can replace the greats that got us started. See what I mean? What's happening in Hollywood today, this is just my opinion. It's an image being put out there that is *hurting* the minority race of people.

See, this country was built on greed, and greed has taken us over, to the point where I don't even let my grandchildren—if they could do rap music with a different kind of image, but see, young people see this stuff today and they think that's the way they supposed to be when they grow *up*. Ain't no way in the world they going to dress like that and walk into anybody's place and get a job. See? That's misleading.

Ain't nobody going to hire nobody that if you go walking in there looking like you going to hold them up? And then they going to hire you? *No!* See what I mean? And it's sad that it seems like the whole United States is wrapped up in this thing. And it brings back memories to me about how the drug thing first got started, see? Our government didn't seem to care, long as the drugs stayed in the *ghettos*. It seemed as soon as the drugs started getting to the suburban areas, then they started getting close to the White House, then they want to do something *about* it but now it's too *late*. They can't stop it. Seem like they don't want to stop it.

But I don't know. It is sad the way the music thing has turned. It's more than just making a hit record. It has affected a whole lifestyle, a generation of people. You and I...all different races of people. You'd be surprised—since Martin Luther King's passing, you would hope things had gotten better. But things have gone *backwards*. Because they have put it on TV, they allowed street gang people that has no values, to record this kind of stuff. And dress that way, they let 'em dress that way in school. And my goodness, you don't know—the average citizen is scared to *death*. Because everybody look like they want to *rob* you.

Mathews: That's the image that has been projected, and certainly a lot of it has to do with what you say. What sells is what's going to get recorded, and that's it. But you know, fortunately there sure seems to be a lively interest these days in the *blues*.

Brown: I'm *happy* for that.

Mathews: I can imagine. Why do you think that is? Blues festivals are being attended in record numbers.

Brown: Thank God for those people. See, like the old saying goes, "You can fool some of the people some of the time, but you can't fool 'em all the time." That's the way things happen. Those special people out there who feel just like I feel. They say, "No, I'm not going to let them shove this type of stuff down my throat. Let me go back to the good old days." See, American people have *finally* woke up. That's our heritage. That's our culture. In other words, the blues is *one thing* where we can say, "This is *ours!*" When we go overseas and play it, people just idolize us, because hey, we are the pioneers. This is *ours*. This is what we started. And America gets credit for that, see? This is our *culture*. What else can we say that is *ours*? What else can America say, "Hey, this is ours?" You, see? And so a lot of people, thank God for 'em, a lot of people have woken up to that fact that, hey…I don't want to listen to that other stuff I'm hearing on the radio nowadays. I want to hear what I heard when I was a *kid*. And they done fell back in love with it. Tradition. There you go. It's clean, it's about *life*, it's about love. It's about *life*. Ain't nothing in there dirty.

Mathews: Maybe a little naughty.

Brown: Yeah, a little *naughty*. Get a little naughty. [laughs] But, hey, that's all right, that's all right.

Mathews: Well, it really has to make all you men and women that were in a sense a big part of the evolution of the music, who in many ways pioneered it. The modern blues tradition. It's got to make you feel pretty good that it's doing well.

Brown: Oh yeah. It's like when the disco thing came out, it hurt a lot of bands. But I was happy that I made a decision to specialize in rhythm and blues. I had a group that was doing "top-forty" music like "Earth, Wind, and Fire," you know. Doing all this stuff, you know? And so, I decided to come back to my roots, so to speak, and specialize in one type of music that appealed to people in their thirties, forties and fifties. And the sixties. See what I mean? I was in Las Vegas when I made that decision. I went up and down the strip, sitting and listening to all the groups in the lounge. I did a survey. I wanted to see what the audience, what did they really like? And all the groups in those different hotels, they were playing variety, you know.

And I was making notation on what songs did the people respond to the most. And how much of a tip did they give the band for playing certain songs. And when I put all that together, it took me about two weeks of going out every night, staying out *all* night, hitting *all* the lounges and listening to *all* the songs.

And when I looked at my notes and saw that, my goodness, people got more excited on the "oldie but goodies" stuff. Well, I know *all* those songs. Why am I playing this top forty, soul, funk stuff? You know what I mean? I was playing the top forty, soul, funk, and I was playing the blues, all that stuff mixed in. But I said, "Let me stick with the 'oldie but goodie' stuff, and I will never be out of work." Now this was back in the sixties, when I made that decision, and I've never been out of work. Been playin' the whole time. Never been out of work. The disco thing didn't bother me one bit. Didn't even touch *me*.

Mathews: Where could you play, particularly in the sixties, where rock and roll was really becoming big.

Brown: I was playing in Las Vegas and Anchorage, Alaska. Most of my time in Las Vegas and Anchorage, Alaska.

Mathews: Anchorage. How did you get hooked up up there?

Brown: Now *that's* a story. That's a story. Can you imagine, we're playing, my band and I, playing in Las Vegas. We're playing at this club. We've been playing at this club for two years, seven nights a week.

Mathews: Did you live down there? I guess you had to.

Brown: Yeah, *yeah*, I *moved* down there, yeah. Been playing there for two years. In the early sixties. In fact, 1960. You know Vegas is a tourist town. And this happen all the time, and when this happened this time, I just took it for what it is. You have people coming up to you saying, "Give me your card. I know a club that would like to have a band like yours." And so, this couple, they happened to be from Anchorage, Alaska. And they were very enthusiastic and showed a lot of emotion. And the time they was in Vegas, they was in the club every *night*. Sitting there listening to the same old songs and enjoying it.

So, they said, "This club in Anchorage, Alaska, we know the club owner real well and we've got to tell him about you. And would you come to Anchorage, Alaska?" And all I'm thinkin' about is igloos and Eskimos, you know what I mean? *Cold*. I said, "My god!" So, not to show that to them, I said, "Yeah, I wouldn't mind coming to Anchorage." And so I forgot all about it and so, two or three months goes by, and on a Wednesday night. I never will forget it. I was on a break and the assistant manager of the club came to me and said there was a phone call for you. And I said, "For me?" Because I hardly ever had a call at the club. They call me at home, you know.

And I got the phone and here is this guy from Anchorage, Alaska, and he said, "Am I talking to "Good Rockin' Brown?" And I say, "Yeah." And he said, "Well my name is so and so... and some friends of mine gave me your card and they said that you got a good band and I got a club up here and I want to know if you would come to Anchorage and play in my club?' I say, "Well, you know I'm on my break right now, let me give you my home phone number and you call me at home and we can talk, OK?" It's about time for me to go back out on the stage and I say, "My goodness. This guy called me from Anchorage, Alaska." *The last place I want to go.*

I'm having fun in Las Vegas, I'm working every *night*, you know what I mean? And so, lo and behold, this guy called me at the house the next day and he said, "I'm very serious. Would you consider coming to Anchorage, Alaska?" I say. "You know, I got an unlimited stay here in Vegas, I've been here at this for over two years. I'm working seven nights a week. And I'm making so and so and so." The guy tells me, "So what would it take for you to come to Anchorage, Alaska?" And then I perked up a little bit, you know what I mean? I stretched the price on him and he didn't flinch on that, you know. And so I said, "Well let me think about it. I definitely don't want to work no seven nights because I'm almost getting ready to tell the club owner here that I want to back off. I got to have at least one night off." And so, he said, "Well, I can offer you six nights out of a week, and I will pay you boom, boom, boom, boom." And what he said was almost *double* what I was getting in Vegas.

Then, as keen as I was when I was on the road and knowing what was going by, I didn't show my excitement over the phone about that figure because I wanted him to turn up the *ante*. All right! Oh, my goodness! So, after I had talked it over with my wife, and told her I had got this offer and I said. "This guy is offering me a one-year contract, he never ain't seen me or heard me and he offered me double the money that I'm making here. And also, he gonna throw in a house for us to stay in. If I accept it, after three months, then I can send for you and the kids to come on up."

So, after we tossed it around, I said, "Well, I really put this guy to the test. I'll get myself a big raise here and up it and see will he jump on that. If he jump on that, then I'll *go*." So, I called him and I said, "I don't mind coming to Anchorage, Alaska, but first tell me about Anchorage, Alaska. How big it is? And how is the people up there?" And so, he ran everything down to me and told me that the town really do need a good band, playing what we were playing. See, because up there, all they was getting was country and western, and rock and roll type groups. They was just in and out. What this man was looking for was a good, versatile rhythm and blues band that could entertain the people. His club hold about three hundred people, see?

Mathews: What was the name of this club?

Brown: The Club Oasis, out on Seward Highway.

Mathews: Is it still there?

Brown: Oh, I don't know, now. But I know the last time that I was up there playing, was back in the eighties, it was still there.

Mathews: So, you left Vegas and went up there.

Brown: So, look here now. This was during the wintertime, OK? We went up there three different times. The first time we went up was in the summertime. I was going to tell you a story about the second time, because when did that guy send me my deposit and I picked it up at the Western Union office? It started to snow in Vegas. That's right. And it hardly ever snow in Vegas. But that was the second time, it was in the month of November, I think. That was a *calling* sign. [laughs]

But it was in the month of July when we opened up in Anchorage, Alaska. I never will forget it. It took us five days to drive up there, from Las Vegas, five days, I never will forget that. I had a van, and I pulled a trailer behind the van, and we was *loaded* down to the max, you, see? I never been to a place where in the summertime it's *daylight* about twenty-two hours, you know. Daylight. So, going to work at ten o'clock at night and the sun is shining.

We were playing from ten o'clock till four o'clock in the morning, all right? Six nights a week. We had to back up strippers. They had about three dancers on the show. We were doing three shows a night. And it was just *unbelievable*. The place was just *packed* every night. And the money that I saw, no *wonder* the guy offered me the money he offered me. My goodness, he was selling people them cheap bottles of champagne for, oh, my god, *fifty* dollars a bottle. Fifty dollars a bottle. And he bought those bottles of champagne for about five dollars a bottle or something a bottle. Yeah, and every table that you look at, my goodness, they had at least a half a dozen bottles of champagne, to almost around about ten or eleven bottles on every table. And plus, all the other mixed drinks, you know? And my god, it was unbelievable.

Mathews: With the pipeline going, all these guys are making money and nowhere to spend it.

Brown: Now, when the pipeline came in, oh, my god. But you had guys working out in the bush, they'd be out there for three months. And then they'd come into town with all of this money on 'em. And they're only gonna be in there for two or three days, and they wanted to *party*. I'm telling you, those girls *cleaned up* up there! I'm telling you. We were seeing hundred dollar bills like we would see *five* dollar bills down here. See what I mean? All you see up there was fifties and hundreds.

Every Monday, I had to put money in three different banks. Every Monday, those showgirls, those little old makeup kits they used, they'd be full of hundred-dollar bills. They'd go on the bank. I'm telling you. It was a crazy scene.

Mathews: I can imagine. That goes along with a lot of other stories that give that kind of an impression about that wild nature. A lot of people with a lot of dough that were stuck out there and they come in, man.

Brown: You know what my biggest hit was up there in Anchorage? The first week I was up there they put me on TV. "Please, Mr. Custer, I Don't Want To Go." Can you believe that? People took to that song up there. I *really* acted it out, I really acted it out. It was really something to see. It's just like "Walking the Dog"—now "Walking the Dog" is my hit, even though Rufus Thomas, he did it, but my goodness. When I go in person overseas and everywhere, "Walking The Dog" is my song, see, because, I *acted* it out. People pay big money to see "Walking The Dog." [laughs]

Mathews: Well, that's OK with me. I'd like to ask, just in closing here, Earl. I'd like to ask you about your feelings as you look back, as you look back over a long and productive career, one that clearly is very much alive and well. But you've covered a lot of ground. I'm wondering if you could say what some of the things are that you are most proud of and or thankful for over the years. I know you've made a list of references now, but looking back and having had a chance to reflect on it from time to time, some of the things that maybe stand out.

Brown: Number one. I am so blessed and proud that the good lord provided me with a wonderful wife. The wife that I'm married to now, Rose Brown, I thank God for her coming into my life. Because, from the marriage, forty-three years ago, I was twenty years old and she was eighteen. Eight children, twelve grandchildren developed from that.

See, I didn't drink or smoke, didn't get into drugs. At that young age I was looking for a woman who loved children, who did not drink or smoke, and loved to travel– *loved* the things that I loved. You know, I was blessed to find this woman in Lodi, California? Out of all the places, Lodi, California. At the Spot Club. Yeah, lord. 1953. Yes indeed. Isn't that something?

Mathews: Was she in the audience?

Brown: At the time I had Bryce Robinson playing guitar for me. White guy. He was going with a Mexican girl named Rose. Her name was Rose also. So at the age of eighteen, my future wife had just left home to get out in the world on her own. She had got a job, and this Mexican girl, and my wife is Filipino, decided to rent a house together. They was friends, OK? So the Mexican girl was going with my guitar player. And so she was telling Rose about the band, "You got to come out. I want you to meet Earl. You got to see Earl, because Earl has so much *energy*."

I did the unexpected. Back in those days you just didn't see musicians doing what I was doing. I was, not like, I was going to say Dennis Rodman laughs. So, you know how flashy he is. I wasn't flashy, but I was just an entertaining individual with a lot of energy in my plan. And see, in the average band you just didn't see this. You wouldn't see a guy playing the saxophone and all of a sudden run off the stage and jump up on somebody's table and shock 'em, or run to the bar and start running up and back and playing, *playing* all at the same time. Jumping here and jumping there, running all outdoors and people would get up from the tables and follow me outside. I'm playing down the street from the club. And the band is in the *club* playin' and I did all these crazy things, see?

I would stop traffic, just to draw attention to sell. I learned this at the Apollo Theater, I learned that while you're performing, that if you do something out of the ordinary, it would shock people. People will *remember* that. This is why at the Paramount, you saw me go down. You saw me jump down off the stage and walk just a few minutes in the first row of people and blow. Mark Naftalin, he didn't know I was going to do that. See, at practice, we didn't do that, see what I mean? So, he was shocked when I left the mike and went down in front of the people, see?

I've learned that if you want people to remember you, you've got to do something that they will remember. See what I mean? If you are just going to stand up on the stage and just play, well then they'll soon forget that. But if you do something going to *shock* 'em, "I didn't know he was going to do that, you know, then they will remember. That's why I try to create an image for myself, like Mr. T, that TV guy. For a long time, that's the way I would be dressed, with a lot of jewelry and stuff, so I could be *different* from the other entertainers so people will remember that.

And so, my future wife Rose came to the Spot Club in Lodi. She was eighteen, so the club owner wasn't going to let her in. I was sitting back in the club, so I had to come out in the front and talk to the club owner because he was sitting at the front door collecting the money, see? I had to talk to him to let her come in. So, when I went out in front and saw this woman standing there, with a *knit coat* on that was buttoned up from the neck *all the way down* past her knees, I looked at her and I said to myself, "That's going to be my wife." That's right. I tell all the kids that story. I knew, just looking at her. All I saw was her eyes, because she was covered up from her neck all the way down. Beautiful coat, she had on. It was one of those fitting types of coats, OK?

But I knew. I was twenty years old, she was eighteen. And when I talked to the club owner, I say. "Look here. They told me she did not drink, so I'll make sure that the other Rose would not set no drink in front of her." And so, we had to go back and play, and I did a set and as soon as I took a break, I was over there in front of her face, talking with her. And I came on too strong. She didn't want to have nothing to do with me. See? But I knew that she was the one, and I knew that she had to be my wife, OK? She was just like a lot of other people, seeing this crazy guy running all over the place, jumping up and down. She thought I was on *drugs*. She didn't want anything to do with that.

Other women were chasing me, and I was chasing her. So, to make a long story short, it took me a whole year. *Yeah!* I was coming from Oakland to Stockton, and trying to take her out, you know what I mean? So, over the period of one year, she saw me for what I really were. And after a whole year, then she decided to let me take her out. That's right. I was almost ready to give up on her, after a whole year. But that piano player, Lawrence Busby, thank him today. He's the one who told me, "Brown, hang in there. Don't give up yet. Don't give up yet." And I didn't, I'm telling you.

And so, like most people, they married in church or have a big wedding, when she finally saw me for who I really was, and she knew that I loved her and that my intentions was genuine, and that I just didn't want a fling. I wanted to be married, I wanted children, a whole lot of 'em, we went to Reno and got married. A lot of people said, "That ain't gonna last, that ain't gonna last." I'm telling you.

Mathews: Well, forty-three years later...

Brown: There you go. Never been separated.

Mathews: Yeah, well, that's admirable and I congratulate you; that's a wonderful thing.

Brown: So that's what I give thanks to. I give thanks to God for giving me the talent, because it had to be Him. Because there ain't no way in the world, musically, you know what I mean? That's one of the things I regret. I wish I could play like Kenny G. And have that kind of musical ability. But I've been very blessed to see the world, to make pretty good money, and be in pretty good health, and have a wonderful wife, kids, you see their pictures up there. All eight of them were up there. And then, all the grandchildren. And I was blessed with my *first wife*. A beautiful daughter happened from that marriage, but that marriage only lasted three years, see, because we were both young. And right today, my wife and my ex-wife are good friends. So, I have a whole lot to be thankful for.

Mathews: And you're playing. And musically, you're doing something right, you're doing it right.

Brown: I hope so.

Mathews: You don't have to play like Kenny G. to capture the heart and soul of somebody, that's for darn sure. I mean, you're playing is where it is.

Brown: And so, my good friend Cool Papa, he just passed away. See, I gave Cool Papa his start in California. Yeah, he was a guitar player and singer, and I owe this to Cool Papa. He played with my band for a long time in the fifties, OK? And the early part of the sixties. He's the one that is responsible for me being inducted into the Blues Hall of Fame, see? He's the one that let the society know about me and my background and all of the things that I did in music and the blues. And so, they got in touch with me, and they researched and looked and saw, because overseas they gave me a lot of good write-ups. So, they inducted me into the Blues Hall of Fame, along with Little Richard and Lowell Fulson and Ray Charles. We all got inducted the same night at the Oakland Auditorium there, in 1990. I want to show you his picture, the guy that gave me my trophy. He was a movie star years ago, he was in a lot of movies. That was a memorable night for me. This guy here, Herb Jeffries.

Mathews: Herb Jeffries! He used to sing with Duke Ellington. The Bronze Buckaroo.

Brown: *Yeah!* yeah. That was in the Oakland Tribune paper. So out of all the other entertainers that were walking across the stage, they decided to use my picture and put it in the Oakland paper. That was a blessing *too*.

Mathews: Yes, Herb Jeffries is on the record as saying that what was going on down on Central Avenue in the forties was "our Harlem Renaissance," all that wonderful artistry, down there.

Brown: Yes, indeed.

Mathews: Well, Earl, I can assure you that this has been a wonderful privilege for me.

Brown: Well, same here, it's good meeting *you*, you know.

Mathews: So, I'd just like to thank you on the record for again, having me in and being such a generous host and offering such a nice overview.

Brown: Can I offer you a Pepsi? [laughs]

[End of interview]